100 THINGS SOUNDERS FANS
SHOULD KNOW & DO
BEFORE THEY DIE

Geoff Baker

TRIUMPH
BOOKS

Library of Congress Cataloging-in-Publication Data available upon request.

This book is available in quantity at special discounts for your group or organization. For further information, contact:

Triumph Books LLC
814 North Franklin Street
Chicago, Illinois 60610
(312) 337-0747
www.triumphbooks.com

Printed in U.S.A.
ISBN: 978-1-62937-567-0
Design by Patricia Frey
Photos courtesy of AP Images unless otherwise indicated

For Sounders fans

Contents

Introduction

It was deathly silent inside the cramped locker room at BMO Field as the Sounders dissected their stunning December end to the 2017 season. They had just lost the MLS Cup final 2–0 to Toronto FC but knew the final score should have been at least double that.

Jordan Morris and Cristian Roldan, two of the team's brightest young stars, were among the last to finish dressing and gathering their things. Roldan would go on to be named the team's Most Valuable Player after a standout third season, but had been shut down completely by Michael Bradley and an unyielding Toronto transition game that never allowed the Sounders more than a few seconds with the ball.

As for Morris, he'd gotten on the field in the second half, but his night was as forgettable as his injury-plagued season in moments that didn't involve U.S. Men's National Team heroics. Both Morris and Roldan knew there could be greater moments ahead, with most of the team's lineup poised to return in 2018.

But the Toronto side had exposed shortcomings in the defending champion's game. And now, reality was sinking in that the Sounders were no longer on top of the Major League Soccer world.

For the Sounders and their fans, it was a devastating end to a remarkable two-season run atop that MLS universe. As is so often the case in sport, the reign from above had been fleeting. In the Sounders' case, their championship in 2016 had been so unexpected it seemed they spent most of the 2017 season having to justify it.

The reality is few teams in any sport make it to back-to-back championship matches. Fewer return to the finals a year after winning it all, the trappings of success so often claiming many top squads early on the following season.

That wasn't the case with the Sounders, who finished 2017 tied for the most points atop the Western Conference standings and then held their playoff opponents without a single goal until the second half of their championship match in Toronto.

For a while, it had seemed that goalkeeper Stefan Frei might duplicate his MLS Cup heroics of the prior year. He'd stood on his head for sixty-plus minutes once again, deepening the panic amongst the sold-out throng at BMO Field fearing their talented-but-snakebit team could again fall victim to its former netminder. Alas, it was not to be as Jozy Altidore, robbed by Frei in extra time a year earlier, put away his breakaway chance this time around for the only goal that would be needed.

The rest of the match was a coronation for the Reds and their hometown fans. The Sounders never got close to equalizing before a late Toronto insurance strike. It was about as dominant and lopsided a finals victory performance as anyone could remember. And not the way the Sounders ever imagined their magical run concluding.

Indeed, it would take time to get over such a defeat. Plenty of soul searching would occur, by players and a self-critical head coach Brian Schmetzer alike. Even general manager Garth Lagerwey, heralded the week preceding the MLS Cup final for his brilliant moves positioning the team for a repeat title run, would come under fire for bringing in relatively few new players in the weeks that ensued. Not until Lagerwey signed Norwegian midfielder Magnus Wolff Eikrem in late January, with 2018 training camp already started, did he quell some of the uneasiness.

That's to be expected. Of all the people jolted by Toronto's dominance in the final, the fans might have been hit the hardest. Where players, coaches, and executives continued to insist they largely hadn't "shown up" for that championship match, the fans had no way of knowing whether this was true. To many, what the Sounders seemed to be attributing to failed execution was looking more like evidence of a lack of talent relative to the team that dethroned them.

Time will tell.

And over time, once the sting of the finals loss fades, their two-season stretch is one I believe will grow in legend. It will be appreciated ever more by a fan base already treated to 44 years of special moments throughout the franchise's MLS history and prior incarnations.

The idea of preserving those moments and portraying them comprehensively against a professional soccer backdrop spanning decades in Seattle is what attracted me most when I was first approached to do this book in July 2017. History means little if not preserved and guardians of Seattle soccer—men like Alan Hinton, Jimmy Gabriel, Schmetzer, Adrian Hanauer, Dave Gillett, Pete Fewing, and Frank MacDonald—have done their utmost to keep spreading the word.

Now, with help from some of those men, my hope is this book preserves that history on a wider scale. The story of the Sounders is about more than the MLS team that began play in 2009. It's also about more than just the players on the pitch. I wanted this book to appeal as much to fans who remember a stunning, last-minute comeback goal by Roger Davies in the 1982 North American Soccer League semifinal as to newcomers who leapt from their seats when Roldan's late strike in July 2017 delivered a 4–3 victory over D.C. United from 3–0 down.

This book tells the story of Frei's save off Altidore in the 2016 MLS Cup final, while at the same time reliving Marcus Hahnemann's penalty round stop of Lenin Steenkamp at Memorial Stadium to deliver the Sounders an A-League title in 1995.

It describes 40-plus years of bonding between the Sounders and their fans. From the magical moments of the 1974 franchise debut to today's Emerald City Supporters and their organized, dedicated passion.

The history of professional sports teams matters little if the stories behind the games and personalities are forgotten. My hope is that much of it is preserved here. And that the two-season run by the Sounders just completed will hold its own within that history regardless of what happens from here on out.

1 Roman Torres Has a Championship at His Feet

Roman Torres was the most unlikely pick to score a championship-winning goal in MLS history. But on a frigid December 2016 night in Toronto, with neither the Sounders nor the hometown Reds able to score in regulation or overtime, it came down to Torres on penalty kicks.

The hulking defender from Panama, captain of that country's national team, had appeared in only 13 regular season games over two seasons with the Sounders. He'd torn the anterior cruciate ligament in his knee only weeks after coming over from Colombian side Millonarios midway through 2015, ending his season and limiting his play the following year. But his game picked up late in 2016, helping the Sounders make the playoffs and advance through each round with a rock-tight defensive strategy to offset a weakened attack.

That strategy held up in the championship match, with the Sounders keeping things scoreless despite failing to register a single shot on goal in regulation play or overtime. Torres was a monster throughout the match, outmuscling Toronto star Jozy Altidore throughout and limiting him and Sebastian Giovinco to a handful of opportunities. Like all others on the field, Torres was exhausted by the end. But after the teams made it through five rounds of penalty kicks tied 3–3, Justin Morrow hit the crossbar during the second sudden death round and opened the door for Torres and the Sounders to steal a title.

The Sounders hadn't used Torres among their first five shooters when penalty kicks began. Then, as the sudden death segment began, he didn't know whether he'd be called upon.

Despite a hulking physique, Roman Torres played striker until switching to defender at age 15 in a bid to make his country's national U17 team.

"All of a sudden, I see them signaling over 'two-five,'" he said. "And I go 'Really? Two-five? Number twenty-five? Okay.'"

Torres had yet to score a single MLS goal. But growing up in Panama, he'd played as a forward on his youth team.

Playing professionally in Colombia, he'd scored 44 goals over parts of 11 seasons. In the semifinals of the 2015 CONCACAF Gold Cup, he'd scored the opening goal on a header.

But he'd need to use his feet this time, as Toronto keeper Clint Irwin stared back at him from 12 yards away.

"I had no idea where I was going to shoot," Torres said. "I was just saying, 'God, you're going to tell me where to put this ball and it's going to go where it goes.' And it did and thank goodness for that."

Once his shot hit the back of the net, Torres let flow a tide of emotion. His teammates stormed the field to greet him, champions at last.

For Torres, it capped a long journey that began in Panama City. Torres was just three when the U.S. invasion to overthrow dictator Manuel Noriega occurred. Though Torres was too young to remember much, he sensed things gradually improving in his Central American country. By age 15, he was still playing as a striker, far bigger and taller than most boys his age. He attended a national U-17 tryout camp with about 200 to 300 other teens, looking to qualify. At one point, the coaches began splitting the youngsters into positional groups. They called out for all forwards to raise their hands.

"There were a lot of kids with their hands raised," Torres said. "Then…they called for defenders and I noticed there weren't a lot of them. And I was like, 'I'll play defender!' because there really weren't a lot of people to compete with.

"And so, from that moment on, I was a defender, and I was learning and learning and getting better at the position. And I decided that was going to be what I adopted as my position. I just kept learning how to play defender as much as I could."

His MLS Cup–clinching goal would turn out to be a warm-up act for Torres. Less than a year later, playing a World Cup qualifier for Panama against Costa Rica, Torres would score in the 88th minute to snap a 2–2 draw. Moments later, when the final whistle sounded, he was a national hero. Panama was going to its first FIFA World Cup and his goal had put them there.

Understandably, that moment outranks even his Sounders exploit. Torres ripped off his shirt in celebration immediately after his goal. "The stadium was just in pure happiness and euphoria over what happened," Torres said. "It was a historic moment for our country and our national team."

For now, his rare goal-scoring has secured milestones on two continents.

2 A Hollywood Beginning

Hollywood film producer Joe Roth had grown up playing youth soccer on Long Island. He later played a season at Bowling Green University and then another at Hofstra University.

Back then, in the late 1950s, a professional soccer career wasn't imaginable for those playing it. There was no pro league in the United States, and even the best players on the country's national team knew they had no chance of making it in any top circuit overseas.

In Roth's case, he had a fallback plan in movies. He would go on to produce more than 40 films and direct six of them, including *America's Sweethearts* with Julia Roberts and Billy Crystal in 2001. Roth had co-founded Morgan Creek Studios with James

G. Robinson in 1988, later became chairman of movie studios at 20th Century Fox and Disney, then started his own production company, Revolution Studios.

But he never got over his soccer bug. He'd coached his oldest son, Zack, for 15 years starting in the 1990s and until Zack played for Boston University. By then, Major League Soccer was getting launched on the heels of a successful 1994 World Cup hosted by the U.S. By 2007, when David Beckham joined the Los Angeles Galaxy, Roth could see the sport was gaining serious traction.

"It felt like a turning point," Roth said. "Maybe not *the* turning point, but a turning point."

And he wanted to be a part of it.

He called his friend, Tim Leiweke, who ran the Anschutz Entertainment Group company that owned the Galaxy and several MLS teams. They got together, along with AEG chief financial officer Dan Beckerman, for lunch at The Palm steakhouse in Los Angeles, a block from the Staples Center.

"They showed me a spreadsheet of what the math was," Roth said. " I said, 'Okay, I'm interested in doing this.'"

Leiweke phoned MLS commissioner Don Garber in New York and arranged an introduction. Roth and Garber met at a Galaxy game.

"I told him I'd like to own a team and I think I can help in other areas because there's this whole entertainment side to it," Roth said. "He said 'Great,' and to look in the Pacific Northwest."

Roth visited Seattle, Portland, and Vancouver, all of which were preparing MLS expansion bids. But Portland and Vancouver already had their principal owners, and Roth wasn't interested in being anything other than top dog.

Also, while Roth visited Seattle with Leiweke alongside him, the NBA Supersonics were in the midst of being duped out of their franchise, which eventually moved to Oklahoma City. Roth sensed a strong business opportunity.

Leiweke's younger brother, Tod, was president of the Seattle Seahawks and had already been talking with Adrian Hanauer—owner of the second division Sounders franchise in the USL—about vying for an MLS expansion team. But the league was interested in higher profile ownership, and Hanauer didn't quite fit that bill.

So Leiweke arranged for his younger brother and Roth to have dinner at the SkyCity restaurant atop the Space Needle. "That's really where I think the plot began as far as ownership goes," Leiweke said.

The younger Leiweke gave what his brother describes as a "passionate" business pitch to Roth.

"Tod doesn't get as much credit probably as he should get for that," Tim Leiweke said. "He was dead right on that one and completely understood what Adrian [Hanauer] had in terms of pent-up demand. And Joe [Roth] was smart enough to get in."

Roth didn't need much convincing from there. He met Hanauer through Garber at the 2007 MLS All-Star Game in Colorado. "I actually did some research and it didn't take much," Roth said. "[Hanauer's] minor league team was outdoing everybody else's minor league team. Then I did some homework and found that Washington was, per capita, the biggest youth soccer state and also had a very vibrant adult league at night."

Roth figured that he, Hanauer, and the Seahawks would make a solid partnership.

"I realized that I live in Los Angeles and know nothing about the infrastructure of a soccer team," Roth said. "But I knew how to run movie studios. It seemed to me that here, you had the two prongs you typically have at a movie studio—which is the creative and the business sides. So the Seahawks were the business. To get that entire staff—which didn't have a whole lot to do because they were selling out every game anyway—and Adrian became the basis upon which I decided to move forward."

Hollywood pal Drew Carey joined the partnership soon after and the Sounders were officially announced as an expansion franchise on November 13, 2007, with Roth as the majority owner.

"I started out of passion and as a hobby because it was a sport I loved," Roth said. "And I could just feel it was going to grow because we can't be that different here than everybody else in the world.

"So it was just a feeling. And we turned it into a real business."

3 Sounders Play First MLS Game

Sounders owner Adrian Hanauer admits he didn't sleep much the night of March 18, 2009. The very next day, his new Major League Soccer entry was playing its very first match, against the New York Red Bulls.

"I was about as nervous as you could possibly get," Hanauer said. "You wonder how the team will play, will anybody show up? Will they like what they see? Will they like it enough to come back? I was probably just as nervous about the same thing for the next three years, but that night was particularly bad."

Olympia native Kasey Keller, who'd left his overseas goalkeeping career behind to try to make soccer work closer to home, was also feeling some pressure. He knew a faceplant against the previous year's MLS Cup finalists could undo a lot of the hard work that had gone into launching the new franchise.

"I really wanted to make sure that wasn't the case where we'd fall flat and people would leave that first game going, 'What? This is what we were excited about?'" Keller said.

As it turned out, Hanauer and Keller needn't have worried. His Sounders put on as good a performance as any expansion debut side could have hoped for. A crowd of 32,523—officially deemed a sellout with the upper levels at Qwest Field closed off—gave the team a rousing welcome as it walked onto to the pitch. Washington State Governor Christine Gregoire presented MLS commissioner Don Garber with the team's first ceremonial Golden Scarf.

And once the game began, the city was introduced to a new sports star as Colombian forward Fredy Montero quickly took over. Montero needed fewer than 12 minutes to score the franchise's first goal, taking a cross from Sebastien Le Toux on the right side of the box and firing a shot past New York goalkeeper Danny Cepero. Even today, Montero remembers that goal as his finest Sounders moment.

"I just couldn't believe how loud the crowd was," Montero said. "I'd never really heard anything like that before."

And it would stay that way. In the 25th minute, Montero led Brad Evans with a pass in behind the defenders and watched him slip a shot past Cepero for a 2–0 lead. "I had never played in front of a crowd like that before," Evans said. "And I'd gotten to do it in my first game for an expansion side at 23 years old. It was pretty incredible. And to score a goal on top of that and win—it was a special day for everybody involved."

The Sounders cruised from there, outshooting the visitors 14–8 and only allowing a couple of tough chances against goalkeeper Keller. Montero brought the crowd to its feet with his second goal of the night in the 75th minute, intercepting a pass deep in New York's half, carrying the ball into the box and faking out Cepero with a couple of juke moves.

Keller had received the loudest ovation from fans during pregame lineup introductions. He'd been an integral part of Hanauer and majority owner Joe Roth's plans to market the team during the lead-up to the launch. At one point, Keller had toyed with skipping the team's first training camp in Argentina and playing the 2008–09 season in England. He'd just helped Fulham avoid English Premier League relegation and he could have returned to Germany, where he'd captained Borussia Mönchengladbach in 2006–07.

But Hanauer and Roth both let him know they felt it important for public perception and overall team unity that he be there. They didn't want people thinking the team was second rate and that star players would just show up when their schedules allowed it. They also wanted to use Keller as an ambassador for the game locally and have him appear at public events.

So Keller agreed upon signing his August 2008 deal that he'd stay and be there full-time and ahead of the franchise opener. "Being able to beat New York, which was a finalist the year before, 3–0 at home and make it exciting and special for all the fans that showed up was very important," Keller said.

"It wasn't really until I drove home with my wife after the game that we both really kind of came to the conclusion that it really was the right decision to make. To come home, to stay, to be there for that first game. To be a part of that. And if I hadn't been a part of that, if I'd come back in July because I was playing somewhere in Europe, it just wouldn't have been the same.

"That's when I knew all the decisions I'd made, to come home, to be there for the first day of preseason, to be there for the first game, that I'd made all the right decisions."

On that drive back from the stadium, Keller could finally put his mind at ease. And for that night, at least, team owner Hanauer could get himself some sleep.

4 Fredy Montero Becomes First Sounders Star

Brian Schmetzer could hardly believe his ears as he sat down for dinner in Colombia with the player who would become the very first Sounders star. Schmetzer, an assistant under head coach Sigi Schmid, had traveled to South America in 2008 with team vice president Chris Henderson to acquire a key piece for the squad's inaugural 2009 campaign.

Fredy Montero was only 21 back then but had just scored 16 goals for Deportivo Cali in his native country's Copa Mustang circuit. Now, as Schmetzer sat across the dinner table from Montero, he wanted to get to know a player in whom the Sounders were prepared to invest significant money.

But he couldn't get a word out of him.

"It was almost uncomfortable," Schmetzer recalled. "We couldn't get a peep out of him. He was so quiet and deferential, it was hard to believe this was the guy we were hoping would be our star player."

Years later, Montero laughed when recalling that night.

"That's my personality," he said. "Sometimes I just need time to get comfortable around people and the environment of where I'm living. But then, when I get comfortable, I can talk to people."

Montero let his goal-scoring do the talking upon his arrival in Seattle.

After nine goals in as many preseason games, he made his regular season debut on March 19, 2009, in his franchise's first MLS match against the New York Red Bulls at Qwest Field. Just 11 minutes in, Montero took a pass from Sebastien Le Toux at the top right corner of the box and put a wonderful ball along the ground into the far left corner of the net.

Fredy Montero let his scoring do the talking en route to piling up a team-record 47 goals over four seasons.

The crowd of 32,523 erupted.

"I couldn't believe how loud it sounded," Montero said.

Montero would assist on a second goal, then scored himself in the 75th minute to seal his team's 3–0 victory. He earned MLS Player of the Week honors for that feat, then Player of the Month accolades after adding another goal in his second game versus Real Salt Lake.

And a Sounders star was born.

"When I first came there, people didn't know very much about Fredy Montero," he said. "They weren't expecting all that much. But we knew we needed to do well to help [the Sounders] draw big name players to Seattle, so I was happy to help contribute to the team."

Montero went on to score 12 goals and added seven assists that season to be named MLS Newcomer of the Year.

"At 21, I didn't want to put extra expectations on myself," he added. "But as players, we felt bad when we didn't do well. We knew the team needed to win that first year, so when I could help them, it made me feel good."

Montero endured somewhat of a sophomore slump his second season in 2010 and was even bounced from the starting lineup by Schmid after nine games. But he found his stride and went on to score 10 goals by season's end, getting named top player on the league's 24 Under 24 list.

He added another 12 goals in 2011, as well as three goals the final three games of the U.S. Open Cup to lead the Sounders to a third straight title—getting named Player of the Tournament in the process. Montero scored another 13 goals in 2012. By then, rumors of his pending departure were in full force. Montero had confided to *Sports Illustrated* his rookie season that his childhood dream had been to play in Europe. Almost immediately, rumors of a transfer to Fulham of the English Premier League surfaced and had to be quelled by Montero.

But by 2012, he couldn't contain the rumors—or his desire to head overseas—any longer. The Cascadian King, as he'd come to be known, was loaned to Colombian champion Millionarios in 2013, then loaned again to SC Portugal in Lisbon by July of that year.

He scored a hat trick in his debut and by January 2014 had inked a multi-year deal with the Portuguese squad. His Sounders tenure was officially over.

"I will never forget that time," said Montero, who later bought a home in Seattle's east-side suburbs and lives there offseasons. "The city will always feel like a home to me."

In all, Montero scored 47 goals during his four seasons in Seattle, a mark that stood as the franchise's best until surpassed by Clint Dempsey in 2017. But more importantly to a fledgling franchise, Montero gave his team a true star in which could rally fans around in its search for a marketing toehold.

5 Clint Dempsey Comes Home

It wasn't quite David Beckham heading to the Los Angeles Galaxy back in 2007. But when the Sounders announced on August 3, 2013, that they'd signed U.S. Men's National Team captain Clint Dempsey, the city's soccer community had its own Beatlemania moment.

All of a sudden, the Sounders were leading local newscasts and even national sportscasts as well. The Twittersphere exploded as the rumored deal finally materialized. Speculation had begun two days earlier, when Dempsey bumped into soccer fan Jorge Perea at San Francisco International Airport. Perea later tweeted that the pride of Nacogdoches, Texas, was on his flight and headed to Seattle— setting off a wild 36 hours of coast-to-coast Internet hysteria about whether that was true or false.

For Dempsey, the journey started weeks earlier. He'd let it be known to his agent, Lyle Yorks, that he'd consider returning to Major League Soccer from the English Premier League for the right price and contract length. For Dempsey, that meant a deal worth between $30 million and $40 million, not to mention the transfer fee his Tottenham Hotspur club would need to be paid.

Yorks began putting the word out and got a few hits. The Los Angeles Galaxy, as expected, would play ball. So would the hapless Toronto FC franchise, which, buoyed by new president and CEO Tim Leiweke, was about to embark on a spending spree to lure top international talent.

The Sounders were also interested, and Yorks let Dempsey know they'd claimed they would "move mountains" to get him. Dempsey was in training camp with Tottenham and still had a guaranteed year left on his contract plus another year's option.

But he was intrigued. Seven years into his British foray, Dempsey had attained mixed results. There were early struggles playing for Fulham and dealing with the heightened media exposure that comes with being the highest touted U.S. star to set foot on English soil. But now, playing for the storied Tottenham squad and more secure with his transition overseas, Dempsey felt no pressing need to go home. He'd been the team's third most productive attacking player during the 2012–13 season, scoring 12 goals in 43 all-competition matches.

And yet, word began creeping out that summer that Tottenham would indeed sell Dempsey's contract for the right price. Dempsey was also looking for long-term security—and there was that whole "move mountains" thing the Sounders had pledged.

"They started talking a little bit more about it and we tried figuring out whether it was going to be possible," Dempsey said. "How much was it going to cost to buy me out of my contract? What kind of a contract was being offered? What teams are you going to go to?

"For me, I ultimately wanted to be in the States," he added. "So it was either going to be the L.A. Galaxy or Seattle."

Dempsey had watched some Sounders games on television and caught a glimpse of what the fan support was like. "I was excited about the opportunity to go there. And as time went on and talks became more realistic to make it happen, I was excited about going there, progressing the game in the states and being closer to family."

The Sounders offered to pay Tottenham a $9 million transfer fee and give Dempsey a guaranteed deal of $24 million over three and a half seasons. Dempsey was 29, and that was more money than he'd dreamed possible. He knew he wouldn't play forever.

"I was 29 years old and at the end of the day, you want to play soccer as long as you can because you love it," he said. "You want to play at the highest level, but also, you want to take care of your family in a good way. The older that you get—I mean, everybody's

Landing forward Clint Dempsey gave the Sounders and their fans their very own soccer "Beatlemania" moment.

different, but for me, it was important to raise my kids here. To keep helping the league grow here was important. And to be closer to my family—even though it's still a four-hour flight to get to Houston—that was a lot easier to make, or for them to come and see me, than to be in England."

MLS executive vice president Todd Durbin, who negotiates such international contracts on behalf of the league, handled the talks. Finally, a deal was reached. Dempsey boarded the plane to San Francisco and then prepared to catch his Seattle connection when he and soccer fan Perea ran into each other. Perea initially tweeted that Dempsey was on his flight, but then retracted it when he saw the star head for another gate.

Unknown to Perea, he initially had it correct. But the fact that EPL squad Everton was training in San Francisco fueled Internet speculation that Dempsey's final stop would be in that city. That bought the Sounders additional time to fly Dempsey to Seattle and have him stay at the Westin hotel in suburban Bellevue. It was a nervous time, since the contract had yet to be signed. Dempsey was due to take his physical the following day before sealing the deal. If Dempsey failed it, or got cold feet, the whole plan could fall apart.

Sounders owner Adrian Hanauer went to meet Dempsey at the hotel. And to his horror, some soccer-savvy fans spotted the star in the lobby.

"I remember being at the hotel and some fans walking up to us and saying 'Hey, ah, man, can I get your autograph?'" Hanauer said. "They started asking him why he was here and he told them he was just visiting friends."

Hanauer was well aware of the prior Internet fuss and worried the fans would take to social media and create a frenzy before the Sounders had their deal. But given it was a hotel, it's possible the fans were out-of-towners unaware of the Dempsey fuss taking place within the city. In any event, they didn't broadcast their sighting of the star.

The Sounders had dodged a major bullet. Dempsey took his physical the following day, then met for dinner with Sounders majority owner Joe Roth, Hanauer, team president Peter McLoughlin, and head coach Sigi Schmid.

Dempsey signed his Sounders deal, and the team and MLS had landed one of the biggest marquee players in its history. Dempsey says he was never told about being expected to promote the league. He just assumed that was part of the bigger money he was given.

"I know they wanted me to help promote the game in Seattle and the league," Dempsey said. "I had no problem with that. Anything I can do to help the sport grow, I'll do."

Putting the ball in the net would be one way. And he's done that. By the end of 2017, Dempsey has scored 46 times for the Sounders. That's only one behind Fredy Montero for the franchise's all-time lead.

And in the postseason, having missed the team's championship run in 2016 due to an irregular heartbeat, he atoned quickly with three goals the first four matches to help lead the Sounders back to the title game.

Never Over Until the Final Whistle

Two of the catalysts for the unlikeliest of comebacks in Major League Soccer history woke up the morning of July 19, 2017, not even sure they'd play that night.

Newly acquired Dutch right back Kelvin Leerdam was in a Vancouver, B.C., hotel room, gathering his immigration paperwork and preparing to drive across the border from Canada into the United States and then two and a half hours south to Seattle. Meanwhile, left back Nouhou Tolo was at home massaging a sore shoulder he'd dislocated during practice five days earlier.

Leerdam hoped he'd complete his drive in time to dress for that evening's game against D.C. United. And Nouhou, the singular first name Cameroonian bruiser Tolo prefers to go by, was hoping the trainers that day would see enough mobility in his shoulder to allow him to dress for the game, as well.

By kickoff, both were indeed in uniform as the Sounders took to the pitch at CenturyLink Field for their first game in 15 days following a layoff for the CONCACAF Gold Cup. And as Leerdam and Nouhou watched the first 45 minutes of play unfold from the sideline, they were likely a tad relieved not to be out on the field.

D.C. United had scored just 14 goals in their first 19 games but somehow potted a quick pair in the opening half. In fact, the cement-footed Sounders were fortunate another two or three more didn't go in. As the halftime whistle sounded, the 42,714 fans in attendance booed the home-side players as they trudged off the field.

In the locker room, they tried to regroup. Sounders head coach Brian Schmetzer wondered to himself whether he could have done more to better prepare his players following the layoff. The ones he'd started the game with, including back line veterans Roman Torres, Chad Marshall, Gustav Svensson, and Brad Evans, looked slow and lifeless, getting burned by speedy midfielders on the two goals.

The attack was already missing star forward Clint Dempsey and second-year homegrown Jordan Morris, both continuing Gold Cup duty with the U.S. Men's National Team. The national side had at least sent back former University of Washington Huskies star Cristian Roldan, but the Sounders remained stuck in neutral on offense. Uruguayan playmaker Nicolas Lodeiro was getting chased around the field by opposing defenders who kicked away at his shins and ankles every chance they got. Midfielder Harry Shipp was a non-factor as well, a recurring theme in recent weeks.

Early in the second half, Schmetzer had seen enough after D.C. United scored a third goal in the 50th minute to go up 3–0.

Schmetzer knew his squad couldn't afford to throw away a crucial three-point opportunity at home against a team with the worst record in the Eastern Conference. At the very least, he didn't want to get blown off the field in front of a hometown crowd that was turning surly in a hurry.

Leerdam and Nouhou both got the call to start warming up. Schmetzer figured the pair could at least inject speed up and down both flanks and perhaps wake up their teammates while catching opponents off guard.

Both players were just about ready to come in when the Sounders finally scored in the 51st minute on a Will Bruin header off a Joevin Jones cross to the box to cut United's lead to 3–1. Schmetzer hesitated, not wanting to put Leerdam and Nouhou in the game when his starters finally seemed to be finding their groove.

But after a few more minutes, they'd reverted to their previous sluggish form. In the 54th minute, Leerdam and Nouhou entered the match, allowing Jones and Evans to bump up to the midfield and Roldan to take on more of an attacking role.

The move changed the game's tempo almost instantly. Where the United defenders had previously repelled Sounders advances like a brick wall, balls were now finding their way behind them.

"We just needed to get more attacking movements up the field," Schmetzer would say later. "I was just basically trying to get more energy and some more dynamic attacking movements out wide, because they were defending inside out. They had the lead and they were protecting their goal. We needed to do something out in the middle channels to break them down, and I think both Nouhou and Kelvin helped us do that."

The crowd also got into it, sensing their team still had a shot. The Sounders had already erased a 3–0 second-half deficit at home a few months earlier, scoring three in the final 15 minutes of regulation for a 3–3 draw against New England.

Now the Sounders had United back on their heels in much the same way. And in the 62nd minute, they struck.

Leerdam heaved an unusually long throw-in to the edge of the box that deflected over to Nouhou on the far left. Nouhou faked right, then passed to Jones on the left flank. Jones, as he does so well, put a perfect cross into the box that Evans headed into the net.

The crowd went wild and the Sounders, down just a goal at 3–2, didn't relent. Wave after wave came at the overwhelmed United side, by now trying desperately to hang on.

But they couldn't.

In the 74th minute, Lodeiro sent a corner kick from the right side to the near edge of the box. Svensson was being marked by Lloyd Sam but broke totally free as the ball arrived. The Swede redirected it into the upper near-side corner of the net with a right-footed flick.

The stadium went berserk, thunderous applause cascading down from all sides. With the game now knotted 3–3, the Sounders never stopped coming. And just four minutes later, Roldan, who'd been slowly taking control of the game, capped the historic comeback with a marvelous run.

Jordy Delem had pushed a midfield header up toward the vicinity of an onrushing Roldan. The ball deflected off defender Kofi Opare and toward the United goal, where Roldan and defender Steve Birnbaum chased after it.

Birnbaum tried to play the ball instead of the man and the agile Roldan—never breaking stride—poked it ahead and deftly skirted by his opponent to earn a clear path to the net. United keeper Travis Worra raced out to cut down the angle but Roldan got to the loose ball first and put it between Worra's legs for a 4–3 lead.

No MLS team had ever come back from 3–0 down to win in regulation time. Not long after Roldan's go-ahead tally, the Sounders had done just that.

"I thought the substitutes made a huge difference," Roldan said of Leerdam and Nouhou. "Everybody was committed to coming back."

Leerdam said his first MLS game was one to remember. Although he'd already been training with the Sounders, he'd been required to leave the country and then re-enter it again in order to activate his work visa. And so, upon leaving his Vancouver hotel room that morning, he and team security chief Gene Ramirez had driven to the Peace Arch border crossing near Blaine, Washington, and sat in a waiting room with other visa holders looking to enter the U.S. to work.

They knew the wait could take a while. But Leerdam got through within an hour and the pair was soon on the road for the drive to downtown Seattle, arriving mid-afternoon.

"For me, it was a crazy day because I'd just come over from Vancouver four hours before the game," Leerdam said in a joyous and relieved locker room afterward. "And then, you play a game three goals down and you still win…. I hope the next game will be a little bit easier because this will not happen again."

And it didn't. Buoyed by Leerdam solidifying the right flank and Nouhou the left, as Jones was pushed up to the midfield late in the season, the Sounders never again allowed three goals in a game. In fact, they didn't get scored on at all for a three-month stretch starting September 10. That covered a span of six games, four of them postseason matchups as the Sounders cruised back to the MLS Cup final for a second straight year.

7 What's in a Name?

The pressbox above CenturyLink Field is named after Gary Wright, the longtime Seattle Seahawks director of media relations. But if not for Wright, the name of the soccer team watched on the field below that pressbox might have been Seattle Alliance, Seattle FC, or Seattle Republic.

Those had been the three ready-made choices offered to fans participating in an online ballot to pick the name of the city's new MLS entry. Apparently, the Sounders name was not to be included initially because MLS officials worried that it conjured up too many memories of a failed North American Soccer League they were eager not to be associated with.

"They felt they had made a mistake when they allowed the [San Jose] Earthquakes to be the Earthquakes," Wright said, the naming decision coming just a few years after the initial San Jose MLS franchise—named after its NASL counterpart—had moved to Houston. "Things weren't going so well at that time. They just felt everybody should have a fresh start."

Even the team's inner circle wasn't convinced Sounders was a good idea. Wright said owner Adrian Hanauer was a staunch supporter of keeping his former USL team's name, but "the rest of us, for the most part, felt we should try something fresh because the name Sounders had kind of a minor league connotation."

But the Sounders name had long been part of the city's soccer lore. Fans were not happy at seeing no mention of "Sounders" among names being offered up to vote on and let the team know about it via an online barrage of emails.

That put the team in a no-win position. It risked either upsetting the league or alienating its own fanbase before it had even gotten off the ground as a franchise. But Wright, hired out of retirement as the fledgling team's head of business operations, had a solution. He proposed adding the write-in option for anyone that wanted Sounders or anything else. That way, Sounders could get in there without MLS objecting.

Not that Wright himself will ever admit to devising the plan. In his self-deprecating way, he insists "a collaborative process" led to the idea. But those supposedly a part of that collaboration say it was Wright who first brought it up.

In any event, the league went along with the whole thing, which wasn't too surprising given write-in votes typically don't add up to much. Given the hundreds of name combinations fans could possibly come up with, the chances of Sounders garnering too high a vote percentage appeared nil. But in this case, a highly organized lobby of fans was prepared to push the Sounders name over the top. Wright admits he knew from the start that Sounders was going to win.

"By then, I kind of figured it was going to be," he said. "I'd just heard from too many people."

And he insists it wasn't a case of pulling the wool over any eyes. Wright had known MLS commissioner Don Garber from their days working in the NFL and says team owners Hanauer and Joe Roth made clear to him in advance that Sounders winning the name contest was a very real possibility.

"It was like, 'Hey, if Sounders wins, we've got to go with this,'" Wright said. "And he was fine with it at that point."

Wright explained that having had nearly a year and a half to prepare for their franchise launch, the team had already vetted numerous ideas. Some were accepted, others rejected. But they were well thought through.

"I think even he understood that if Sounders was to win, then let's go for it because this was going to be a great franchise," Wright said. "We'd already won over his confidence."

More than 14,500 fans registered to vote online. And in the end, when the accounting firm Deloitte & Touche tallied the ballots, Sounders won by a landslide.

The Sounders sought to appease the league by adding the more traditional "FC" to the club's full name in order to differentiate it from the NASL version. And now, the name is recognized as a hallmark of success for the model MLS franchise.

Which wouldn't have been possible without some quick thinking to preserve part of the city's soccer heritage.

8 DeAndre Yedlin Raised by His Grandparents

DeAndre Yedlin didn't find out his parents' true story until he was nearly a teenager. He'd grown up in the Seattle suburb of Shoreline, raised by his grandparents Ira Yedlin and Vicki Walton. His mother, Rebecca, Ira's daughter, would visit as often as she could. But it was his grandparents who'd treated him like a son, provided stability, and shuttled him off to soccer practices.

"I always call him my 'kid' because grandson sounds so far removed," Walton said.

They'd sought permanent custody of DeAndre when he was only 19 months old and obtained it a few months later. And though Rebecca, his birth mother, objected initially, she later put her anger aside and accepted the arrangement.

She'd visit on weekends initially, limited by the distance of her apartment to the Yedlin family home. But by the time DeAndre was six, the visits increased.

"At some point, we started talking about things and her life," Yedlin said. "Then, eventually, I began asking about my father."

DeAndre had long been curious about his Afro and his skin tone, which was darker than the rest of his family.

But Larry Morris Rivers was a taboo subject in DeAndre's childhood home. His mother had met Rivers when she was 16 and he was 21. They'd moved in together a year later, then at age 18 she became pregnant with DeAndre.

Rivers had already been jailed throughout the 1980s on various assault and robbery charges. At one point, he'd nearly beaten a man to death outside Pike Place Market.

"He wasn't a good person," Rebecca Yedlin said. "And I was very young and naïve."

So she left Rivers while pregnant. He got arrested soon after, in June 1993, for distributing cocaine in downtown Seattle and got a 14-month prison sentence.

Two weeks later, DeAndre was born. Rebecca Yedlin struggled to make ends meet and was jailed in the summer of 1994 for writing bad checks. Soon after her arrest, she accepted an offer to move back in with her parents.

Things went well until she paid her only visit to Rivers in jail, bringing along their infant son. She'd planned to smuggle in some marijuana for Rivers in DeAndre's diaper bag but panicked at the last minute and stashed it instead in a jailhouse storage locker.

A guard dog nonetheless smelled the marijuana traces on her and the plot unraveled. She was arrested and would spend much of 1994 and 1995 dealing with the fallout from both criminal cases.

During this time, she'd moved back out of her parents' home, leaving DeAndre in their care. After that, she'd spend years putting her life back together.

Yedlin's father, meanwhile, was arrested again in 2003 for abducting an elderly Cambodian immigrant in his car, robbing him at gunpoint, and pistol-whipping him when he tried to escape.

He was convicted of felony robbery and kidnapping and imprisoned for life as a three-time offender. Yedlin has never met his father and, while once curious, no longer feels any compelling need to.

His mother never saw Rivers again after that jailhouse visit and her arrest. She later went back to school and became a business technology and medical office technology teacher at South Seattle Community College.

Her first teaching job had been in 2004, with inmates at the Kent jail. She taught them life skills.

"Talk about making a 180," she said.

In the meantime, she also raised a daughter on her own, Yedlin's half-sister, Jenea, from a different relationship. DeAndre had been introduced to her right away and the pair remain close.

His mother has tried to make up for lost time with him, as well.

"As I got older, I got a better relationship with her," Yedlin said. "It's been really nice to hang out and get to know her on an adult level."

9 Chad Marshall Solidifies the Back Line

Two-time MLS Defender of the Year Chad Marshall didn't get a good vibe when he walked into the office of his new coach in November 2013. Former Stanford standout Marshall had spent a decade with the Columbus Crew, winning an MLS Cup in 2008 and establishing himself as one of the league's all-time premier defenders.

But the Crew was undergoing a transition that would soon benefit the Sounders as much as any player transaction in their history. Columbus had fired Robert Warzycha and hired Gregg Berhalter to take his place and serve as the de facto general manager in all player decisions. Berhalter came with a stellar reputation as the first American to manage a European club when hired by Sweden's Hammarby IF. Still, he'd gone 11–16 in two seasons in Sweden and lost his job primarily because the team was too defensively oriented.

By coincidence, that was the same knock against the Crew squad Berhalter took over from interim coach Brian Bliss. And for Marshall, the rock of that defense, the proverbial wall had his name scribbled all over it as he walked into Berhalter's office for their first meeting.

"In that meeting he expressed, 'Hey, Seattle's interested, does that interest you?'" Marshall said. "To bring that up in your first meeting with a coach, it didn't really scream like, 'Hey, we want you here.'"

Marshall already had a guaranteed year remaining on his contract, so he wasn't worried about his financial future. But he was the lone remaining member from the 2008 championship squad and sensed even before the meeting the franchise wanted to move in a different direction.

"They had just had an ownership change and brought in a whole new front office," Marshall said. "A whole new coaching staff was in. I was kind of like the last person from the previous team. So it just seemed like the right time."

And it certainly was for the Sounders.

Marshall knew Sounders coach Sigi Schmid from the 2008 championship season and years prior. He'd played with Brad Evans in Columbus, as well.

"I'd obviously played with Brad in Columbus and he'd spoken so highly of the organization and how great the city was," Marshall said. "It was hard not to notice what was going on when Seattle was playing ESPN games every other week with crowds of 40,000 plus. Every player wants to play in that environment."

And Marshall got his chance. Within weeks of that initial meeting with Berhalter, the Crew traded Marshall to the Sounders for Targeted Allocation Money and a third-round pick in the 2015 MLS Super Draft.

And it didn't take long for the Sounders to reap the benefits.

With center back Marshall anchoring the back line, the Sounders won their first and only Supporter's Shield in 2014 with a record of 20–10–4. They also captured the U.S. Open Cup that year by beating the Philadelphia Union 2–1 in the final.

Alas, the magical run ended in the postseason with a loss in the Western Conference Final to the Los Angeles Galaxy. The series actually ended 2–2 on aggregate goals, but the Galaxy advanced by virtue of a lone away goal at CenturyLink Field in a 2–1 loss in the second match while the Sounders managed none in a 1–0 defeat in the two-game series opener on the road.

For Marshall, the season was nonetheless an individual success. He captured his third Defender of the Year award, starting in all 31 games he appeared in as well as playing in four postseason contests.

He scored the game winner in a 2–1 win over Philadelphia in May, tying his career high with his third assist of the season in that same game. Marshall made the All-Star roster and was named to the league's Team of the Week three times.

Not only that, his veteran stability also helped soothe a locker room beset by tension late in 2013 largely because of the monetary demands of Eddie Johnson. With Johnson since traded, Marshall helped guide the blossoming Sounders to their best season yet.

He followed up in 2015 by again making the All-Star roster and Team of the Week three times. And the Sounders nearly advanced to the Conference Finals again by coming within minutes of upsetting favored FC Dallas in the semis.

The Sounders had won the first leg in Seattle and needed just a win or a draw at Frisco, Texas, to advance. With the game scoreless in the 84th minute, however, Tesho Akindele headed home a Michael Barrios cross to put Dallas in the lead 1–0.

That set the stage for the biggest goal of Marshall's life. In the 90th minute, with the Sounders desperately needing to equalize, late substitute Marco Pappa put a corner into the box that Marshall found at the far post to tie the game 1–1 and leave the Sounders on the verge of advancing.

But it was not to be. Walker Zimmerman put Dallas back on top 2–1 in injury time and sent the game to extra time with the series tied on aggregate. From there, it went to penalty kicks and Dallas captured the series by outscoring the Sounders 4–2.

A dejected Marshall was nonetheless rewarded with a call-up to the United States Men's National Team in January 2016, playing

The Chad Marshall acquisition from Columbus ahead of the 2014 season solidified the Sounders' back line for years to come.

in a scoreless draw against Serbia in an international friendly. It would be his 11th international cap and first in seven years.

His signature Seattle moment would come the following season, when he helped guide the club on a second-half comeback from last place to the championship that had so long eluded it. Marshall was named the league's Player of the Month in a pivotal September, as the Sounders went 3–0–1, and he scored the winner in a 1–0 victory over Chicago.

He garnered Team of the Week honors four times—two of them during that critical September—as the Sounders went on to make the playoffs and capture their first title. He played every minute of the postseason and was rewarded with a call-up to the U.S.M.N.T. training camp the following January at age 32.

The following season, in 2017, he again anchored a back line that didn't allow a goal the final two weeks of the regular season or in the first four playoff matches as the Sounders cruised their way back in to a second consecutive finals appearance.

10 Born in 1974

Spawned by unexpectedly large U.S. television audiences for the 1966 FIFA World Cup, the North American Soccer League was founded two years later in 1968. But by 1974, it was still largely a semi-pro-caliber league, with players forced to take second jobs to compensate for relatively low salaries.

Amid this backdrop, the NASL expanded in 1974, bringing in eight new franchises while two others folded. The new teams, including a Seattle-based squad, paid the league $75,000 apiece in franchise fees and gave the NASL a needed West Coast presence. The Seattle ownership was led by Portland-born Walt Daggatt, a longtime corporate executive who'd been looking to bring an NFL franchise to the city until Kansas City Chiefs owner Lamar Hunt—also owner of the NASL Dallas Tornado—talked to him about looking at soccer instead.

Daggatt assembled an ownership group from some of Seattle's best-known families and prominent businesses. It included Lloyd Nordstrom, Howard Wright, David "Ned" Skinner, Herman Sarkowsky, Lynn Himmelman, and Lamont Bean. The franchise was awarded in December 11, 1973, and by January 22, 1974, fans had voted to go with Sounders over Mariners and other choices as the team's name.

Daggatt's ownership group had a $500,000 budget and promptly began scouring the globe for player talent. Liverpool native John Best was hired as the head coach and Scottish defenders Jimmy Gabriel and Dave Gillett quickly became popular fixtures.

The team's first game was on May 5, 1974, on the road against the Los Angeles Aztecs. A small crowd of 4,107 fans came to East Los Angeles College Stadium for the match, which saw the Sounders defeated 2–1 by an Aztecs squad that would go on to finish with the league's top overall record that year and later capture its championship.

John Rowlands scored the franchise's first goal in what was a competitive contest to the end. The Sounders quickly gained a reputation as a hard-working, likeable bunch commonly referred to as "The Lads" by their fans.

The team would play home games at Memorial Stadium, a facility of roughly 12,000 seats—which was continuously being expanded with bleacher section additions—on the Seattle Center campus in the shadow of the Space Needle. A crowd of 12,132 attended the home opener against the Denver Dynamos on May

12, 1974, with Willie Penman opening the scoring less than two minutes in to what became a 4–0 win.

That was soon followed by a stretch of four consecutive losses and a scoreless draw. But the season turned around from there as the Sounders reeled off four consecutive wins, including two on the road at Toronto and Vancouver. The fourth of those victories came at home against the Philadelphia Atoms in front of 13,876 fans on June 22, 1974, a match in which the Sounders became the first NASL team in history to sell out their stadium.

"We had a lot of fun that first year," defender Adrian Webster said. "We were a pretty competitive team and the fans really took to us."

It was the first of six sellouts that season for the Sounders, who ran their unbeaten streak to seven games before losing at home 1–0 to Dallas in front of another standing-room-only sellout and season high 14,876 fans.

"That stadium was really rocking, man," said Gillett, a defender on that 1974 team. "We had a really good team and we hardly ever lost a home game for the next two seasons. It never rained, so it was summer nights, big crowds, and a packed atmosphere.

"The stadium became a bit of a fortress," he said. "If I was another team, I would have hated to play there."

Goalkeeper Barry Watling would earn a first-team All-Star nod that season, as would forward Rowlands. The Sounders would rack up 10 wins—second most in the league that year—as they pressed to make the playoffs.

But the league's playoff format and scoring system weren't helping. Nor was the fact the Western Division was the league's toughest—the only one to have three teams finish with more than 100 points.

Only two teams from each division made the playoffs, so the Sounders and San Jose Earthquakes were in a dogfight behind the first-place Aztecs for that final spot.

A San Jose loss at home to Washington on August 3 opened a playoff door for the Sounders. They still had three games remaining compared to just one for the Earthquakes and trailed San Jose by 13 points. But in a league with the potential for nine-point victories, a 13-point gap wasn't as formidable as it sounded.

The Sounders would play their final three games over just a five-day span. It didn't help that they played to a scoreless draw at St. Louis on August 7, earning just three points to narrow San Jose's lead to 10. Two nights later, though, the Sounders defeated Rochester 3–0 at home for a nine-point win that narrowed the Earthquakes lead to just a single point.

The season would come down to the final weekend.

San Jose would host the first-place Aztecs at home on August 10, while the Sounders would play the following day at home against the archrival Vancouver Whitecaps. Anything but an Earthquakes victory in which they scored three goals or more would guarantee the Sounders had something to play for the following day.

With an Earthquakes loss, the Sounders would need just a win or likely only a draw to advance.

Alas, it was not to be.

"I remember it was out of our hands whether we were going to make the playoffs," Gillett said. "And I think San Jose beat somebody 5–0 or 5–1, so we couldn't make it."

Indeed, the Earthquakes routed eventual champion Los Angeles 5–0 to move 10 points up on the Sounders and guarantee they couldn't be caught. Sounders fans were heartbroken and in tears the following day, with Memorial Stadium again packed to capacity at 14,876 fans to witness a 2–1 victory.

"It was a pretty successful season for the first time," Gillett said.

The Sounders finished with 101 points, two behind second-place and playoff-bound San Jose.

"What I remember most from that first season was the fans and the bond we shared with them," Webster said. "Those were special times and the feeling inside that stadium was something else.

"It really helped set the tone for what became the Sounders of today. That bond is still there."

11 Alan Hinton Becomes Mr. Soccer in Pacific Northwest

For more than a dozen years, playmaking left winger Alan Hinton graced English Premier League pitches for Wolverhampton, Nottingham Forest, and a pair of championship squads at Derby County. But in 1976, his 9-year-old son, Matthew, died from a rare form of cancer, devastating Hinton and his wife, Joy. Unable to focus on the pitch, Hinton retired from playing.

Soon, the couple left England altogether. Al Miller, then head coach of the Dallas Tornado of the North American Soccer League, paid Hinton an unannounced visit in his tiny village of Wednesbury and convinced him to try playing in the United States for a six-month spell.

"We were thinking we could rebuild our lives," Hinton said. "And then, we just loved it."

Hinton joined the Tornados at age 35 and went on to score four goals in 24 appearances, helping them win their division and serving as team captain the final three matches.

At that point, he retired again. But the Vancouver Whitecaps offered Hinton a job as an assistant coach. As his wife and 7-year-old daughter, Tonya, were enjoying life overseas as a pleasant distraction from their prior turmoil, he took it. Then the

Whitecaps talked him out of retirement and into playing again. He scored a goal and added an NASL record 30 assists at age 36 while also launching a coaching career that took him to Tulsa as head coach the following season.

During a Vancouver game at Tulsa, Roughnecks keeper Colin Bolton, Hinton's former Derby teammate, asked him if he wanted the head coaching job. Hinton met with the team's general manager the next morning and was offered the job immediately.

But Hinton turned it down. His Whitecaps were playing brilliantly and would go on to tie the New York Cosmos for the league's best record at 24–6 before being upset by Portland in the quarterfinals.

Hinton retired for good after that and took the Tulsa job. A year later, he was offered the same gig by the Sounders and quickly jumped at the chance to return to the West Coast.

He led the Sounders for three seasons, guiding them to the 1982 Soccer Bowl and a 1–0 defeat at the hands of the Cosmos.

The NASL folded in 1984. But Hinton took a job coaching the indoor soccer Tacoma Stars from 1985 to 1990, his family settling permanently in the Seattle suburb of Bellevue. Hinton began a real estate career after that and stayed heavily involved in youth soccer with the Crossfire organization, earning his "Mr. Soccer" nickname for his work with the sport around the Puget Sound.

By 1994, the Sounders were being resurrected to play in the A-League and Hinton was offered a job as their team president. He soon appointed himself head coach and helped the team win the championship by its second season.

12 Stand with ECS Members at a Game

While taking in a Sounders game, it's tough not to notice the rowdy, slightly inebriated, singing, chanting supporters in the South End of CenturyLink Field. Several sections in what's also known as the Brougham End of the stadium are reserved for members of the Emerald City Supporters. And if their singing and chanting appears slightly choreographed, that's because it is.

The group deploys "capos," or captains, who stand at the head of each section and yell out on bullhorns what the next song is going to be. A majority of those in these general admission sections 121 through 123 are paid ECS members. But not all of the seats are occupied.

"There are sometimes single tickets for our section," ECS co-president Heather Satterberg said. "The organization is also a season ticket holder so we have a number of tickets we make available to current members, but you can buy those for other people. And frankly, if an old face gives me a call and says, 'Hey, I'm in town,' I'll be like, 'Great, let me find you a ticket.'"

The team posts warning signs at the section entryway that the seats are mostly occupied by ECS members and that anyone entering them should expect an experience different from the rest of the stadium. Fans purchasing single tickets to those sections through Ticketmaster get the same type of warning.

And whether that's having a view obstructed by ECS members standing all game, or being expected to chant, sing, and cheer on command, the general message is the same: fans should not expect to sit in these sections taking selfies all match long.

"Somebody's going to hand you a song card and say, 'Hey, instead of taking pictures, why don't you help support the team?'

The thousands-strong Emerald City Supporters group welcomes newcomers prepared to actively participate in cheering on the home side.

Someone might say it a little stronger than that," Satterberg said. "We do really try to encourage people to be a part of it. Because there are 40 other sections where you could stand, or eat, or sit, or take selfies for the entire game."

ECS rules dictate that members follow what each capo tells them to do. If they yell, "Scarves up!" when players first enter the pitch, ECS members must hoist theirs above their head and keep them up until told otherwise.

"Participation is the expectation," ECS co-president Tom Biro said. "You will sing, you will chant, you will jump up and down. Flags will be waved in front of you. That's not to say it's an obstructed view per se, but it kind of is.

"Most of us watch the game at home later," he added. "That's not to say we don't know what's going on. But you're literally there to affect change.

"That's not to say we don't want anyone in the section to have seen what's going on out on the field. We enjoy that and revel in it. But you are there with a purpose. And that purpose is not just to say, 'I spent 30 bucks for my ticket and now I'm going to drink a beer.' It's more than that."

Demographics within the section are all over the place, from those in their young teens and twenties to others in their thirties and even forties. There are also plenty of women up yelling alongside the men. The group discourages anyone from bringing small children because of the general rowdiness.

Though alcohol is flowing throughout the match, the capos and other ECS leaders keep an eye out for potential troublemakers. ECS has its own security personnel and they'll often approach a member and tell them to tone things down before it goes too far and regular security needs to get involved. Most of the time, the peer pressure wins out.

But if going to a game, shouting yourself hoarse, and having a fun, non-violent time that leaves you physically drained is your thing, the ECS leaders both say they'd have no problem welcoming you for the day. The group counts just less than 3,000 yearly paid members and is always seeking out new—and younger—talent as older ones inevitably move on. But ultimately, they don't care who you are as long as you follow their rules.

As the group's official website states: "It is much more important to join us in support of the Sounders on game day than it is to buy a membership."

13 Sounders Win Consecutive A-League Titles

Sounders keeper Marcus Hahnemann stood ready in the goal-mouth, staring down the veteran shooter about to take one final crack at him.

About 35 yards away, with more than 5,000 fans roaring in the Memorial Stadium stands, Atlanta Ruckus forward Lenin Steenkamp was all that stood between the Sounders and their first championship of any kind. It was the decisive Game 3 of the 1995 A-League championship series, and the Sounders had scored late to tie the match to force this shootout round to decide the winner. With the Sounders having grabbed a 2–1 shootout lead, Steenkamp was his team's final shooter and hope.

For Hahnemann, one of a plethora of Sounders to hail from the Seattle Pacific University Division II national championship squad of 1993, this moment was one he'd never thought possible. It was only the prior year that the Sounders were revived from the decade-old ashes of their North American Soccer League predecessor franchise to play in the A-League—back then still the top professional outdoor circuit in North America.

Hahnemann had grown up in the Seattle suburb of Sammamish, worshipping the NASL Sounders and feeling heartbroken when they folded in 1983. They'd actually spent their first two seasons playing at the aging Memorial Stadium facility where Hahnemann now stood in his crease, staring back at Steenkamp.

The possibility of a pro soccer career seemed remote to Hahnemann while he was starring at Newport High School in Bellevue, Washington, then helping SPU steamroll NCAA opponents from 1990 to '93. But then, all at once, the Sounders were revived in 1994 under their former NASL coach Alan Hinton and put together a juggernaut of local talent. Besides Hahnemann, they had SPU scoring stars Peter Hattrup and Jason Farrell in the midfield, Jason Dunn up top, and his brother James on the back line, not to mention forward Chance Fry, who'd signed with the original NASL Sounders right out of high school in Bellevue, and Peter Crook from the Seattle suburb of Kent.

"It was an unbelievable time for soccer to come out," Hahnemann said. "At the time, SPU was just dominating everybody and we had all these guys ready to go pro at the same time."

They also had old-time pros like original Sounder Bernie James and his fellow British countryman Neil Megson.

Indeed, by 1995 the second-year team under Hinton was beating most comers. They went 19–5 to finish second overall behind arch-nemesis Montreal, which was upset by Atlanta in the playoffs. That set up a best-of-three showdown between the Ruckus and the Sounders for the A-League title.

The Ruckus took the opener at Adams Stadium in Atlanta. The game was decided in the shootout round where, unlike penalty kicks, the shooter had to dribble the ball up on a keeper from the 35-yard line. "There was skill involved and at least the keeper had a chance," Hahnemann said. "Where on penalties, you're guessing which side to go to and there's not as much skill."

The Sounders were down but had the luxury of two final home games if they could square the series in Game 2.

And that they did, with local product Fry scoring twice and Jason Dunn adding late insurance for a 3–0 win in front of 4,626 ecstatic Memorial Stadium fans to set up a winner-take-all Game 3.

A season-high 5,115 fans attended the nailbiter finale. Atlanta opened the scoring and clung to their 1–0 lead until Farrell rocketed home the tying marker in the 81st minute to electrify the crowd and set the stage for another shootout round to decide a champion.

The Sounders scored a pair of shootout goals and were up 2–1 when Steenkamp—sixth in A-League scoring and a shootout master—had his turn against Hahnemann. If Steenkamp scored, the shootout would be extended. If he missed, the Sounders would have their first-ever title in any league.

Steenkamp moved the ball forward, but Hahnemann cut down his angle and made the stop. The Sounders were finally champions. Hahnemann raced toward the sideline and was immediately mobbed by fans.

"As a goalkeeper, of course I knew I was going to save it," Hahnemann said. "So then I saved it, and we won it. Then I ran out and there was Nate Daligcon and Todd Stauber—guys I'd played with at SPU—they were the first guys to get to me because they'd jumped out of the stands.

"The whole field erupted and everyone piled on to the field. It was awesome."

Hinton—who'd lost the 1982 Soccer Bowl with the previous Sounders incarnation—now had his first championship as a pro coach.

"The camaraderie on that team was very good and we had a lot of talent," Hinton said. "We could compete with just about anybody."

And they did again the following year, repeating as A-League champs in somewhat less dramatic fashion.

They finished third overall in a seven-team league but upset the Colorado Foxes in the best-of-three semifinal with a pair of road wins. In the newly formatted one-game final, against the Rochester Rhinos, the Sounders drew a huge crowd of 7,027 to Memorial Stadium, and once again their Pacific Northwest-laden roster prevailed.

Joey Leonetti, from Portland, Oregon, opened the scoring at the 25-minute mark. He then added insurance in the 85th minute. As they had the previous year, the jubilant fans stormed the pitch in celebration.

"It wasn't as big as it is today, so we were all pretty tight," Hahnemann said of the team. "We had, like, three guys on our whole office staff. So you become friends for life with all those guys."

Major League Soccer was starting up the following year and began draining away talent from the Sounders and other A-League teams. But Hahnemann, to this day, insists those Sounders could have played in MLS and done well.

"We were good," he said. "We were really good. When you think of Brendan James, Neil Megson, Billy Crook, and James Dunn—that was our back four," he said. "And it was as good as any MLS team. I guarantee you."

14 From Walmart to a New Life

Growing up in Communist Cuba, Osvaldo Alonso couldn't contemplate one day leaving a sports mark on a place like the Pacific Northwest. Just getting out of Cuba was his main preoccupation as his country's national team prepared to play in the 2007 CONCACAF Gold Cup.

Alonso began preparing. He started in Cuba's first two games at Giants stadium in East Rutherford, New Jersey, before flying to Houston to prepare for the next contest. He was out shopping with teammates when they headed into a Walmart. There, amid the shelves lined with groceries and products he'd never have access to back home, he simply walked out of the store.

"I was mentally prepared to do it," he said. "That day at the store, I said, 'This is the moment that I have to walk away.' And I walked away."

One block passed, then two. He stopped a passerby in the street.

"I asked him, 'Do you speak Spanish?'" Alonso said. "And he said 'yes,' he spoke Spanish."

Alonso explained what was happening, borrowed a phone, and called his friends in Miami. Then he hopped a bus for the ride across multiple states to Florida. He had with him only a backpack tote and light jacket. He was alone and worried but convinced in what he was doing.

"At the beginning, I was scared," he said. "I thought, at that moment, that I'd never see my family again. I knew I could never go back to Cuba. It was a scary moment for me."

Alonso trained with the Chivas USA team, then joined the Charleston Battery of the USL and played a full season there in 2008—getting named the league's top rookie. In 2009, the expansion Sounders aquired his rights.

Never did he dream things would go the way they have. Alonso is now the team's all-time leader in MLS games played and in total minutes. He scored a memorable goal against Chicago late in a 2–0 win that clinched the Sounders third straight U.S. Open Cup. In 2012, he was an All-Star named to the MLS Best XI for the first time.

By September 2016, he'd been named team captain. But something even more memorable happened. Alonso was finally allowed to have a visit by his father. They hadn't seen each other in eight years. Alonso's dad flew up to Seattle and saw Alonso at a Sounders game.

Nowadays, his parents live in Miami. But Alonso still has a brother and sister in Cuba. He is also now allowed to travel back there without consequence and has done so.

In early 2017, the Sounders returned to Charleston, South Carolina, for training camp. Alonso reflected on his life there nearly a decade earlier, living alone in an apartment with no friends except for teammates that occasionally dropped by and took him out. "When I came here I didn't go anywhere because I didn't speak English," he said with a laugh. "Now that we're here, we stay downtown and I can walk around a little bit and see more of it."

The beginning was tough for Alonso. But with the Sounders, the ending got better.

15 Sounders Lose 1977 and 1982 Soccer Bowls

For all of their North American Soccer League success, the Sounders kept running into one championship obstacle—the New York Cosmos. They were the equivalent of baseball's Yankees when it came to soccer, backed by a formidable payroll that could lure top talent from around the world.

And in both games, Italian star Giorgio Chinaglia would be the difference-maker that denied the Sounders their moment.

The 1977 final seemed almost like a home game, played in front of a mainly Pacific Northwest crowd of 35,548 fans at a packed Civic Stadium in Portland. Thousands of Sounders fans made the three-hour drive from Seattle and spurred their side to control play early on.

Sounders goalkeeper Tony Chursky remembers the game well. His team started off strong, but then disaster struck when Chursky played a ball and then prepared to boot it back upfield. As he was setting the ball down, Stevie Hunt of the Cosmos came out of nowhere, knocked it from Chursky's hands, and scored the game's opening goal. What most fans in the stadium didn't know was that Chursky was completely deaf in his left ear after a childhood bout with the mumps.

As he was playing the ball, he looked back toward his goal and couldn't see Hunt sneaking up behind him from his left. "It was actually my fullback, Mel Machin, who was screaming to me that [Hunt] was coming up behind me," Chursky said. "But because I was facing my goal, Mel was on my left and that's my deaf side. I didn't hear him at all."

Chursky also had an astigmatism in his left eye and some depth-perception issues that prevented him from noticing Hunt's blur until it was too late.

The Sounders did tie things up on a Tommy Ord goal minutes later and headed to halftime tied 1–1.

But 40 years later, the team's captain in that game, Adrian Webster, recalls that first half being a missed opportunity. "I can remember at halftime we were all a little bit disappointed that we weren't out in front," said Webster, known as "The Shadow" to Sounders fans. "We'd had a goal disallowed and then Tony made that error. At the time, I felt a little bit sorry for him but in typical Chursky style he went on to have a tremendous game. But I think those were little turning points."

Things stayed tied until the 78th minute, when Hunt took a throw-in and sent a cross to the box that Chinaglia headed home. And that would be enough to give the Cosmos the 2–1 victory in what turned out to be the final meaningful match of Brazilian star Pelé's career. He would retire following an exhibition game two months later.

"We thought we were good enough to win on the day, but sometimes it doesn't work out," Sounders defender Dave Gillett recalls.

Even more than his Sounders losing the game, Gillett feels the Cosmos victory was a lost opportunity for a league that ultimately failed because of runaway spending on name stars often past their prime.

"The message they sent—which I thought was the wrong message—was that you could buy a championship," Gillett said.

"Rather than you can get a bunch of average players, coach them better, and you can be successful without spending a whole lot of money."

While Webster was disappointed, he says the opportunity to play against Pelé and former Brazilian teammate Carlos Alberto ranked as a career highlight. The Sounders weren't even supposed to make the final that year, needing a string of upsets largely on the road to qualify.

"I think the pinnacle was the semifinal when we had 56,000 in the Kingdome," Webster recalled of a two-game series win over the Los Angeles Aztecs. "We'd gone to L.A., beaten them 3–1, and then came home and finished the job. It was just electric, the crowd. And I think that was always one of the highlights for me—the relationship with the fans. It was incredible."

But five years later, when the Sounders next made the Soccer Bowl, the league was already on a downward spiral.

Chinaglia and Alberto were still around for the Cosmos in 1982 when yet another upstart Sounders squad qualified for the championship game and the first rematch in Soccer Bowl history. This time, the game was played at Jack Murphy Stadium in San Diego, a cavernous venue of more than 52,000 seats where only 22,634 fans showed up. It was the smallest Soccer Bowl crowd ever.

Looking up at the stands that night, Sounders coach Alan Hinton today remembers feeling disappointed before the game had even begun.

"The game was in San Diego and it was one of the worst decisions ever by the North American Soccer League to take it there," Hinton said. "There were 20,000 people there if we were lucky and the game should have been a double-header. A game in New York would have sold out and a game in Seattle would have sold out. It was the worst decision ever."

The 1982 Sounders had finished 37 points behind the league-leading Cosmos during the regular season. New York, meanwhile, had won the title in 1977, 1978, and 1980 before losing in 1981 to the Chicago Sting. Now, out to retake their throne, they'd finished 23–9 and were clearly the class of the league.

Yet just as they had five years earlier, it was the Sounders that controlled the early parts of their championship match. Jeff Stock nearly scored in the 15th minute and then Steve Daley in the 29th.

"You could see it in their eyes," Stock said. "They knew what they were up against with our team and they didn't want any part of it. We were all over them."

Hinton agrees. "We actually pummeled them for the first 20 minutes, should have gone ahead. We outplayed them. But in the end, they found a way to win."

Chinaglia scored the game's only goal in the 31st minute, on a play started by Alberto. After taking a pass from midfielder Julio Cesar Romero, Chinaglia turned and unleashed a right-footed kick that sailed past goalkeeper Paul Hammond.

The Cosmos took over the game after that, with Chinaglia ultimately collecting the MVP award to match a previous one from the 1980 Soccer Bowl.

"It was a very good experience," Hinton said. "I was disappointed because I like to win. I like to say, [then-coach] Jimmy Gabriel got beat in a close one in 1977, then I got beat in 1982. And that's why I like to call [current Sounders coach] Brian Schmetzer 'Sir Brian,' because Jimmy Gabriel and I didn't win it. We don't qualify for 'Sir.'"

But looking back, Hinton says those two Soccer Bowl appearances "mean more because of what's happened since with this club. That's why I'm so protective of the former players. They did contribute so much to the importance of the club today. It's a brand…a very positive brand. And now, the ownership and players have taken it to another level."

16 Garth Lagerwey Changes Team's Approach

Garth Lagerwey the player didn't look like anybody's idea of a general manager. With a bandana wrapped around his head, the scowling, onetime goalkeeper looked more like an *Easy Rider* extra than a suit-and-tie boardroom member.

But the former Duke University undergrad who'd ultimately construct the Sounders team that won the franchise's first championship had always excelled in the classroom. And when his five-year MLS playing career ended with the Miami Fusion in 2000, he immediately enrolled at Georgetown University Law School. By 2004, he had earned his degree and been hired by the prestigious Latham & Watkins firm to work on contract law in their Washington, D.C., office. For the next three years, he worked in a variety of divisions, including mergers and acquisitions.

It was there, in 2007, that Lagerwey was called on to assist Dave Checketts, founder and chairman of SCP Worldwide, in acquiring a minority share of the St. Louis Blues NHL team. For several months, Lagerwey and Checketts worked closely together until the deal went through. The two men had something else in common: Checketts just happened to be the majority owner of the Real Salt Lake MLS franchise—which had fired its coach and general manager that summer.

The timing proved fortuitous. Once the Blues purchase went through, Checketts told Lagerwey he needed a GM for his soccer team and wanted him to throw his hat in the ring.

"Life is luck and timing," Lagerwey said.

During a round of interviews for the Salt Lake job, Lagerwey got called in for a meeting with the Latham law firm's longtime managing partner, Eric Bernthal. Latham was known as a firm that ran its lawyers ragged but also rewarded them for success and expected loyalty in return. Lagerwey worried he was about to be fired for considering a job offer elsewhere.

"I go to his office and I'll never forget it," Lagerwey said. "He goes to me, 'What are you doing?' I told him I had an opportunity in sports and it's what my background is. And he said, 'Well, what is it? General counsel?' And I said no, it's not just to be a lawyer. It's like general manager.'

"And he says, 'You mean, like pick the players?' And I'm like, 'Yeah, a real general manager.'

"And he's like, 'Okay, I'll make you a deal. You let me negotiate your contract for you and in exchange, I'll use you on every piece of recruitment literature we use.'"

Lagerwey wound up getting the Salt Lake job. Two years later, in 2009, his team won the MLS Cup in an upset over the Los Angeles Galaxy. Coincidentally, the title match was played at Qwest Field, where Lagerwey's next career move would take him five years later.

By the 2014 offseason, the Sounders were still reeling from being knocked out of the playoffs by the Galaxy after winning the Supporters' Shield for the best regular season record. The Sounders that year had also begun distancing themselves from the Seahawks business operations and venturing out on their own.

Sounders owner Adrian Hanauer had served as the team's GM since its inception. But now, having moved from minority owner into a managing partner role with the team, he knew his attentions were needed elsewhere.

"I knew we were sort of heading to this transition of running our own business operations," Hanauer said. "And I knew that was probably where I needed to spend more of my energy to make sure that went smoothly."

It was tough for Hanauer, who loves soccer, its tactics, and camaraderie. The team's Alliance Council of fans thought he was doing a good job, having reconfirmed him as GM by a 96 percent vote of support. But he put in a call to Lagerwey, who took the job.

Lagerwey was ready for a new challenge in a bigger soccer market. He spent much of 2015 evaluating what the Sounders had and shoring up their second division S2 team and youth academy. He sensed the Sounders were getting older and needed more depth, but there were some delicate politics required. After all, they'd also just enjoyed their best regular season ever.

"We were too old and I knew it wasn't sustainable," Lagerwey said. "But keep in mind coming in, in 2014, the Sounders had won the double: the U.S. Open Cup and the Supporters' Shield and they'd made the conference final. So sometimes, if it isn't broke, you can't really fix it."

Instead of making wholesale changes, he simply let the 2015 season play itself out and reveal the shortcomings he'd already sensed were there.

"We had rough patches during the 2015 season and my personal opinion was that if we lost either Clint [Dempsey] or Oba [Martins], we fell apart," he said. "We needed to systemize how we played and acquired players. We needed to systemize our depth chart and our profiles at each position so that if any player went down, we knew their replacement's role within the system and could use them to replace the injured player."

The surprising departure of Martins for the Chinese Super League on the eve of the 2016 season also proved fortuitous. It created an opening for the team to use rookie Jordan Morris up top and freed up designated player money Lagerwey would use that year to acquire Uruguayan playmaker Nicolas Lodeiro from the Boca Juniors in Argentina.

All of a sudden, the Sounders' youth movement was underway. And it would result in a transition from last-place team midway through 2016 into an MLS Cup champion before the season was over.

The youth movement continued just days after the Philip Anschutz trophy was hoisted. Lagerwey would either move or allow 13 veterans to leave before the 2017 season kicked off, replacing them with younger players. But it wasn't all youth. He also added veteran striker Will Bruin from Houston and Swedish midfielder Gustav Svensson from the Chinese Super League. Each would make a case for themselves as the team's MVP throughout the campaign. Then, midway through the season, he bolstered the lineup by adding right back Kelvin Leerdam from The Netherlands and midfielder Victor Rodriguez from Spain. And by December, the team found itself back in the MLS Cup final for a rematch with Toronto FC.

For Hanauer, who still stands on the sidelines at team practices, the temptation to second guess Lagerwey prior to the 2016 championship was always there. By July of that year, the team had sunk to its lowest depths ever and fired longtime head coach Sigi Schmid.

"I try to be another voice, but not an overpowering voice," Hanauer said.

17 Sounders Make It to Champions League Semifinal

Sounders defender Djimi Traore had plenty of experience playing big-time soccer matches on a huge stage. He'd been in the starting lineup for English Premier League powerhouse Liverpool when they won the UEFA Champions League final in 2004–05 against AC Milan on penalty kicks after overcoming a 3–0 deficit.

So French-born Traore, his career winding down after a decade in Europe, wasn't all that fazed in March 2013 when his new Sounders team faced their own two-goal aggregate deficit in the second leg of a CONCACAF Champions League quarterfinal series against Tigres UNAL of Mexico. No MLS team had eliminated a Mexican opponent since the Champions League format was revised in 2008, and Tigres had already won the opening leg of the series 1–0 in Mexico.

Now playing the second leg at CenturyLink Field, they'd scored in the 23rd minute to take a 1–0 lead and put the Sounders two down on aggregate heading into halftime.

There are three ways for MLS teams to qualify for CONCACAF Champions League play: win a U.S. Open Cup, make the MLS Cup final, or win a Supporters' Shield. The Sounders have qualified via all three routes but have typically experienced a rather short exit from the tournament of the top teams from North and Central America as well as the Caribbean.

That changed in 2013. They'd qualified by virtue of their third consecutive U.S. Open Cup title in 2011, then ran the table in Group play against teams from Honduras and Trinidad & Tobago. That put them in the path of Tigres, leaders of the Liga MX at the time.

By halftime of their second game, the Sounders weren't at all pleased with themselves. The Tigres had actually brought over a "B" squad of sorts with a small roster and only three holdover players from the first leg game. But since they now led 2–0 on aggregate, the Sounders, just like Traore's former Liverpool team against Milan years earlier, now needed to score at least three times.

Traore listened in the locker room as Sounders coach Sigi Schmid gave the team an earful.

"I wasn't too happy with how we played in the first half," Schmid would tell reporters later. "I wasn't too happy in terms of some individual efforts, which we sort of identified at halftime very directly, but we also said, 'This is how we're going to play in the second half. This is what I need.' I thought you saw definitely Steve Zakuani step up in the second half. I think DeAndre [Yedlin] definitely stepped up. We said, 'Three goals is very possible. Three goals is not impossible for us in the second half. Let's score three goals; let's go do it.'"

It helped that the Sounders had caught a break just before halftime when Manuel Viniegra was sent off with his second yellow card. That meant the Sounders would play one man up and Schmid wanted them to seize the moment, not roll over because they were convinced they couldn't beat a Mexican squad.

"He was telling us, 'Don't give up on the game,' and, 'It's only the second half and we can still come back,'" Traore said.

Traore could feel the butterflies inside, just as he had pregame. Not because he felt a comeback was unlikely—he knew better. But he'd wanted to make a good first impression on his new team and fans and felt he hadn't quite done it to that point.

That would soon change.

Playing a man up, the Sounders tied the score in the 54th minute when DeAndre Yedlin—also playing his first match for the Sounders—fired a partially deflected laser from 35 yards out to beat goalkeeper Jorge Diaz de Leon.

"To be honest, it was a massive lift when he scored that goal," Traore said. "We started to gain confidence. And after that, a lot of things happened."

But the Sounders needed more goals in a hurry. They got one quickly from Traore, who put them ahead to stay with a 60th minute cannon blast from distance that rocketed just underneath the crossbar. The crowd erupted and the Sounders went wild as well, mobbing Traore in celebration.

"I think it was a great strike," Traore said, adding he'd hit the ball about as hard as he possibly could. "But more importantly, it really helped us out. And that was big for me. It was my first game at CenturyLink and there's pressure on you. The fans expect a lot of things. It was the first time they'd seen me play live. And of course, that goal made my life easier."

Still, his goal merely tied the aggregate series 2–2. And if the score held, the Tigres would advance by virtue of their away goal. The Sounders kept on pressing and, with 15 minutes left in regulation, Eddie Johnson found himself sprinting for a Steve Zakuani ball down the left side. Johnson got behind the defenders, reached the ball at a near impossible angle, and then somehow tucked it short side behind keeper de Leon.

"In the first half I got in the same position and I tried to shoot it across to the back post," Johnson would later tell reporters of how he fooled de Leon into committing early. "I looked at the replay and saw he leans and cheats a little bit. I was able to sneak it in near post."

The Sounders held on from there for what was arguably the greatest comeback in their history up to that point. The stunning victory enabled the Sounders to advance within four games of winning the tournament—something no MLS team had managed in a decade.

"It's amazing," Yedlin told reporters afterward. "It is a story you can pass on to your kids and grandkids and it makes the city proud. It's good for us."

Although the Sounders would ultimately lose to another Mexican side, Santos Laguna, in the semifinal, they'd proven to themselves they could match up against a top international club.

Traore agreed with Yedlin about the impact of the victory on the franchise. "It was massive," Traore said. "When you think about it, Clint Dempsey wasn't there yet, Oba [Martins] was there but he didn't play in that game. And for the club, it was huge because they didn't have a whole bunch of trophies. To beat a Mexican club like that was very important."

18 Stefan Frei Makes "The Save"

Stefan Frei had no idea the defining moment of his career had just happened. On a frigid night at BMO Field in Toronto, the Sounders were desperately staving off Toronto FC in a scoreless 2016 MLS Cup final. As the last minutes of extra time ticked away, Frei managed to get his left hand on a Jozy Altidore header that appeared certain to find the back of the net.

"Even after I got to it, I thought that it was nothing," Frei said. "The rest of the stadium saw a chance denied and there was a bit of an 'oooohhh!'"

But it wasn't until a few moments later that Frei realized the save was much bigger than he'd initially suspected. One of his teammates was fouled further up the field, leading to a delay in the action and a chance for the stadium's video replay board to show Frei's save once more.

"They showed a replay of it and you could hear the entire stadium just go, 'Ugh!'" Frei said. "And I looked over to the bench and I see [assistant] Djimi Traore vigorously high-fiving our keeper coach. And I said, 'Oh, that's probably a good sign.'

"And then they showed it again and I felt that the stadium was very deflated after that. Which is another good sign that it was somewhat of a big moment."

Indeed it was, as the Sounders had posed no offensive threat of their own all game. They became the first MLS Cup champion to fail to register even a single shot on net. But when the penalty kick round came, Roman Torres did indeed put the ball away to secure the first ever Sounders championship, cementing Frei's save in MLS Cup lore.

Sounders goalkeeper Stefan Frei got the best of Toronto FC and forward Jozy Altidore throughout an iconic 2016 MLS Cup performance.
(USA Today Sports Images)

The defining moment of Frei's career began innocently enough. Toronto FC's Tosaint Ricketts had sprinted to a ball near the endline, keeping it in play and lobbing a rather innocent-looking cross to the box. But nothing is ever innocent with only minutes to play in a scoreless final. Players on both sides were frozen and fatigued, yet Altidore found enough leg strength to leap up and redirect the ball toward the net.

"It looked like it was going to go over him. It wasn't the best of crosses," Frei said. "But he made a solid effort for it. And the fact that he was able to almost kill it, or dampen it a little bit to get it down again, was very impressive."

The fact Altidore could not get a full thrust into his header also helped buy Frei "a split second more" to get into the proper position. "You're taught to try to get into the middle as much as you can and then react. It can go left, it can go right. You're hoping it can go right because your momentum carries you there."

But the ball went left.

Frei had to re-adjust, helped by the header being somewhat softly struck. He focused on moving his feet in the most efficient way possible, using a cross step to head left and then one more to load up for a spring off his left foot. He almost stumbled a bit. But he got his left hand up just high enough to reach backward and redirect the ball out of harm's way.

"I always preferred when I can to use my lower hand," he said. "I know the rule is to try to use your top hand because there's less distance to the ball. But I think that with the lower hand you get more control and that was particularly crucial on that play.

"Had I used my right hand, I wouldn't have been able to arch it behind my body as much as my left."

The rest is history. Frei's save was captured in an iconic shot by *Seattle Times* photographer Lindsey Wasson. Frei has since seen fans with tattoos of the photographic image on their bodies and wearing it on T-shirts. Like Wasson, he's never received a dime for any sales of the image.

"I saw there were squabbles over who has rights to it and to make prints and this and that," he said. "I find it interesting that nobody ever asked the object of it about any of this, but I'm okay with that."

After all, the save garnered him the game MVP award, an MLS Cup ring, and an immortal moment nobody could take away.

19 The Greatest Sounders Game Ever

Things were looking desperate for the Sounders on a sweltering night in Fort Lauderdale. Their dream 1982 season in the North American Soccer League was on the verge of ending, down 3–2 to the hometown Strikers with less than a minute to play and the ball deep in their end.

At stake was a trip to that year's Soccer Bowl in San Diego. The Sounders had already been stunned 2–0 at the Kingdome in the opener of the best-of-three series. Now in a wild second game being televised nationally on USA Network, the Sounders had seen the lead change three times in the second half and not in their favor.

But the final act of what many consider the greatest game the Sounders have ever played was about to take place. Featuring heavily in it would be Roger Davies, the British midfielder and arguably the first true superstar the Sounders ever had. Davies had been urged over to the Sounders from England in 1980 by new head coach Alan Hinton—his former Derby County teammate who'd assisted on his first career goal years earlier—and responded by scoring a league record 25 times to earn NASL Most Valuable Player honors.

Now, two years later, his skills diminishing at age 31, Davies had been reduced to coming off the bench late. His team had entered that muggy September 8, 1982, night at Lockhart Stadium a confident bunch, though many Sounders fans had their doubts.

The Strikers, led by top-scorers Brian Kidd, Branko Segota, and Bernd Holzenbein, had gone 18–14 overall but were 12–4 at home in front of their rabid Striker Likers supporters. Lockhart was a small, cramped venue and it felt as if the fans were literally on top of the players. On this night, even with the start time pushed back to 8:00 PM to accommodate the TV broadcast, it was 88 degrees at kickoff with the humidity making it feel like triple digits.

As if that wasn't enough, the charged-up crowd of 15,196 was bringing even more heat, smelling blood after the Strikers' surprising win in Game 1. The Sounders had started the season just 3–9 but had gone 15–5 the rest of the way and been nearly unbeatable at home.

Now their armor had been pierced.

Sounders defender Jeff Stock remembers heading into a hot and "hostile" environment, where the Strikers had been talking things up for the hometown fans. "They were talking smack," Stock said. "They were already talking about how they were going to be in the final."

And that more than anything, he said, ticked off the Sounders. Despite the heat, the crowd and the series deficit, they just collectively thought, "There was no way we were ever going to lose this game."

The teams played a tense, scoreless first half in which Strikers scoring leader Kidd was injured in the 17th minute and replaced up top by Yugoslavian-born, Canadian-raised Segota. It would be the 21-year-old Segota who finally opened the scoring in the 54th minute, sending the stadium into a frenzy.

But that was only the beginning of a wild 35 minutes to come. Hinton waited until the 65th minute to substitute Davies in along with Victoria-born center back Ian Bridge to generate some late-game offense. And that's exactly what happened. The Sounders stunned the crowd by scoring twice in fewer than four minutes to take the lead, with Peter Ward and Davies striking in the 69th and 73rd minutes.

But with just more than 10 minutes to play, Holzenbein tied it 2–2 and then teamed up with Segota to feed Ray Hudson for the go-ahead goal just 86 seconds later.

Once again, the stadium was in a frenzy. The hometown Strikers had to kill off eight more minutes and they'd be off to the second Soccer Bowl in team history.

"They were getting champagne bottles ready in their locker room with five minutes to go," Stock said. "But we were like, 'Are you kidding me? How are we even behind in this game? We never gave up.'"

As the clock ticked down to one minute remaining, the crowd rose to its feet, urging the team on. The ball was played back to Sounders keeper Paul Hammond. Center back Bridge was by now all the way up the field, as he'd been for most of the final minutes.

"When you're playing your center back that far up, things must be pretty desperate," Stock said. "But we never doubted we could do it."

What happened next has gone down in Sounders lore. "I just felt like something was going to happen," Sounders coach Hinton said. "It was only a feeling. But we never quit."

Hammond booted the ball much of the length of the field and it somehow went straight to Bridge, who flicked it to Ward along the left flank.

"What would have happened if their defender would have headed it?" Hinton said. "We lose the game."

Instead, Ward now moved the ball up to the edge of the box and then flung what Hinton called "a beautiful cross" to an onward-sprinting Davies, who arrived just as the ball got there. Davies unleashed a snap-header past helpless keeper Jan van Beveren to the near post.

The Sounders screamed with delight, an ecstatic Davies pumping his left arm in triumph in what would ultimately be his final goal for the team. The stunned Strikers collapsed to their knees, knowing a championship berth had just been snatched away. Van Beveran sat in his crease, head between his hands.

Only 43 seconds remained on the clock.

"It was quite unbelievable," Hinton said. "I've described it as, 'Some things that are not going to happen just did.'"

Stock remembers barely being able to move as he raced over to Davies to celebrate. "I must have lost eight pounds that night," he said. "We left our guts out on that field the final 10 minutes."

But as depleted as the Sounders felt, the Strikers were crushed. In the stands, the Striker Likers were deathly silent, so much so that the Sounders' whooping and hollering could be heard above the din. But the game wasn't over yet. The Sounders, given new life, carried that momentum into sudden death overtime when, just four minutes in, Ward put another cross over from the left side that Davies again struck with a header. The ball might have found its way in on its own. But just in case, Kenny Hibbitt was there at the goalmouth to head it home for one of the easiest scores of his career.

The Sounders erupted in celebration, storming the field after their 4–3 victory. The shocked home fans trudged slowly to the exit, barely comprehending the turn of events.

"Everybody went nuts," Hinton said. "I said to Peter Ward after the game, 'I've never thought you were a great crosser of the ball. But today, you proved you were one of the greatest crossers of all time.'"

The emotion of the night had taken a toll on both sides, with the exhaustion evident in their faces. It would carry over to two days later, when they played a far less intense Game 3 in front of more than 28,000 fans at the Kingdome. Scoreless after regulation, Hibbitt would add another sudden death goal—this one from distance—to propel the Sounders to their second Soccer Bowl.

Although the Sounders would lose the Soccer Bowl to the New York Cosmos, the excitement of their playoff run—especially the thrilling Game 2 semifinal—would remain etched in the minds of fans for decades to come. And when naming the game that's stood out above the rest, those familiar with Pacific Northwest soccer will often point to that night when Davies came off the bench for one last hurrah.

Davies was traded that offseason to—of all teams—the Strikers. He'd play out 1983 in Fort Lauderdale and then head back to England for several lower-tier seasons before retiring in 1987.

But the contributions by Davies, Hibbitt, Ward, and others that hot night in Florida have never been forgotten by those who witnessed it. Decades later, Stock remembers it as if it were yesterday.

"It was just great players doing great things."

20 Talk to Players at Practice

Sounders fan Martin Kastner Jr. has figured out something that many are still not aware of—that if you show up to the team's training facility at the Starfire complex in suburban Tukwila, Washington, it's fairly easy to meet and talk to the players. In fact, it's far easier than doing it at MLB spring training facilities or NFL training camps, where hundreds of screaming fans usually line cordoned-off security barriers competing for player attention.

Things at Starfire are about as informal as it gets. The club does have signs at an entryway to the practice pitch beyond which only players and staff can pass. And there is sometimes a temporary steel barrier lining the walkway out to the parking lot for when players come off the pitch and head for the dressing room.

But the later into the season it gets—with children done with summer holidays and back in school—there can sometimes be only a dozen or so fans at each workout. The Sounders usually start weekday workouts at 10:30 AM and come off the field about noon. Also, on bad weather days, there might be only two or three fans watching. One of the good things about the Sounders is they encourage players to interact with the fanbase whenever possible.

So if you want to meet Clint Dempsey, Jordan Morris, or Stefan Frei, especially on a cool, damp day, chances are you can have him all to yourself. Kastner, 21, a University of Washington communications major, knows this very well, having chatted up all of the players over the past couple of seasons.

"A lot of fans that come out here like to get a lot of autographs," Kastner said. "But I'm not an autograph savvy person. The thing with autographs is, you kind of have a piece of the memory but it's not a genuine memory.

"Having a conversation is a very good memory to have."

Kastner said no Sounders player has ever brushed him off. Nor has the team's staff or security chief, who is present at every practice to make sure fans behave and don't get too aggressive with players. But generally, the security chief will keep his distance and let fans engage—especially a known commodity like Kastner, whom every player and coach has seen and spoken with before. They know he isn't a professional autograph seeker. Kastner says the conversations with players can vary.

"We talk about what's going on, or I'll compliment them on an impressive goal," he said. "We don't really discuss too much about tactics."

On this particular day, only 24 hours before the Sounders play in a critical 2017 Western Conference semifinal match against Houston, Kastner has only two other fans competing with him for player attention. Kastner tries to make it down once per week, but it sometimes means driving an hour in morning traffic from his home near Graham, Washington. So far, he's yet to be disappointed by any trip.

"I wanted to connect with this team," he said. "I've really enjoyed this."

21 A Red Card Wedding with No Bouquet

Back before the Sounders and Cascadia rivals the Portland Timbers had each won an MLS Cup, the Lamar Hunt U.S. Open Cup took on added significance for the franchises. By 2015, with the Timbers only months from their first MLS Cup title, they met the Sounders on June 16 in the tournament's fourth round at Starfire Stadium.

The significance of the U.S. Open Cup games then, compared to now, was such that both sides featured much of their regular lineups rather than filling them with prospects and bench players. Portland also wanted to jumpstart its season after a difficult opening, while the Sounders had never lost a U.S. Open Cup match at Starfire. Since the Sounders and Timbers already didn't like each other, those regulars meant that this had the makings of a powder keg even before Major League Soccer allowed referee Daniel Radford to work the match.

By the time the night was done, what became known as the "Red Card Wedding" would go down as a dark moment in Sounders history and the professional career of U.S. soccer legend Clint Dempsey.

Radford to that point had been just a fourth referee in MLS games. The Sounders had even argued beforehand that he shouldn't be assigned to the game. But the league defended using him, saying its officials had to be tested in bigger matches at some point. Radford had already shown a penchant for being quick to card players and would quite memorably continue that trend on this particular night.

The dimly lit, poor quality field, surrounded by 4,000 fans, made for a confined, hostile environment for the visiting Timbers. An element of confusion was thrown in since the Timbers were wearing their dark green home uniforms while the Sounders were dressed in black. With the early evening sun starting to set, it made the jerseys appear identical. Players could barely tell who was on their side. The Sounders eventually changed into their white kits at halftime.

From kickoff, referee Radford seemed to be micromanaging the game. Instead of setting a disciplinary tone, he seemed more preoccupied with accurately marking the location of throw-ins and other secondary aspects.

The Sounders took two yellow cards in the first half, one of them by right back Brad Evans that would come back to haunt him later on. The teams were scoreless at halftime, but Diego Valeri's goal in the 48th minute gave Portland a 1–0 lead. Then in the 69th minute, fireworks erupted when Evans tried to kick away at a ball that a Portland player had fallen on top of. Several kicks later, Radford blew the play dead and reached for a second yellow card for Evans—ending his night with an automatic ejection.

More than two years later, Dempsey, who was on the bench as a substitute at the time, remembers the Evans ejection as the point where his blood started to boil. "I didn't agree with it," he said.

The entire Sounders sideline was incensed. As Evans walked off the field, he dismissively waved his arm as if to say the call was a joke. The fans were irate and the game's tension ratcheted up. The Sounders hadn't wanted to use Dempsey much, if at all, preferring to save him for the MLS season. But not wanting to lose at home to its archrival, the Sounders put Dempsey in at the 71st minute and Obafemi Martins equalized off a cornerkick while shorthanded in the 78th to make it 1–1.

Just moments later, Martins fell to the turf and had to be carted off on a stretcher. As the Sounders had used all three substitutions already, they were now down two men the rest of the way. Dempsey admits now that the Martins injury, on top of the Evans red card, left him increasingly frustrated and set the stage for what was to happen next.

"That ref has a history of giving out a lot of cards," Dempsey said. "And for me, I think that there are ways you can manage the game without having to do that. If you set the tone early, then you don't have those types of issues."

The game went to overtime, where Rodney Wallace scored off a rebound in the 100th minute to put Portland up 2–1.

At that point, the game got out of hand. Michael Azira was given a straight red card 10 minutes later for elbowing Gaston Fernandez in the face. Azira was typically a mild-mannered sort and the play looked somewhat inadvertent, but Radford was having none of it. Dempsey took exception and got in the referee's face, berating Radford until he was given a yellow card. That set Dempsey off completely. He circled around the pack and grabbed Radford's notebook out of his pocket while the referee was distracted. Dempsey proceeded to tear the notebook to pieces and fling it to the pitch. By then, Radford realized what had happened and pulled out a red card for Dempsey, as well.

Dempsey now admits he just "lost it" and did the first thing that came to mind in grabbing the notebook. "You have to hold yourself to a higher standard."

The fans went ballistic and so did Dempsey, who kept circling around, trying to get at Radford as Tyrone Mears, Chad Marshall, and even some Timbers players tried to pull him away from the official. Finally, as Dempsey started walking off the field, he made a dramatic hand-clapping gesture in the face of an assistant referee as he passed him.

Fans pelted the pitch with debris. Somebody even tossed an empty trash can into the back of the end zone that remained there after play resumed. Sounders coach Sigi Schmid was so disgusted he headed down the field toward a corner flag and watched the remainder of the match from there. Afterward, he told reporters,

"I didn't want to get thrown out, so I just walked away from the bench because I was maybe going to choke a referee. I figured I'd walk away before I did something stupid."

The Sounders, now down to just seven men versus Portland's 11, gave up a third goal in the 116th minute and suffered a 3–1 defeat.

The bigger tally was the three red cards to the Sounders and a possible suspension for Dempsey. The question was how MLS would view what the Professional Referees Association was calling "referee assault" and "abuse" for Dempsey allegedly having threatened Radford.

MLS suspended Dempsey for only three games, which the referees' association denounced as a "step backward" for the league. Dempsey was also fined $20,000 and banned from the U.S. Open Cup for at least two years or six matches. The referees' association was further upset that Schmid wasn't disciplined for his postgame comments that appeared to threaten an official, even if made in a somewhat joking manner.

More than two years later, Dempsey isn't proud of what happened. "Looking back on it, obviously you would go back and change it," he said. "But what happened, happened. You live and you learn. That's what life is. Everybody's always trying to live and learn. I learned from it."

22 Brian Schmetzer: Four Decades of Work Ethic from Player to Coach

Brian Schmetzer learned early on the value of a strong work ethic. His German immigrant parents had run a sporting goods shop in the Lake City neighborhood of Seattle and insisted their son help out. Schmetzer's father, Walter, was also always tinkering with various handyman projects in the back of their home, and his son would do what he could to help and learn how to work with tools.

Walter had also played professional soccer in Germany's lower divisions, and he instilled a love for the game in his son, starting up the Lake City Hawks youth team. It was while a teenage Schmetzer, then still attending Nathan Hale High School, was playing a game that newly minted Sounders coach Alan Hinton spotted him from the stands. Hinton was scouting another player but liked the strong technical skills Schmetzer had spent hours honing with his neighborhood friends.

Schmetzer was immediately signed by Hinton. However, since Schmetzer was only 17 at the time, it was his parents who had to ink the contract. Thus, Schmetzer's 11-year pro playing career began as a reservist with Hinton's team. He played indoor for the Sounders that winter, then in the Trans-Atlantic Challenge Cup, making his outdoor pro debut against Celtic as a late-match substitute.

Head coach Brian Schmetzer has carried the historical load—and the hardware—of Seattle professional soccer through multiple incarnations of the Sounders franchise.

It wasn't until 1982 that Schmetzer saw his first NASL action, playing in six games. By 1983, he was a regular and scored his lone NASL goal in a 2–0 win on June 25, 1983, against the San Diego Sockers at Jack Murphy Stadium.

"I was a very average player that was able to help his team in some of the smaller ways," Schmetzer said.

He moved on to the Tulsa Roughnecks in 1984 after the Sounders folded. But the league itself collapsed after that season and Schmetzer would spend most of his remaining career playing indoors. During this time, he kept watching and learning more about the game's strategies and tactics.

"I was always thinking the game through, trying to figure out different ways of doing things," Schmetzer said. "Because my one gift when I was much younger and we were playing outdoors was that I could run all day. I'd go up and down and up and down. I could run. I didn't have a God-given talent of blazing speed and I wasn't a big guy, so, I had to do something to keep my job. It was survival."

In the late 1980s, he was both a midfielder and assistant coach for the indoor soccer Tacoma Stars.

By 1991, he decided to call it quits. After playing indoor soccer for the St. Louis Storm that year, he retired and moved his family from Missouri back up to Seattle where he started working in construction.

"All that time spent helping my father out taught me to be pretty handy," he said. "And I had no choice. Playing soccer professionally wasn't going to be enough. I had to do other work."

And that he did for the next three years until the Sounders were revived as an A-League team in 1994. Schmetzer was talked out of retirement by his former NASL coach Hinton and spent the 1994 season with the team.

Later, Schmetzer played the 1995 indoor season with the Seattle SeaDogs at age 32 when the team drafted him, then moved into coaching full-time as an assistant with them in 1996.

Schmetzer remained in coaching with various local teams until Adrian Hanauer became managing partner of the Sounders' A-League franchise.

One of the first people he interviewed for the team's vacant coaching position in late 2002 was Schmetzer.

"He was the guy in the area everybody was telling me I had to go get," Hanauer said.

Schmetzer guided the Sounders to a 23–4–1 record his initial 2002 season and was named the league's coach of the year. The Sounders lost the USL final to Montreal in 2004 but then won the championship in 2005 and 2007.

"I was always proud of the fact that those players worked," Schmetzer said. "Even back then, you look at those teams and they never quit. They never gave up. They always had an honest effort. Those are all still hallmarks I'd like to keep with this team. We don't quit. We try and win trophies, we try and win every game. There are some similarities there."

After the Sounders were awarded an MLS franchise late in 2007, Hanauer kept Schmetzer on a short list of coaching candidates. After the job went to the higher profile Sigi Schmid, Schmetzer was hired on as his assistant. And when Schmid was ultimately fired in July 2016, Hanauer knew he needed to look no further for his replacement.

"I had a comfort level with Brian where I knew what his thought process was on things," Hanauer said. "We didn't need this long learning curve to get to know one another and where we were as a franchise."

Indeed, Schmetzer knew the team's legacy better than most. He set about trying to instill that throughout the organization, reinforcing the importance of a strong work ethic to achieve results. That he did, watching as the Sounders rallied from ninth place to make the playoffs on the season's final day, then win the organization's first MLS Cup on a Roman Torres shootout goal.

"What makes Brian so special is the way he communicates with the players," former coach Hinton said. "I'm very proud of what he's managed to do for all of these years. And now look at him. He's accomplished something none of us were able to do as coaches. He's won a championship at the top level."

Getting It Done

For Sounders veterans like Clint Dempsey, Will Bruin, Chad Marshall, and Stefan Frei, their locker room had added tension the final night of November 2017 because of the unassailable truth before them—they could only blow it from here.

Outside, more than 45,000 fans awaited them at CenturyLink Field for the second leg of their Western Conference championship against the Houston Dynamo. The Sounders had beaten the Dynamo 2–0 in Houston and thus owned two critical road goals in a series to be decided on aggregate.

In other words, they could only blow it from here.

They'd heard the stats about how no team had ever blown a two-goal lead in the conference final after opening with a road win. About how only three teams in Major League Soccer history had overcome even a one-goal conference final deficit after losing the first game at home.

Houston had never won at CenturyLink Field. Hadn't even scored there since March 2011, back when Bruin was a rookie with them. The Sounders hadn't yielded a goal in five consecutive games and an MLS record 557 playoff minutes.

They all knew the truth. They could only blow it from here.

And in sports, sometimes, the hardest thing can be getting the job done when everybody on the planet expects you to do it. But that's what champions do and on this night, with a return trip to Toronto for an MLS Cup rematch against the Reds at stake, the Sounders went out and got it done.

"It was professional," Frei said afterward. "Very professional."

The Sounders, almost surgically, dismantled their opponent with pinpoint passing and textbook finishing. It was an artistic display, starting with Bruin's terrific flick to send in Victor Rodriguez alone for the game's opening goal just 23 minutes in.

The stadium exploded. The Dynamo could have made things interesting had they scored first, reviving the Sounders' worst fears about blowing a series everyone assumed they'd already won.

A two-goal lead in an aggregate series is hardly insurmountable. But a three-goal gap? Not against this Sounders team at home—and everybody in the stadium knew it.

The rest of the night was a celebration of where the Sounders had been and where they were headed. Repeat trips to the championship game are increasingly rare in any sport. The difference between the Sounders doing that and getting knocked out in the semifinal one year after winning it all was infinite.

Rather than take the rest of the night off, they instead kept pouring it on. Any relief they felt at Rodriguez widening the gap was used to enhance their focus and continue their jaw-dropping creativity on attack.

"You don't think about it," Bruin would say about the team's composed state. "You just try things."

It was possibly the finest display of soccer the Sounders had produced during their two-season run at the top. Joevin Jones would feed Dempsey with a perfect pass at the goalmouth that was converted by Deuce for a 2–0 lead in the 57th minute. Then in the 72nd minute, Bruin raced after a good ball by Harry Shipp, then went in alone and scored to make it 3--0.

It could have been 5–0 or 6–0. But it didn't matter. The Sounders were back in the MLS Cup final and had given their devoted hometown fans the chance to celebrate and hoist the conference championship trophy with them in a lengthy on-field celebration.

Sounders coach Brian Schmetzer, in his first full season as head coach, watched with emotion. He knew he had just guided the Sounders back to the title game. There would be no further talk about his inheriting a talented squad from the fired Sigi Schmid the prior year. The 2017 version had a plethora of new faces all over the field.

As a USL coach, Schmetzer had won a title with the Sounders in 2005 and 2007. But in 2006, the team had come apart because Schmetzer felt he hadn't done enough work preparing them for what life after a championship could feel like.

From the first day of training camp, just weeks after his team's 2016 MLS Cup win, he'd been urging them to leave the past behind and focus on the present, all in an effort to get back to a championship game he knew was possible.

With that return trip within reach going into the critical second leg against the Dynamo, Schmetzer switched his approach and insisted his players forget the future this time.

It had been a mental high-wire act. But the job had gotten done. And with the MLS Cup final still nine days away, it was Schmetzer this time who opted to focus on the present. He was nearly overcome in talking about how Osvaldo Alonso had carried the conference championship trophy over to a section of fans. The fans stayed and cheered for each Sounders player that raised the trophy high.

"The relationship between the fans and the players is what makes this club so special," he said. "The energy in the building from the opening whistle was good. Houston came to play and we were ready to play."

Indeed they were. With nothing left to do but blow it, the Sounders made sure they didn't and got the job done.

24 Native Son Returns

Kasey Keller had been born in the Washington state capital of Olympia, grew up in nearby Lacey, and had become the first American goalkeeper to play as a regular in the German Bundesliga, the English Premier League, and the Spanish La Liga.

So naturally, when the Sounders were set to launch an MLS expansion team in 2009, Keller was high on their list of targets. He'd played off and on for English side Fulham in 2007–08, teaming with future Sounders forward Clint Dempsey. Prior to that, he'd spent three seasons for German side Borussia Mönchengladbach and four with English mainstay Tottenham Hotspur. But then he got a call from the Sounders and began to talk.

"This was actually home," Keller said. "It wasn't coming back to MLS. It was actually coming back to the Northwest and coming back to where I saw myself winning."

One of the big influences for Keller, who'd played at the University of Portland, was a conversation with midfielder Claudio Reyna about his own time in MLS. Reyna had captained the U.S. Men's National Team alongside Keller, but in 2007–08 Reyna left his longtime EPL stint for two seasons with the New York Red Bulls.

"I'd spent 20 years with the national team but not kind of ever really playing here," Keller said. "Those were the majority of the factors in deciding."

After extensive conversations with Sounders owners Joe Roth and Adrian Hanauer, Keller, then 37, also had to decide how long a

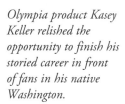

Olympia product Kasey Keller relished the opportunity to finish his storied career in front of fans in his native Washington.

hiatus from soccer he wanted to take. They both wanted him in training camp with the Sounders the very first day and not finishing off the season in England.

So Keller skipped the 2008–09 EPL campaign and focused solely on his new club. It went without saying—though Roth and Hanauer did say it—that Keller was expected to take on a soccer ambassador's role in addition to minding the net.

"It didn't hurt having a few months off and to be able to continue the training without the pressure of actually playing," Keller said. "And also to be able to do some of that ambassador role as well during the lead-up to when the team got going."

Keller admits he didn't know where things were headed when he'd signed in August 2008. But the team already had about 15,000 season ticket subscriptions so "we knew it was going to be something."

But Keller knew he was taking a risk. There had been so many incarnations of one soccer league after another in the United States that a dozen years of relative MLS stability was no guarantee of anything.

"None of us really knew what was going to happen," he said. "I mean, the franchise was investing money, but at the same time you had to be conservative. Where the league is now compared to where it was in 2009, I mean, they weren't going to invest $10 million in a training facility, just because you didn't know where the league was going to be."

Keller hoped that once the team got through the season opener, things would stabilize. And a 3–0 win over the New York Red Bulls at Qwest Field didn't hurt. He'd worried beforehand that the team had been put together a little late and might embarrass itself in front of unprecedented media coverage.

"There was as much press there ready to get alongside with us, [but] I think there was a group of press that was ready to come down on us as well," he said.

That didn't happen. The Sounders and Keller went on to have a highly successful season. He was 12–5–11 with 10 clean sheets and only 26 goals allowed in his 29 starts. In his three seasons, he was 44–22–25 with 30 shutouts and 97 goals allowed in 93 starts.

But for Keller, he knew things would fall into place after that successful opening game.

"If I'd come in that July because I was playing somewhere in Europe, I wouldn't have been a part of that," he said. "It wouldn't have been the same. That's when I knew that all the decisions I'd made to come home, to be there for the first day of preseason and for the first game, that I'd made all the right decisions."

25 Sounders Win First Supporters' Shield

A disappointing end to 2013 for the Sounders had been capped by a playoff loss to the archrival Portland Timbers. There had been tension in the locker room as well, much of it caused by an increasingly unhappy Eddie Johnson, who had taken his request for more money in front of the television cameras during a game at Columbus.

The Sounders quickly began shedding some of the baggage they felt had prevented them from claiming any silverware a second straight season following years of U.S. Open Cup dominance. Johnson was traded to D.C. United, with the Sounders having already cast their Designated Player lot with Clint Dempsey, Marco Pappa, and Obafemi Martins and having no salary room to meet the mercurial Johnson's demands for a raise.

"We just needed to change things up," Sounders owner Adrian Hanauer said. "We felt we were a team on the rise, and we didn't want anything preventing us from getting to where we should go."

Dempsey had also not produced as expected after returning to MLS play from England. He'd scored just once in nine league games and would head out on a two-month loan to Fulham ahead of the upcoming 2014 season, hoping to smooth out some rougher edges.

But it wasn't all bleak.

The Sounders knew they had something special in Shoreline product DeAndre Yedlin, who had dazzled in his debut season, becoming the first rookie since 2005 to be named to the MLS All-Star team. Combined with a full season from Dempsey, the always dangerous Martins and new goalkeeper Stefan Frei in his comeback season, the team had high hopes heading into 2014.

"We knew we had the talent," team vice president of soccer operations Chris Henderson said. "It was just a matter of us living up to what we were capable of."

The team got off to a sluggish start. After a 1–0 win versus Sporting Kansas City, the Sounders were stunned 2–1 at home by a new-look Toronto FC team that had loaded up on star players, including British footballer Jermain Defoe. Defoe scored twice before the match was even 23 minutes old and the Sounders never recovered, though Dempsey managed a second-half strike that signaled good things ahead for him.

By the time the Sounders headed to Portland for the season's fifth match, they were a pedestrian 2–2 and destined for sub-.500 once the Timbers took a 4–2 lead into the game's final six minutes. But Dempsey came out of nowhere to score a pair of goals just two minutes apart to complete a hat trick and salvage a 4–4 draw.

All of a sudden, things weren't looking so bad. With Dempsey now doing what everybody expected, the Sounders took off, winning their next five games in a row before suffering a team record 5–0 loss at New England. But that faceplant against the Revolution would prove an anomaly as the Sounders went unbeaten in their next five matches, winning four of them. By the time the Los Angeles Galaxy showed up to CenturyLink field for a July 28 clash, the Sounders had gone 10–2–2 their previous 14 league games and also qualified for the U.S. Open Cup semifinal.

The team was riding a wave of confidence, leading the conference standings. But as would be a recurring theme for much of that season, the Galaxy brought the Sounders back down to earth, winning 3–0. The Sounders surrendered three goals the first 36 minutes and never mounted much of a challenge at all in front of their home fans.

The loss took the Sounders a while to get over. They went 1–3–1 their next five matches and had won only twice in two months by the time the Colorado Rapids paid a visit to CenturyLink on

August 30. But by then, the Sounders had also routed the Chicago Fire 6–0 to reach the final of the U.S. Open Cup, something the entire team would later say helped them regain some lost swagger.

The Sounders beat Colorado 1–0, then defeated Chivas USA 4–2 on the road before returning home to edge Real Salt Lake 3–2 for a third straight win. Four days later, the Sounders defeated the Philadelphia Union 3–1 in overtime at Chester, Pennsylvania, to claim their first U.S. Open Cup title since 2011. Though the hefty schedule caught up to them with losses their next two matches, the Sounders were a confident bunch as they headed into the season's stretch run.

Coincidentally, the schedule had them finishing with two games against the dreaded Galaxy, who had gone 2–0–2 in their four prior games against the Sounders. It would be a winner-take-all clash for the Supporters' Shield and a possible Western Conference championship preview.

Both home-and-home games were akin to a playoff series. The opening match, in front of a packed house of 27,244 at the StubHub Center in Carson, California, saw the Sounders fall behind 2–0 by the 50th minute on Galaxy goals by Baggio Husidic and Marcelo Sarvas. But Dempsey got the comeback started in the 69th minute, burying a Yedlin cross that was flicked by Martins in the box. The stunned crowd was finally silenced as momentum swung the Sounders' way. Just three minutes later, Lamar Neagle raced for a good ball from Martins along the right side and beat goalkeeper Jaime Penedo to the far post.

The improbable result left the teams with 61 points apiece and meant the Sounders—who had two more victories than the Galaxy overall—needed just a draw at home to claim the regular season title. Six days later, a crowd of nearly 60,000 filed into CenturyLink to see the Supporters' Shield decided. A tense match carried on scoreless through the first 70 minutes when Gonzalvo Pineda became involved in a shoving match with Marcelo after his hard tackle of Dempsey.

A melee erupted as Osvaldo Alonso stormed over and shoved Marcelo away, then aggressively shoved A.J. DeLaGarza back several feet. The roaring crowd helped ratchet up the emotion even higher as referee Mark Geiger tried to contain the powder keg.

With just under six minutes to go and the stadium poised to explode, the Sounders were awarded a free kick and quickly put the ball in play before the Galaxy could set themselves. Martins took a flick from Dempsey and split the defense with a pass through to Pappa, who had been streaking down the left side. Pappa coolly beat sliding goalkeeper Penedo to his right and set off possibly the loudest eruption ever heard at a CenturyLink Field soccer match.

The cheering crowd still hadn't settled down by the time regulation play ended. An additional four minutes were added in which the Galaxy needed two goals to take the title. As the Galaxy futilely pressed forward, a ball was played back dangerously toward keeper Penedo, who had to dribble past a sliding Pappa. But instead of immediately kicking the ball upfield, Penedo inexplicably kept on dribbling. That gave Pappa time to sneak up behind Penedo and steal the ball away.

Pappa and Martins had a breakaway on an empty net. And though defender DeLaGarza raced back to cover, Pappa scooped the ball by him and into the net for the game-clinching goal.

The celebration was on as the Sounders claimed their first Supporters' Shield to go along with their U.S. Open Cup. Their record of 20–10–4 was their best ever. For a while, fans dreamed of completing the unprecedented treble with an MLS Cup victory, as well. Alas, the Galaxy got their revenge in the conference final, defeating the Sounders on aggregate and later going on to claim the MLS Cup title.

For the Sounders, their MLS Cup hopes would have to wait two more years. But on that final afternoon of the regular season, their team had its first regular season crown and another franchise milestone.

26 The Most Memorable Sounders Tifos

Alongside singing, chanting and cheering, the primary efforts of Emerald City Supporters members during every home match is to unfurl a giant Tifo banner from their seats in the South End of CenturyLink Field. And it takes plenty of planning and work beforehand.

"It's a big thing from a membership attraction and retention standpoint," said ECS co-president Tom Biro. "Once you make it, you want to stand up for it and be a part of it. Players notice it. [Sounders coach] Brian Schmetzer talks about it."

Fellow ECS co-president Heather Satterberg says the group uses any space it can to make the Tifos. She works as a commercial real estate manager and can sometimes find empty office space not being used.

"We go wherever we can," she said. "If there are real estate professionals who can give us a floor somewhere in a building, we'll borrow it for a game. We have a couple of property managers with us.

"We'll also do it in the stadium if they have days available. Or, in the [events] hall next door, or in parking garages. Wherever we can."

Among Tifos generally recognized as the group's best is "Tonight we go all in" from an October 7, 2012, match against Portland in which Sounders coach Sigi Schmid is depicted at a card table. That Tifo was voted best in all MLS that year.

Another is the Brougham Cathedral that the ECS unfurled in October 2017 ahead of the regular season finale against Colorado. It portrays seven players—Osvaldo Alonso, Stefan Frei, Nicolas Lodeiro, Clint Dempsey, Jordan Morris, and Joevin Jones—set against stained glass cathedral window backdrops and depicting what it means to be a Sounders player. It uses the words *passion* and *loyalty* and *hope* and *defiance* and *desire* and *resolve* and *growth* to define characteristics those players bring. The Tifo is already considered by many ECS members to be the greatest they've ever done.

Another all-time great is the Build a Bonfire Tifo unveiled before the August 2013 home debut of Clint Dempsey against Portland. The words are off the name of a popular ECS chant in which their Cascadian rivals from Portland and Vancouver are tossed into the bonfire to feed its flames. The Tifo featured midfielder Alonso, forward Eddie Johnson, goalkeeper Michael Gspurning, and right back Brad Evans riding horseback as the proverbial Four Horsemen of the Apocalypse.

By far, the consensus worst ECS Tifo was the "Rickroll" of August 21, 2016, in which a video of 1980s British pop star Rick Astley was put up on the big screen while ECS members held signs that spelled out the lyrics to "Never Gonna Give You Up." The Timbers, meanwhile, demolished that effort by unfurling a stellar Away Day Legends banner with a gold star reminding fans they were the "'15 MLS Cup Champs."

Biro notes that some of the location-switching when Tifos are being created is intentional, geared towards secrecy. The last thing ECS wants is for a member of Timbers Army or the Vancouver Southsiders to stumble upon their Tifo by accident. If word leaks out beforehand about a group's Tifo plans, it can lead to embarrassing moments that linger for years.

"If we get wind of somebody else's Tifo, then we'll make a competitive Tifo making fun of theirs," Satterberg said.

"Or," Biro said, "we'll unveil our Tifo before they can put theirs up."

Before the very first MLS clash between the Sounders and new Timbers expansion franchise in May 2011, a battle of Tifos erupted inside what was still known as Qwest Field. Right after "The Star

Spangled Banner" had been played, the Timbers Army dropped three Tifos reading We Are, The Timbers Army, Who Are You?. But then, a two-pronged response by the ECS and a smaller supporters group, the North End Faithful, delivered an epic knock-out punch.

The ECS unfurled in multiple layers a Decades of Dominance Tifo covering the entire South End and depicting several Sounders from over the years including Jimmy Gabriel, Preston Burpo, Marcus Hahnemann, and Brian Schmetzer. Then, a bannered fist dropped down from the upper deck and appeared to crush a Timbers logo, followed by the unveiling of a smiling banner image of Roger Levesque and the words 48 seconds—a reference to his opening minute U.S. Open Cup goal in Portland the previous year in which teammate Nate Jaqua pretended to chop him down like a tree.

The massive display overwhelmed the Portland effort and is widely considered one of the best Tifos the ECS has ever produced. But then, in an artistic *coup de grâce*, the North End Faithful at the other end of the stadium simultaneously released their own Tifo that appeared to be a direct response to the Timbers "Who Are You?" jab.

It depicted Fredy Montero and said: We are Faithful, We are Sounders.

It was the perfect comeback.

"It's like, 'Yeah, that's who we are,'" Satterberg said. "I don't know if they knew what the Timbers' guys were bringing or what, but it was great."

Original ECS co-president Greg Mockos says when the group first began creating Tifos, it tried to achieve three points: First, inspire the home players. Second, inspire the home fans. And third, take a dig at the opposing team and fans.

"If you can get all three of those in the Tifos," he said, "you'll find that those are the most successful."

27 Sigi Schmid Fired

Sounders owner Adrian Hanauer woke up the morning of July 26, 2016, resigned to the unpleasant task on his immediate to-do list: firing the only head coach his soccer team had ever known.

Sigi Schmid had jumped to the Sounders in 2009 after winning the MLS Cup with the Columbus Crew the prior season. He'd taken the Sounders to the playoffs in each of their first seven seasons, winning four U.S. Open Cups and a Supporters' Shield in 2014 as the team with the best regular season record. But now, with the Sounders languishing in last place and differences of opinion about how to move forward, Schmid, 63, no longer fit the vision of where Hanauer wanted to go.

"It sucked because I loved Sig as a person," Hanauer said. "I guess the only thing that made it a little bit easier is that we'd had some conversations prior to the day—some heart-to-hearts about things not going very well. It was pretty obvious."

Hanauer also had "some level of certainty" he was making the right call. He'd bandied it about in his mind after watching the Sounders slog through several July matches. Then the Sounders headed in to Kansas City and got demolished 3–0 on a muggy afternoon with temps in the triple digits. The Sounders didn't register a shot until the 88th minute and the final score actually flattered the visitors in what was a completely as lopsided contest.

"It was just about the worst game I've seen us play," Hanauer said.

But it wasn't the tipping point. Hanauer said "the results over a period of time" were more of a determining factor. He'd also talked to a number of players and observed their interactions with Schmid. "My gut told me they were ready for a new voice," Hanauer said.

It helped that Hanauer had a high degree of trust in assistant coach Brian Schmetzer, who he'd known since his days owning the second division Sounders of the United Soccer League. Hanauer suspected Schmetzer's voice might be the right one, as opposed to hiring a brand new coach Hanauer was unfamiliar with.

And his general manager was on board. Garth Lagerwey had been hired the prior year to replace Hanauer as GM so Hanauer could step aside and focus on his increased business responsibilities as majority owner.

Lagerwey was brought in to shake things up in terms of club thinking. And while he didn't say much in 2015, preferring to watch and take mental notes, the sluggish start to 2016 confirmed many of his fears about where the organization was headed.

"It wasn't any one thing," Lagerwey said. "I know that many people circle the Kansas City game, but if anything, that was the straw that broke the camel's back. It wasn't a determining factor. I just don't believe in that. It was 103 degrees and we played like crap. But it's not like it was the first time we'd done that."

Lagerwey wanted more consistency. He felt the team had "cratered on a colossal scale" in both the current and prior season. In 2015, the Sounders had scored just three goals over an 11-game span, and now he felt the exact same thing was happening again.

Lagerwey and Schmid differed over the need to have a "more consistent approach" to matches.

"I don't think Sigi had ever before had a general manager in the way that I envisioned the role," Lagerwey said. "Look, he was literally inducted into the Hall of Fame when I was here, so it wasn't just a track record of success. It was phenomenal success. I get it. I understand why we weren't necessarily looking for new ideas and how to improve upon things. So, was there maybe a different world view? Sure. But it doesn't mean that mine was better than his. [It's] just that, at some point, we needed to pick a new direction."

And that's what the Sounders did.

Hanauer invited Schmid into the office that morning and informed him of the decision. "I think I just said, 'Look, Sig, I've decided we're going to make a change.'"

Schmid handled it well and shook his hand.

"It was not a shock," Lagerwey said.

It was a busy morning for Hanauer and the team, as Nicolas Lodeiro had just arrived from South America to sign his new Sounders contract. His coach at Boca Juniors in Argentina had known Schmid and told Lodeiro to say hello for him.

That led to an awkward moment, as Schmid was still in his office gathering his things. Lodeiro had asked, "Where's Sigi?" in broken English and had to be told what had just transpired. Lodeiro still went and delivered the message to Schmid. Soon after, the Sounders held a press conference announcing Lodeiro's arrival. In many ways, Lodeiro would prove the catalyst that transformed the team's second half and helped lead it to an unexpected first MLS Cup title.

And that left Hanauer pondering what might have been had he not made the coaching change. He's a big Schmetzer fan, but he also wonders whether it was simply the team's talent and overall health "regressing to the mean" of where it became the playoff-caliber squad envisioned all along.

"Sigi was there for seven and a half years, and he was able to change his voice and the messaging enough to get through to players over that period of time," Hanauer said. "And who knows? Maybe after that Kansas City game, he could have found a way to change that voice again. And if he does that, who's to say it couldn't have been him winning an MLS Cup championship? You never know."

28 Chris Henderson Goes from Youth Phenom to Top Executive

Growing up in Edmonds, Washington, Chris Henderson couldn't help being a fan of the Sounders in their North American Soccer League incarnation. After all, his older brother, Pat, played for the team under then-coach Alan Hinton.

Pretty soon, it was Chris, the middle of three soccer-playing boys from Edmonds, who was generating all the family attention. He became a star at Cascade High School in Everett, making the U-16 national squad and eventually capturing the 1989 Gatorade National Player of the Year Award.

By 19, he was the youngest player on the U.S. Men's National Team roster. He'd soon become only the second player in this country to represent the U.S. national team at all levels, including U-16, U-20, Olympics, Youth World Cup, and World Cup.

When an 11-year professional playing career ended in 2006, Henderson spent a season as an assistant coach in Kansas City. He was about to take a job as sporting director of the Colorado Rapids—where he'd begun his MLS career in 1996 and spent six seasons—when his younger brother, Sean, phoned with some news. Sean had played for the Sounders in the United Soccer League under Brian Schmetzer and had recently bumped in to the team's owner from those days, Adrian Hanauer. He told Chris that Hanauer, then minority owner of the newly awarded Seattle MLS expansion franchise, was about to begin hiring front office personnel.

"Sean said, 'Hey, why don't you give Adrian a call? I hear they're trying to bump things up for the team in '09,'" Chris said. "And so I called him, we started talking, and things just started from there."

It was right near the end of 2007 when Chris Henderson flew back to his hometown to meet with Hanauer.

"Within 15 minutes, I could see it was going to be special," he said. "The plans were good. The ownership group was amazing. Adrian was committed. You could tell it was going to be big. I knew that if I came here, I could really have an impact on how the team was built."

By January 2008, Henderson became the first player hired by the MLS Sounders, named vice president of soccer and sporting director. He'd assist the team's general manager in all aspects of soccer operations, including scouting, coaching decisions, player personnel, and the squad's youth system.

"I think part of it was the 20-year career I had and the relationships internationally, playing in MLS, understanding our league," Henderson said.

After all, Henderson had represented the U.S. on 79 occasions as a player, including the 1992 Summer Olympics in Barcelona and as an alternate at the 1994 and 1998 World Cups. After leading UCLA to a national championship as a collegiate all-American, he'd begun his pro career with Germany's FSV Frankfurt in 1994 and then moved on to Stabaek in Norway before joining the Rapids in MLS.

"The thing I'm most proud of is that I played for five different coaches during all those years with my various national teams at different levels," he said. "To be able to last as long as I did and adapt to what those coaches expected in their various systems was something I think helped me."

And his contacts around the world paid off immediately for the Sounders. Henderson was on the 2008 trip to Colombia with Schmetzer and Hanauer in which the Sounders convinced Fredy Montero to sign with them. Henderson was also instrumental in getting Obafemi Martins to sign in 2013, watching him later go on to become the team's second all-time leading scorer.

Early on, Henderson helped convince Cuban defector Osvaldo Alonso to sign with the Sounders for their 2009 debut season after Alonso's inaugural pro campaign in 2008 with the Charlestown Battery. Alonso went on to become the Sounders' all-time leader in games played.

And the team's youth academy, under Henderson's stewardship, has become recognized as among the league's best. It developed Shoreline product DeAndre Yedlin, who became the MLS Rookie of the Year in 2013.

Henderson's own playing days as a youth phenom has given him perspective on what it takes to transition successfully to a pro career. And he looks for those traits within players coming up under his watch.

"There are a lot of players who were maybe more talented than me when I was 14 or 15," he said. "But for one reason or another, it just doesn't stick. There has to be a dedication, a commitment, and passion inside of you. Perseverance is part of it. If you don't make it once, it's like, 'Okay, I'll make the next team.'

"You've just got to keep going."

29 Lodeiro Backs Up Big Money with Big Results

Eyebrows raised midway through a disastrous early 2016 season when the Sounders decided to go on a spending splurge. For several months, they'd targeted Uruguayan midfielder Nicolas Lodeiro of the Boca Juniors in Buenos Aires, Argentina. But the owners of one of South America's best-known clubs weren't in the mood for handing out gifts. Lodeiro came with a stiff price tag attached, and the Sounders were prepared to pay it.

By the time the smoke had cleared off their collective wallet, the Sounders' ownership had paid a whopping $6 million transfer fee for a player few outside of Seattle felt was worth it. The fee was the sixth highest in Major League Soccer history—$2 million more than the team had paid for Obafemi Martins in 2013 and just $3 million less than they'd shelled out for Clint Dempsey that same year.

The Portland Timbers had paid just $3 million for superstar Diego Valeri. Lodeiro's cost was also greater than the $5.2 million the Los Angeles Galaxy had splurged on Irish national team captain Robbie Keane. So there was certainly pressure on Lodeiro to live up to that initial cost, plus his $6.1 million salary over three and a half seasons through 2019.

"You never know how a player like this is going to work out," general manager Garth Lagerwey admitted. "We certainly knew the kind of player he could be. But with everything that wound up happening, he exceeded our expectations."

Lodeiro had walked into a minefield. The day he showed up at Sounders headquarters in Pioneer Square, the team had just delivered the news to longtime head coach Sigi Schmid that he was being fired.

"The team was out of sorts," Lodeiro said. "A lot of things were going on within the club. But for me to integrate myself and right the ship with these guys and return to our winning ways—which we started doing in August and September—it allowed us to gain a lot more confidence and prepare us for the playoffs."

Lodeiro had been looking for a challenge. He'd already twice won the Eredivisie title with Ajax in The Netherlands and had captured the domestic double in his first season with Boca Juniors in 2015.

Playing in Argentina felt as close to home as he'd ever been. He'd grown up in the town of Paysandu, on the Uruguay-Argentina border. Buenos Aires was less than four hours' drive away from his large family on a highway that bypasses the La Plata River.

But still, his global soccer journey wasn't done.

"Boca is a team with a lot of history that goes way back," Lodeiro said. "Seattle is a new club in a growing league, a maturing league. It has talented players, but it's part of an infrastructure that's maturing. I wanted to be part of a challenge like that.

"This team is trying to write new history. And I wanted to be part of a team that was trying to write history like that."

Lodeiro wasted little time doing so.

He made his debut on July 31, 2016, and it quickly became clear the playmaker was to be the focal point of his team's attack. Clint Dempsey was on the verge of having his season end due to an irregular heartbeat, a development that would normally devastate any team already near the league's basement.

But Lodeiro was there to take over. He picked up two assists the following week in a 3–1 win over Orlando City. Then, on August 14, he scored his first goal at home against Real Salt Lake with a brilliant left-footed finish inside the box.

About 13 minutes later, Lodeiro floated a cross that Jordan Morris headed home for what proved to be the winner in a 2–1 victory. All of a sudden, the Sounders were on a roll. Lodeiro would go on to record either a goal or an assist in eight consecutive games. He was named MLS Player of the Month for August with two goals and six assists. His Sounders would lose only two of his 13 matches to squeeze into the Decision Day regular season finale.

In all, Lodeiro scored four goals and added eight assists in those 13 regular season games. But there were still the playoffs to come.

And what a ride those six matches became.

His brace in the first leg of the Western Conference semifinal against Supporters' Shield winner Dallas FC gave the Sounders a stunning 3–0 victory at home. Lodeiro then scored a critical away marker in the second leg of the series, enabling the Sounders to advance to the conference final against Colorado.

In the first match, with a howling rainstorm beating down upon the turf, the Sounders fell behind 1–0 on a Kevin Doyle goal in the 13th minute. But Morris equalized just six minutes later and the teams remained tied until the 61st minute. That's when the Sounders were awarded a penalty kick and their designated shooter, Lodeiro, made sure not to miss.

His fourth goal in only four games gave Lodeiro the Sounders' all-time playoff scoring record.

The Sounders won the second leg 1–0 in Colorado to secure their first ever MLS Cup appearance. Lodeiro would convert his attempt in the penalty kick round of that contest, enabling the Sounders to eventually defeat Toronto FC to win their first championship.

As the champagne flowed that night, no one doubted that the Lodeiro purchase had been worth it. His mid-season addition had arguably the greatest one-player impact on a team in MLS history.

Lodeiro was named MLS Newcomer of the Year, garnering 36.5 percent of the vote and easily outdistancing the 18.9 percent garnered by second-place finisher Ola Kamara of Columbus.

"I wanted to learn more about myself and grow on a larger stage," Lodeiro said. "I think I did that."

30 From Dancing Bear to a Muted Celebration

Will Bruin earned a nickname he'd rather forget courtesy of his very first goals scored for the Houston Dynamo as a rookie in 2011. He'd notched a hat trick against D.C. United and, after each effort, celebrated with an arm-flailing jig akin to a bear waving its paws.

His Dynamo teammates had already seen Bruin flail his arms in similar fashion during a finishing drill the previous day. His teammates told the strapping 6'2", 194-pounder he looked like "a dancing bear" when he did that. Prior to the D.C. game, Dynamo scoring legend Brian Ching told Bruin, "If you score, you've got to do the 'Dancing Bear' celebration."

Like all good rookies, Bruin did what he was told—and immediately regretted it. He'd never been the showboating type. But the "Dancing Bear" moniker stuck and Dynamo fans clamored for a repeat whenever Bruin scored for the home side.

And score he did. Bruin notched 50 goals over his six seasons in Houston, second all time for the franchise behind only Ching. Bruin went to consecutive MLS Cup finals his first two years with the Dynamo, losing both times to the Los Angeles Galaxy.

Then the lean years hit and playoff runs stopped coming. Bruin got banged up in the box and was slowed by nagging hurts throughout 2016 as the Dynamo looked to rebuild. By early 2017, he'd been traded to the defending champion Sounders.

It was one of the best things that could have happened when it came to the Sounders making a return MLS Cup trip.

They initially planned to use Bruin as a second-half substitute to spell 2016 MLS Rookie of the Year striker Jordan Morris. Sounders general manager Garth Lagerwey and coach Brian Schmetzer felt limiting Bruin's minutes would help preserve his body for the long haul. But the team struggled to score early on, and Bruin kept putting the ball in the net regardless of his limited playing time.

Finally, with Morris slowed by ankle problems and struggling on attack, the team began starting Bruin up top and flanking Morris out wide. Still, the team was reluctant to stick with the arrangement too long, fearing it might hamper Morris' development and wear out Bruin. He had already suffered a dislocated elbow in a game at Colorado and was taking his usual pounding.

But the issue was resolved in September, when Morris tore his hamstring and was deemed out for the rest of the regular season. Now, it was Bruin up top the rest of the way. He relished the challenge, wanting another shot at the MLS Cup title that had eluded him in Houston.

"I was like, 'Oh, I went to the MLS Cup in both of my first two years, so this is pretty easy,'" Bruin said. "And then, the last three years, I didn't even make the playoffs. So I definitely appreciate where we're at right now. I don't take it for granted as much as you do maybe when you're younger."

Bruin's solid play down the stretch helped the Sounders finish tied atop the Western Conference standings and earn the No. 2 playoff seed. He finished with 11 goals, second on the team only to Clint Dempsey's dozen and with far less playing time.

After a conference semifinal win over Vancouver, the Sounders—as luck would have it—faced Bruin's former Dynamo squad for a shot at a second consecutive conference title. In the opening leg at Houston, Gustav Svensson provided the Sounders

Sounders forward Will Bruin has kept his scoring at a maximum and "Dancing Bear" celebrations to a minimum.

an early lead. Then, late in the first half, Bruin, as he had done so often at BVAA Compass Stadium while playing for the home team, made a break for the goal as a Joevin Jones cross came his way.

And Bruin, the career 60-goal-scorer, finished the play like he naturally can. He leaped high in the air and—in one neck-twisting snap—used his head to redirect the Jones ball to the far corner of the net.

"That was a really, really good goal," Sounders coach Schmetzer would say days later. "I mean, Joevin's ball was good, but Will had some work to do. He had to get up and guide it—direct it into the upper corner."

Bruin promptly turned and headed for the sideline to his right where the Dynamo bench sits. For a split second, he pondered some type of celebration. After all, it was the same corner of the field where, so often, Dynamo fans had implored him to break out the "Dancing Bear" routine one more time.

But Bruin hit the mute button.

"It was kind of weird because I've had a lot of celebrations in that corner before with the Dynamo bench right there," Bruin. "I realized that wasn't my bench I was running to celebrate [there], so I was kind of by myself."

And remembering his good times in Houston—knowing he'd just delivered a dagger to Houston's title hopes—he figured it classiest to leave the celebration to a bare minimum. He'd learned from the "Dancing Bear" experience six years earlier that simply scoring the goal is the ultimate statement.

The Sounders left Houston with a 2–0 win and two huge away goals that could determine the winner of any series tied on aggregate. With the Sounders near unbeatable at home, the series was all but over.

Nine days later, Bruin and company wrapped it up at home and prepared for a return trip to the MLS Cup final.

31 Eddie Johnson Tells Sounders, "Pay Me!"

Eddie Johnson was as solid an acquisition as the Sounders could hope to have made in 2012, coming over from the Montreal Impact for Mike Fucito and Lamar Neagle. Johnson had spent six years in Major League Soccer before heading overseas in 2007 with Fulham of the English Premier League and continuing on until a stint in the Greek Super League ended in 2011.

The Impact drafted Johnson when he signed with MLS but immediately made the trade to the Sounders. Johnson followed by scoring 14 goals—including a league-leading nine of them on headers—to earn MLS Comeback Player of the Year honors. All seemed to be going well, until Johnson started demanding more money the following season to keep the good times rolling.

And he didn't just do it at the negotiating table. On August 31, 2013, the Sounders were playing the Columbus Crew in Ohio when, in the 14th minute, Johnson deftly headed home a free kick by Mauro Rosales that had angled its way deep into the box.

The early goal would be the game's only one. But it was memorable for what happened afterward as the dyed-blond Johnson looked up toward the team executive suites, rubbed his fingers together, and mouthed the words, "Pay me!" several times.

Fox Sports television cameras caught the whole thing. In fact, as a celebrating Johnson approached the sideline, he looked straight into a camera inches away and again rubbed his fingers—this time directly into its lens—and repeated the "Pay me!" phrase.

Johnson wanted seven-figure, designated-player-type money and was scoring goals well beyond his $156,333 salary. But the Sounders were unimpressed, having let Johnson know that they were maxed out on designated players between Rosales, Obafemi Martins, and Clint Dempsey.

It didn't help that Martins had tweeted nearly a month earlier that Johnson "deserves a new contract ASAP," causing ownership to fear Johnson might become the center of a rift spreading to other players on the team. Dempsey, who'd teamed with Johnson at Fulham, had just transferred over to the Sounders from Tottenham Hotspur.

Johnson added fuel to that Martins tweet a few days later when he gave an interview to MLSSoccer.com while overseas with the United States Men's National Team to play an international friendly match against Bosnia-Herzegovina in Sarajevo. When asked whether he'd consider playing in Europe again, Johnson replied that he was happy to revive his career in Seattle. But he added he was open to opportunities. "I want to give myself every opportunity to make as much money as I can to help provide for my kids," he said. "And whatever situation comes up, I'm open to look at it. But I keep reiterating, I'm happy in Seattle. They gave me a second chance to resurrect my career and things are going well."

After the Columbus "Pay me!" moment, he took to Twitter and got into it with fans protesting the move. Two weeks later, after speaking with coaches and team management, Johnson sounded contrite when discussing the Columbus incident with reporters for the first time, reiterating that he enjoyed playing in Seattle.

But the die was cast. Team fears about Johnson creating a locker room distraction and rift became realized by late October and he was held out of training. By November, the Sounders—eliminated by archrival Portland in the playoffs—were shopping Johnson around the league.

The following month, he was dealt to D.C. United for allocation money. At long last, he seemed headed toward the payday he coveted.

But it was short-lived. Johnson played only one season in D.C. before being diagnosed with an irregular heartbeat during the 2014 playoffs. A year later, he retired without having played another match.

32 Fredy Montero Rape Allegation

The first true superstar of a fledgling franchise almost had his MLS career end before it even got off the ground. Just five days before the Sounders played in their MLS debut, a 23-year-old woman went out partying with Montero and some friends.

The woman was recently employed by the Sounders as a Spanish-language translator working with some of its foreign players. Montero was one of them, and he got to know the woman, who was from his native Colombia.

They wound up back at Montero's townhouse in Bellevue that night. From there is where accounts differ.

According to police reports, one of Montero's teammates and another woman had seen him and the complainant kissing. The teammate told police it looked like the woman was "happy" with Montero.

But the woman told police Montero was sexually aggressive and kept trying to have sex with her. She said she stayed at his house because she'd had too much to drink and slept on the floor next to him.

After leaving the next day, she says she realized she'd left a necklace at his townhouse. She says she texted him about it but he didn't return the text until a week later, telling her he'd found it.

By then, Montero had already scored a pair of goals in the team's MLS debut and been named the league's Player of the Week. Having scored nine goals in nine preseason games prior, he was quickly becoming known to Seattle soccer fans while playing an instrumental role in helping the fledgling team market itself to the greater sports fanbase in the city.

It was 2:30 AM on March 22, 2009—three days after the team's MLS opener—that police reports say Montero returned the woman's texts and invited her over to get her necklace back. The woman told police she reluctantly went there, knowing that a teammate of Montero's would be at the house, as well.

But the woman said the teammate soon left, after which time Montero dragged her up the stairs and raped her. The woman told police she screamed and cried for help, but a 16-year-old son of Montero's host family—who was also at the townhouse visiting that night—claimed he'd heard no screams or cries.

Later that day, the woman went to police and reported the rape accusation. Montero was arrested and forced to surrender his passport.

The team did not have Montero travel with it for its game in Toronto that week, claiming he had the flu. But Montero returned to action the following game against Real Salt Lake, scoring once to help secure himself MLS Player of the Month honors.

Meanwhile, police and prosecutors continued to investigate the rape allegation. By mid-April, after the woman and her legal team held a press conference to make the case public, King County prosecutor Dan Satterberg announced that no charges would be filed against Montero.

Among the reasons given the media was that the woman herself could describe no forced sexual contact and also said when she'd told Montero "no" that first night, he'd complied with her request.

Montero, years later, says the experience changed the way he handled himself off the field at a young, impressionable age.

"It changed my life and all of my relationships with my friends and with my family," Montero said. "I felt they supported me more than anybody, and I grew closer to them.

"It taught me a lesson as a human being," he said. "You never know who to trust. At the end of the day, I knew I didn't do anything wrong. But it was something that I couldn't handle."

33 March to the Match

For thousands of fans, attending a Sounders match typically begins about 90 minutes before kickoff. Dressed in Sounders garb and waving team scarves, they gather at Occidental Park in Pioneer Square where they listen to tunes belted out by the team's marching band, often chanting along.

The team's halftime emcee, comic and broadcaster Ken Carson, is there to host the show and get the crowd revved up.

About an hour before kickoff, the half-mile March to the Match begins. The tradition was actually popularized in soccer nations abroad, where entire towns would sometimes gather in the local square and march off to the stadium.

The march proceeds down Occidental Avenue and past the stadium to the south-end entryway of its events center. All the while, the crowd sings team fight songs like, "Take 'Em All" and "Born in 1974" and—when they play a Cascadia Cup match against Portland or Vancouver—"Build a Bonfire."

The march began as a local tradition in 2005, started by the Emerald City Supporters (ECS) group for the second division Sounders of the United Soccer League. Back then, the group was more of an informal gathering of about 20 or so buddies who'd meet for pre-game drinks at Fuel Sports, a bar in Pioneer Square, before heading over to the stadium as a well-imbibed group.

"We were so small that we'd just get up from the bar and walk over all together," said Greg Mockos, who became the first official ECS co-president in 2009 along with Keith Hodo.

It was Mockos who, just ahead of the team's inaugural 2009 MLS season, made a suggestion that the Sounders formalize "a march" ahead of their home opener. Mockos had grown up an Army brat in Italy and became a huge fan of the Juventus squad before going to college in California and taking a civil engineering job in Seattle in 2007.

He knew that Sounders celebrity owner Drew Carey wanted a marching band for the team. That flew in the face of soccer tradition, but Mockos felt there was a way the band could be incorporated into what he and his ECS friends were already doing pregame.

"I thought, 'Hey, here's a way we could combine our style and the way we support a team—which is with songs, chants, etc.—and the marching band,'" Mockos said. "I was like, 'Let's get a march going.' I think it was also very fortunate that the downtown and the landscape of Pioneer Square is conducive to it, with tons of bars where people can jump on the Sounders hype train as it marches on by. It's pretty dense, with not too many major streets to cross."

The team got involved to a limited degree. They wanted to keep the tradition in the hands of fans and not sanitize it too much by team involvement. Sounders owner Joe Roth remembers co-owner Carey insisting on as much when the team was debating how to approach it in 2009.

"He said, 'It's theirs, don't try to take it from them,'" Roth said.

Initially, the team planned to have Budweiser become an official sponsor of the march—until Mockos and his fellow ECS members intervened and asked them not to do it.

The team quickly abandoned the idea.

Carey envisioned more of an organic process where fans could appreciate the experience without official sponsorships or too much corporate involvement. Mockos admits some of the idea came from his soccer experiences in Italy and seeing similar marches there.

"What it's used for over there is really just marking your territory," he said. "So if you're a supporter group, you march around the stadium chanting, sort of to let the away fans know that this is Sounders territory. So it was definitely inspired. We weren't the first to do it, but in the United States, sure, we were."

The Sounders wanted to avoid the violent clashes such marches have led to in Europe. They've worked with ECS leaders to avoid such incidents. Participating fans are obliged to adhere to the team's code of conduct prohibiting smoke bombs, flares, and other flammable objects.

Thus far, there's been no violence attributed to the ECS or the march itself.

"The whole idea is you can get up and go have breakfast at a local bar," Mockos said. "And then you've got this big, fun party you can go to an hour or so before the game that gets you pumped up and kind of blends into the match."

34 Clint Dempsey Sidelined by Irregular Heartbeat

Clint Dempsey just couldn't get himself to feel right. It was February 2016 and Dempsey was preparing for the upcoming Major League Soccer season via on-and-off-field training. While exercising off the field, however, he starting getting heart palpitations and couldn't figure out why. He alerted the Sounders to it, but the feeling went away once the games began.

As the games progressed, the palpitations came and went. Dempsey admits he was somewhat fearful of something he'd never before experienced. He underwent a stress test, an EKG, and an MRI of his heart, but nothing definitive was diagnosed. He tried to focus on the season, which was getting away from his club. By July, the team was in last place and longtime coach Sigi Schmid was fired. In the midst of that, the team signed Uruguayan midfielder Nicolas Lodeiro to play up high with Dempsey and newcomer Jordan Morris. And for a trio of brilliant games, they appeared unstoppable.

In a critical August 7 game at Orlando, Dempsey notched his first hat trick in two years to lead the Sounders to a 3–1 comeback victory. The three goals in 59 minutes for Dempsey equaled his season output to that point. From the outside, things seemed to be looking up.

But privately, Dempsey was worried. He'd had to sub out of the match when the palpitations returned. He'd first started feeling them again during the final game of the Copa America Centenario tournament in July. His efforts had helped the United States Men's National Team reach the tournament's semifinal, losing out to Argentina.

When he had to leave the Orlando game early, his team injected a "loop recorder" device in him to monitor his heart readings during a match.

"It's difficult to try to explain," he said of how he felt physically.

He notched a brace against hated Portland on August 21. That gave Dempsey five goals in a three-game span playing alongside Lodeiro. But that would be his final game of 2016. Five days later, Dempsey was diagnosed with an irregular heartbeat and sidelined for the season. The medical condition he had was actually more specific, but Dempsey has chosen to keep it private. He was told he could go get the problem fixed or continue playing and risk it flaring up again.

Dempsey chose to take care of the problem.

"It puts things into perspective for you," Dempsey said. "I'd always kind of approached things in the same way of being competitive when I played and trying to make the most of it. Yeah, you look at life. But by the same token, what I had was not life threatening. It was career threatening."

Dempsey knew the difference. His older sister, Jennifer, died of a brain aneurysm when he was 12. When he was in college, his friend, Victor Rivera Jr., who was training to be a policeman, accidentally shot himself in the head while bending over to pick up an earplug.

Dempsey's condition, damaging as it was, wasn't going to kill him. And Dempsey accepted whatever might come of it.

"Maybe you think about things a little bit more because you don't know how long you have until it will be over," he said. "But my mentality has always been competitive. You try to win and set goals for yourself and try to accomplish those."

Dempsey watched from the sidelines as the Sounders went on to win the MLS Cup without him. He kept waiting during the brief offseason, hoping for another chance to play. A bevy of doctors kept watch over his training and results. The Sounders were not about to let him back on the field if he'd be harmed.

Finally, after extensive consultations, he was given the green light to resume training. He worked out daily at the team's Starfire facility and then, by late January, ran out on the field with the team for the start of training camp.

"I'm at peace with what I've done in my career," he said at the time. "I'm happy, married, with four kids. So I've got to enjoy life. Hopefully, there's more life to enjoy. But I'm happy and at peace with my career. I think there's more years to play."

The Sounders were cautious. They had a strict plan to introduce Dempsey back into action and weren't about to deviate from it.

"We're not going to throw him out there unless we're 100 percent sure, the doctors are 100 percent sure, and he's 100 percent sure," Sounders coach Brian Schmetzer said.

Dempsey didn't mince words. He wanted to play "a couple more years" and was confident he would.

"It has been difficult," he said as camp opened. "Throughout my career, this is the longest I've ever had to be out."

But he was taking better care of himself, largely by getting more sleep—something he admitted was "a big key" to resolving his issues.

Dempsey was eased into preseason games, then he started the team's season opener in Houston. In the 58th minute, Dempsey slammed home a rebound. It was his first scoring strike in six months. He played the full 90 minutes plus three minutes of stoppage time.

"I felt good," he said afterward. "I'm still trying to get to my top level. I'm not there yet. But I think if you watched the preseason it's been a steady progression and I look to be hopefully better next game."

Indeed he was. Dempsey went on to lead the Sounders in scoring with 12 goals and was named MLS Comeback Player of the Year. And by early November, in his first playoff game in two years against Vancouver, his brace eliminated the Whitecaps. In the Western Conference final, his second-half conversion of a Joevin Jones feed at the goalmouth helped the Sounders eliminate the Houston Dynamo to advance to their second MLS Cup championship game in as many years.

"Just to be able to contribute again has been a thrill for me," Dempsey said after qualifying for his first final in more than a decade.

His team was just as thrilled. The man they called "Deuce" was back at age 34, ready to keep on playing like he'd hoped he would.

35 The Unofficial Team Historian

Frank MacDonald attended his first Sounders game as a young teen at Memorial Stadium in 1975. The North American Soccer League team was in just its second year of existence, but already the young MacDonald had the sport in his blood.

He would go on to become a season-ticket holder in college, making the 160-mile round trip from his hometown of Centralia to the Kingdome. By 1981, he became an intern for the franchise, began working on-staff a year later, and also as a stadium vendor until the franchise folded in 1983.

From there, he moved on to handle media relations for the FC Seattle Storm semi-pro franchise and also wrote articles about them for *Soccer America* magazine until the squad dissolved in 1995. MacDonald kept detailed notes and files on all of it.

"I learned from the first Sounders that sometimes things are headed for a dumpster real fast and you don't know where the files are," MacDonald said. "And if you don't intercede, history would be lost. I've always had an appreciation for history, even when I was fairly young. And so I kind of rescued some of the stuff from the NASL days [and] when FC Seattle went under, I did that, too. I was able to get a lot of their files and their photos."

MacDonald was already the city's de facto soccer historian. As the mid-1990s approached, he was part of an initial effort to gain an MLS expansion franchise for Seattle ahead of the league's debut 1996 season. That didn't work out, but his soccer interest drew him to Seattle Pacific University to help with its fabled program. By 2000, he'd become the school's sports information director and assistant athletic director, a role he'd hold for the next seven years.

That's when, in late 2007, the MLS version of the Sounders hired MacDonald to do their website content. He did it for a year, then, in September 2008 he morphed into a role as the team's media relations director through its first three seasons.

MacDonald left the Sounders in 2014 to work in a corporate role for a company selling scarves. But his passion for the game and recording its local history never left him.

"Even when I drive on I-5, I think of all the things that needed to happen for me to drive on I-5," he said. "I try to be aware of all the things that happened so that I can live the life I'm living. So, that I can share with 40,000 people on a regular basis a great soccer atmosphere in Seattle."

MacDonald has worked with former players to establish a group—Washington State Legends of Soccer—devoted to the state's soccer history. It's been a labor of love up to now, supplemented by an online blog written and maintained by MacDonald.

But the goal is the creation of a full-fledged online soccer museum. MacDonald needed funding to do that, but he caught a break with the 40th reunion in 2017 of the first Sounders team to play in the 1977 Soccer Bowl.

He got former players such as Adrian Webster, Davey Butler, Dave Gillett, and Jimmy Gabriel to agree to participate in a VIP suite experience where fans could pay to sit with them and watch a Sounders game. That raised enough funds for MacDonald to hire a local website-building company to expand the group's online museum idea and introduce digital elements to it.

"They are working with us to partner on a platform to tell the history in a cool way," he said. "And so, we are in the mode of putting the skin on it, doing some test cases on it…. We'll take users down the rabbit hole. They might go in there looking for X and they'll wind up learning about Y and Z and back to A again.

"We've been very immersive about it. We think it's kind of fun."

The plan was to launch the upgraded version of the website during the first quarter of 2018.

"People need to realize that this didn't happen overnight," MacDonald said. "Our club and players and fans now are the beneficiaries of a community that was being built layer by layer since the 1950s. This isn't just some overnight trip."

36 Stefan Frei Resurrects Career

Stefan Frei knew he was viewed as damaged goods when the only MLS team he'd ever played for traded him to Seattle after the 2013 season. For five seasons, Frei had manned the goal for Toronto FC, his career sliding slowly downhill from Defender of the Year in 2009 to an injury-plagued, seldom-used backup role by the time it was done.

Frei had broken his fibula during training in March 2012, underwent subsequent surgery to repair two ankle ligaments, and missed the entire season. The following year, in training camp, he got hurt again and backup Joe Bendik took over and went on quite a run. By then, the Reds staff was reluctant to pull the hot Bendik and the result was Frei appeared in only one match all season.

With just that lone game played in two years, Frei needed a fresh start and somebody to believe in him. He found those believers—after the December 2013 trade for a conditional pick in the 2015 MLS SuperDraft—in Sounders keeper coach Tom Dutra and head coach Sigi Schmid. They needed a full-time replacement for departed keeper Michael Gspurning, though it wasn't immediately apparent they'd found one.

"I think I had proven I could be a good goalkeeper but at that point in my career, it had been over a year since my injury and since I'd gotten solid playing time," Frei said. "As you know, with athletes, confidence plays a tremendous factor. I knew that I wasn't in the same state of mind that I'd been in before."

Frei began the 2014 season rather tentatively, allowing eight goals in his first four matches—including four in one game against Portland. But the team around him was good enough to mask most of his weaknesses, scoring four of their own to survive the Timbers game with a 4–4 draw.

Then in May, playing against the Vancouver Whitecaps, Frei raced about 25 yards out of his goal to the far corner of the field for a loose ball. He could have allowed it to go out of bounds for a corner kick, or booted it out to the sidelines for a Vancouver throw-in. But instead, he played it back toward the midfield. Unfortunately, Whitecaps midfielder Gershon Koffe trapped the ball with his chest and sent a lobbed shot back toward the wide open net.

Frei knew instantly he'd gone too far out and wouldn't get back to the ball in time. The result was a 40-yard goal for Koffe in a game that ended 2–2. It was an example of Frei still feeling rust from his nearly two years of being sidelined; he was unable to make the split-second judgment calls every keeper must make on multiple occasions throughout each match.

But keeper coach Jutra kept imploring Schmid to be patient and give Frei time. After all, there had been positive signs—such as Frei making a season-high five saves in a 2–0 shutout win at Montreal.

"I went through some growing pains that first year, but I don't think there was any way around it," Frei said. "There was no way to get back to a decent level without making mistakes, without feeling okay to be making mistakes. It helps when you have people around who trust in you and your ability.

"They constantly would remind me of that."

Things picked up for Frei in June, when he helped lead the Sounders to their fourth Lamar Hunt U.S. Open Cup championship. After posting a shutout against Chicago in the semifinal, his late save from close range in the 88th minute of regulation kept Seattle tied 1–1 with the Philadelphia Union. Clint Dempsey then scored in overtime, while Obafemi Martins added an insurance marker for a 3–1 win in front of a hostile, pro-Union crowd at Chester, Pennsylvania.

The tournament win helped Frei's season take off. He would post a league-high 20 victories and the Sounders would capture their first ever Supporters' Shield. Frei wound up a nominee for MLS Comeback Player of the Year, yielding 50 goals after starting in all 34 games.

"I've always enjoyed working hard and this is the perfect environment. Because Tom [Jutra] puts in a tremendous amount of work and he's always there to share his feedback on what he sees, but also to listen to how I feel and what I feel I want to work on," Frei said.

The following season, Frei started in 31 games and allowed a career-low 33 goals, establishing himself as one of the game's premier netminders. He was named the team's Defender of the Year. One year later, he proved instrumental in the team's first MLS Cup championship, his iconic save in overtime off Jozy Altidore header helping him secure the game's Most Valuable Player honors.

"They allowed me to resurrect my career," Frei said. "And for that, I will always be grateful."

37 New Attendance Record on Opening Day at Kingdome

As the nation's summer bicentennial loomed, all of Seattle was abuzz with anticipation for the opening of the city's first indoor stadium. The Kingdome would propel the city into the sports universe big time, leading to expansion Seahawks and Mariners franchises by 1977.

But on April 9, 1976, the very first team to play a game inside the Kingdome was for a sport many in the city were lukewarm about. The stadium had held its grand opening just 13 days prior, with more than 6,000 performers from various schools, Boy Scouts, armed forces color guards, bands, and drill teams participating in front of a crowd exceeding 54,000.

But the first sports event would be a much bigger test. Sure, the Sounders had already played two years in the North American Soccer League. But it was one thing to sell out 13,000-seat Memorial Stadium, quite another to generate enough attention to play in an NFL-sized venue.

On this particular day, the Sounders didn't even have the city's undivided attention, since the defending NBA champion Golden State Warriors were in town to play the Supersonics. But for the Sounders, their exhibition game would contain a star power opponent as well—none other than legendary Brazilian star Pelé and his New York Cosmos. And though many in attendance that day had never seen a soccer match, they were lured by the intrigue of an indoor stadium in the normally drizzle-bound Seattle springtime. It had been rainy and foggy all week, but game day was clear with a high of 61 and low of 39. And none of that mattered as fans piled into the room-temperature facility.

As kickoff approached, most of about 4,000 remaining tickets were sold to walk-up spectators to form what would become a near-capacity crowd of 58,128. It would be the largest crowd to see a soccer game in the United States since 46,000 were on hand to watch Hakoah Vienna play at New York's Polo Grounds during a 1926 tour.

The Sounders were coming off an impressive 15–7 finish in 1975, while the Cosmos were establishing themselves as one of the NASL's premier franchises. In another year, the two sides would meet in the 1977 Soccer Bowl. But for now, it was all about seeing the Kingdome and Pelé.

"I remember this massive stadium," recalled current Sounders owner Adrian Hanauer, then age 10, who was at the game with his family. "I'd never seen or been to anything as big or modern as the Kingdome. And I have vague recollections of the excitement in the building, just the energy."

Midfielder Adrian Webster also remembers a charged-up, surreal atmosphere inside the building. "Obviously, it was a big event because it was a new stadium and us moving into a new stadium. It was against the New York Cosmos and Pelé and obviously, on that night, Pelé put on a clinic."

Just three minutes into the match, Pelé gave the fans their money's worth, scoring on a free kick that struck the Sounders' defensive wall and found its way by goalkeeper Tony Chursky. The Cosmos would go up 2–0 on a Dave Clements goal less than three minutes later before the Sounders got on the board in the 65th minute, with Jimmy Gabriel heading home a Tommy Jenkins cross.

The crowd's roar for Gabriel's goal was loud, but Hanauer remembers a distracted tinge to it. "It was loud, but in those days it wasn't as knowledgeable and sophisticated a soccer crowd as we have today. I think that the education, the knowledge is really just miles better now than then."

Instead, many fans continued just to gaze around the Kingdome, happy to be there and not paying too much attention to the game itself. Still, the goal hyped up the fans and made for some good energy the rest of the way. Finally, in the 87th minute, Pelé put things away with a hard shot past Chursky to complete the 3–1 win for the visitors.

"There were a lot of plusses in that game," Webster said. "The biggest was 58,000 people. We were wondering, 'Are we going to be able to maintain this?' With 58,000, you're hoping they're all going to come back. But then, as the season goes along, it all kind of levels out."

The Sounders would average more than 23,000 fans per game at home that season to lead the NASL. For Webster, the biggest disappointment came when, after a 14–10–0 regular season, the Sounders failed to qualify for that year's Soccer Bowl being played at the Kingdome. They were eliminated by the Minnesota Kicks in the division championship round. Minnesota went on to lose the Soccer Bowl 3–0 to Toronto Metros-Croatia in front of only 25,765 fans attending the neutral-site contest.

"I can remember watching the game with my teammates and thinking, 'If we'd been in it, they would have had 58,000 again,'" Webster said. "And who knew that a year later, we'd be in the final? So it was a bit sad that we never got to play in the final at home."

For that season, at least, an exhibition game would remain the highlight.

38 Twitter Feud Turns Foul

Signing international transfer Andreas Ivanschitz in August 2015 wasn't something the Sounders were expecting to create controversy. The midfielder from Spanish club Levante and former Austrian Bundesliga Player of the Year was supposed to bolster the team's depth on attack.

Instead, the team's social media department found itself playing defense. Within hours of the transfer being announced, the Portland Timbers took to their social media feed with a tweet that read: "So, let's get this straight. Ivanschitz and Deuce are on the same club now?"

Deuce, of course, is Clint Dempsey's nickname and also a commonly used slang word for feces. Ivanschitz is pronounced exactly like frat boy humor might suggest. Needless to say, the jab got plenty of social media attention.

Soon after, the official Sounders twitter feed replied to the barb with, "A ___ joke from a ___ club" and filled in the blanks with an emoji of a smiling pile of manure. And that quickly garnered national media attention.

The Sounders took down their tweet, but fans had already taken screen captures of it. The Timbers left their initial tweet posted.

Sounders officials were not pleased with the exchange, which occurred during a transition phase following the departure of the team's digital media boss, Shane Evans. A rotation of staffers had been handling the team's tweets while a replacement for Evans was sought.

The Twitter feud turned out to be one of the highlights of the oft-injured Ivanschitz's season-and-a-half stay with the team. He scored four goals and added nine assists in 34 games but was pushed out of the picture by the July 2016 acquisition of Uruguayan midfielder Nicolas Lodeiro.

After winning the MLS Cup, the Sounders declined their 2017 option on the 33-year-old and he left to play for Viktoria Plzen in the Czech Republic.

39 An Ownership Stake for Fans

Kyle Boyd spent a year after college living in the town of Godoy Cruz in Argentina, marching to soccer games with the rabid fans that support its 96-year-old soccer team. Years later, as a member of the Sounders' Alliance Council, Boyd wanted to re-create that feeling engendered by South American teams through memberships in local sports clubs.

Fans of those teams would buy memberships and literally own a stake in the club. Thus their passion wasn't just bred out of home partisanship—they literally had skin in the game. Boyd and the Alliance Council wanted the Sounders to sell such memberships and give fans a deeper say in club operations.

But that was against Major League Soccer rules and never came about. Still, when the Sounders in 2015 began operating a United Soccer League second division franchise known as Sounders2, the idea was put back on the table. And on October 19, 2014, at a lavish press conference in the famed Chihuly Glass Museum at Seattle Center, the Sounders announced that their S2 affiliate would indeed sell memberships and give fans a type of ownership stake.

Boyd was on hand for that and could not have been happier.

"It's really going to be all about the fans," he said. "[It's] all about creating an emotional attachment to the team."

The degree of actual S2 ownership was debatable. But then again, it certainly surpassed the ceremonial community ownership so often touted by the Green Bay Packers of the National Football League.

For a $250 yearly membership fee, fans got discounted S2 season tickets, choice seat selection, access to players and a members-only club at the team's headquarters at the Starfire complex in Tukwila. The memberships would be to a non-profit entity called the Sounders Community Trust, which would have a 20 percent ownership stake in the new team.

That non-profit status meant that fans couldn't actually share in any S2 revenues. All membership dues money would go to pay for capital improvements at the Starfire facility. So again, it was a limited ownership. The upside was fans wouldn't be hit up for cash calls to pay player salaries like a real owner could be. And they did have a limited say in operations. They would get to elect a board of trustees for the non-profit entity and direct them on how to manage their 20 percent stake in S2.

In June 2016, fan members of the S2 community trust approved a Memorandum of Understanding with the Sounders, calling on them to provide greater support for fundraising efforts, marketing, and branding. The agreement also solidified some of the benefits members would receive.

Sounders owner Adrian Hanauer, who has traveled the world attending soccer matches, says the idea was to get fans more emotionally invested in the USL team. Starting up a USL franchise locally was always going to be a challenge, given it would be drawing from much the same fan base as the bigger MLS franchise. And Hanauer was ready to explore any idea that could heighten that passion.

"If you've ever been to a Boca-River game [in Buenos Aires] or a London derby game, you can feel the passion that fans carry into the stadium," he said.

"There's really nothing like it."

Sounders fan Boyd agreed.

"The fans would gather before a game and thousands of them would march up to this huge stadium, which they'd used for the World Cup [in 1978]," Boyd said.

"And they'd fill it because they were just crazy about their team. They had this attachment to it because it was part of them. They literally owned the team because it was part of the club they belonged to. The place they would work out or hang out themselves.

"I want that here."

40 Make Your Own Tifo

One of the bigger pregame moments for Sounders fans involves members of the Emerald City Supporters unfurling a Tifo in the South end zone.

Tifo is derived from the Italian word Tifosi and describes choreographed fan support. This is commonly done through flags, two-pole banners and other visual displays, some even involving smoke or flares. But the giant Tifo typically associated with the ECS group is far from the only one inside CenturyLink Field. The group actually encourages fans to make their own two-pole banner Tifo and even supplies a tutorial on their official website explaining how to do it.

"We find our members really take pleasure in making their own," ECS co-president Heather Satterberg said. "They feel like they're directly contributing a part of themselves to supporting the team."

The Emerald City Supporters encourage fans to make their own tifos—albeit smaller than the ones they unfurl before every game.

The website tutorial says as much.

"There is additional pride felt when you put the time and energy into creating something from scratch vs. purchasing it from a print shop or other business," the website states. "If you feel your artistic abilities aren't up to [snuff], there are many ECS members that can help you with ways to create a Tifo without being the next Da Vinci."

The website suggests designing an image or adapting something from a graphic they find appealing. All lettering should be kept brief. The website advises purchasing transparency film sheets for inkjet printers at a supply store like Office Depot or Staples, then printing the image on those sheets at the largest size possible to preserve detail.

From there, a pair of 4-to-5-inch dowels—with at least ¾-inch diameter—should be purchased at a hardware store. The website suggests buying a few yards of fabric and fabric paint, or markers, at a local store like Jo-Ann Fabrics, Display & Costume, or Seattle Fabrics.

Once all the materials are gathered, the ECS website suggests finding a space at home or anyplace that offers a few clear feet of wall space to hang the fabric. Also, the room must be able to be darkened, so an overhead projector or computer projector can shine light on it. The printed transparency sheet is then used to project the desired image onto the hung fabric.

From there, a pencil can be used to trace the image's outline on the fabric, which is then taken off the wall and colored in using the markers and paint. The fabric is then attached to the dowels for a completed Tifo.

But the job isn't quite complete. The website explains the next step.

"Drink a beer, you're done."

41 The Science of Winning

As the Sounders morphed rapidly from expansion team to Supporters' Shield winner and, finally, MLS Cup champions, it became clear the team was doing something quite different from most.

Sure, the Sounders had a loyal, rambunctious fan base that gave them arguably the biggest homefield advantage in the league. And yes, Sigi Schmid was one of the most decorated head coaches in MLS history and had a top assistant in Brian Schmetzer and renowned keeper coach in Tom Dutra.

But other teams could say largely the same and weren't close to making the playoffs in every year of their existence. Nor were they neck-and-neck with the Los Angeles Galaxy at having the best win-loss total since 2009. At some point, in dissecting what makes the

Sounders tick, conversation inevitably turns to the team's pioneering sports science department—and to David Tenney, the onetime fitness coach that made it all happen. In fact, Tenney did his job a little too well, as evidenced by the NBA's Orlando Magic hiring him away from the Sounders midway through 2017. But Tenney's contributions are still being felt.

At its essence, Tenney decided during the team's 2009 expansion season that his job was about quantifying athletic prowess and potential and figuring out how to maximize it.

"It's about assessing fatigue," he said, "trying to quantify what happens in the games. [It's about] looking at adaptation to training in games, monitoring sleep, nutrition, what guys do in the weight room."

Everybody sort of knew those things already. But nobody was actually taking a scientific approach to doing anything about it. That's where Tenney quickly differentiated himself, implementing groundbreaking technology like the Catapult GPS and Omegawave systems. The Catapult system measures player movement during training, while Omegawave gauges heart rate variability and readiness before and after games.

It gave the Sounders a huge edge. They now knew which players were fatigued and needed rest and which could be pushed harder. In a sport where the talent level between teams is minuscule, even the tiniest shred of information like that could provide a valuable on-field edge.

And it did.

"The innovative stuff happened more in the beginning when they first started up," Sounders coach Schmetzer says. "All the algorithms that they used to help Sig and then myself measure training mode, game mode, and all that sort of stuff.

"It's a combination of heart rate, body load, velocity load. Their sleep patterns. All that sort of stuff comes in under one formula and then it gives me—at the end of the day—a training load."

And Schmetzer used the data every single day. It literally told him what to do with a player and how hard to push him.

"If today is a hard day, then tomorrow, because we have a game on Saturday, has to be a little less," Schmetzer said. "That training load might seem like a simple number. But there's really a lot of detail that goes into getting me...the information that I need."

The Sounders in 2011 began hosting an annual Sports Science Weekend that showcases the intersection between science and athletics. Tenney was the star attraction, leading discussions on where technology in sports was headed. He was later promoted in 2014 to head the team's quickly expanding, 35-member performance and sports science department.

For Sounders owner Adrian Hanauer, the use of technology to maximize sports performance has always fascinated him. It's something he views as the next frontier to finding undervalued assets like Oakland A's general manager Billy Beane once did, as portrayed in the 2003 book *Moneyball.*

Hanauer had been a gifted-but-undersized soccer player as a youth and abandoned the sport for years because he felt his talents had gone underappreciated by coaches obsessed with only athletic builds.

Not surprisingly, one of Hanauer's current fascinations is attempting to identify "small players" of top quality similarly overlooked. The Sounders' 2017 MLS Cup finalist squad alone had four regulars—Nicolas Lodeiro, Victor Rodriguez, Cristian Roldan, and Harry Shipp—among the smallest players in the league.

"That's one area I'd love to delve deeper into," Hanauer said.

He'll have to do it without Tenney, now a high performance director for the Magic. But the tools of Tenney's work are still in place for anyone with the imagination to take them further.

42 Timing Is Everything

Few American soccer players are good enough to get paid for doing it for 20 years in both Europe and the United States. Although goalkeeper Marcus Hahnemann was one of those rarities, he figures his entire professional career came down to being the luckiest soccer player alive.

Sure, the standout from Newport High School in the Seattle suburb of Bellevue had for years made a mockery of opponents trying to score on him, including during his four seasons spent with the Seattle Pacific University Falcons. Hahnemann managed shutouts in 46 to 78 games played for SPU, winning the NCAA Division II championship in 1993.

But he figured that would be it.

"I thought that would be my path," he said. "Getting a degree there and getting out into the workforce."

The North American Soccer League had folded a decade earlier, one year after the Sounders' demise. From there, Hahnemann had watched the indoor Tacoma Stars and the semi-pro Seattle FC team try to make a go of it. But if offered nothing he considered full-time work.

Until the Sounders were resurrected in the A-League in 1994, the year after he graduated. At the time, pre-dating Major League Soccer by two years, the A-League was the top outdoor circuit in North America.

"It was just absolutely perfect timing," Hahnemann said. "I keep thinking I'm the luckiest person alive coming right out of school and all of a sudden you have a professional team that's just starting up brand new. Which is more important, I think, for a goalkeeper because as a goalkeeper, it's difficult to break into a team."

But Hahnemann did just that with the newly revived Sounders under coach Alan Hinton in 1994. Among his teammates that first year was future Sounders head coach Brian Schmetzer, an "old pro" connection that would serve Hahnemann well years later when he sought out the chance to make a final career appearance in MLS.

"I just learned so much just from having those old pros next to me," he said of Schmetzer, Chance Fry, Billy Crook, and others on those Sounders teams. "I learned so much just from having those old pros next to me and in front of me. That really got my career off to a good start."

The A-League Sounders were formidable, winning the championship in 1995 and 1996. But the onset of MLS meant players were lured away from the A-League for bigger money. Hahnemann was no exception, signing with the Colorado Rapids for two and a half seasons. After that, he'd proven himself enough to head overseas for the start of a 13-year professional career in England.

Not bad for a guy who'd been planning a day job when his college career ended.

"I was living the dream," he said.

He broke in with Fulham, but then spent the bulk of his career with Reading, then Wolverhampton and finally Everton before pondering a move back home. At that point, he'd fulfilled his near-impossible childhood dream of playing in Europe. He'd also backed up U.S. Men's National Team keepers Kasey Keller and Tim Howard in two World Cups. But now his career was nearly done. And Hahnemann wanted one final chance to play in Seattle in front of a home crowd.

"I tried to time my retirement in England and come back," he said.

But the Sounders were lukewarm. Hahnemann said he "spent the summer at the cabin just kind of chilling out" until Sounders owner Adrian Hanauer finally called to ask him whether he still wanted to play.

He started talking to head coach Sigi Schmid and assistant Schmetzer, his former A-Leauge teammate from years earlier. "Schmetzer starts asking, 'So, what if you don't play at all—you come back and you sit on the bench?'" Hahnemann said. "They were wondering what I was going to be like because I'd played for so long. I knew I was a good pro and I just said it plain and simple. I said 'Brian, I've played a lot of games for the Seattle Sounders and I just want to play one more.'"

For Schmetzer, that was good enough.

Hahnemann was signed "just to play one more time," he said. "I mean, that's what everybody wants."

He started four more MLS games, all in 2003. That same year, he played in the CONCACAF Champions League tournament in which the Sounders made it all the way to the semifinal. But by 2014, with Stefan Frei establishing himself as the team's premier netminder, Hahnemann was done.

But he'd bridged the gap between two Sounders eras.

"That was what we always wanted," he said of the Sounders' MLS version. "Fast-forward 10 years and all of a sudden a small crowd was 30,000 where an average crowd for the old [A-League] Sounders was 3,000. I'm happy I got a chance to live that transformation."

43 Teenager Cristian Roldan Says, "No Thanks!"

Cristian Roldan had grown up alongside his high school teammates from Pico Rivera.

By age four, he was playing soccer with them on a narrow strip of grass in the backyard of his family's single-level, ranch-style home in the town adjacent to East Los Angeles. At age eight, the boyhood friends were in the same youth soccer league, with Roldan getting picked that year to star in an Adidas television commercial during the 2006 World Cup.

So when that same group of boys became teenagers with a shot at bringing unprecedented soccer glory to their hometown, Roldan wasn't about to let them down. That's a decision he faced prior to the 2012–13 season as soccer academies run by the Los Angeles Galaxy and Chivas USA were pressuring him to leave his El Rancho High School team to play for them.

But El Rancho had just gone 26–0 in the regular season before being upset in the division title game. There was a sense of unfinished business—that the team had a shot at a division championship and perhaps far more the following year if it stayed intact.

So Roldan did the unthinkable. He told the academies no thanks.

"My family played a big part in that," Roldan said. "We had lived in Pico Rivera all of our lives. My older brother went to high school there and my younger brother was planning to, as well. I made really good relationships there with my coach and my teammates. So I think all of those things played into it."

Roldan's parents, Cesar and Ana, had fled early 1980s civil wars in Guatemala and El Salvador to come to the United States. They'd met within a year of arrival, married in 1989, and the following year bought their house in Pico Rivera and started a family.

The town of 63,000 residents packed in just over nine square miles is about as densely populated and tight-knit as they come. With more than 91 percent of residents from Hispanic or Latino backgrounds, Pico Rivera loves its high school soccer.

But staying to play another season at El Rancho was akin to career suicide. High school soccer was considered a lesser path for elite-level players compared to academies where Roldan—smaller than most on the field—could have his natural skills seen by people that mattered.

Still, Roldan risked it. He went on to score a record 54 goals and add another 30 assists that 2012–13 season to lead El Rancho to the division title and its first California Regional Championship. Given the strength of the region's teams, it was the de facto equivalent of a state title.

Roldan capped it by being named the Gatorade National High School Player of the Year. Former U.S. national team star Alexi Lalas surprised Roldan by walking into his biology class, with ESPN cameras rolling, to present him his trophy.

"It meant a lot to the community and the school because we reached heights we'd never touched before," Roldan's high school coach Dominic Picon said. "Everybody knows who the El Rancho athletes are in the community, and when somebody has the success that Cristian has had, obviously everybody knows who he is, knows about him. He brought true national recognition to a very small community."

Still, the decision left Picon and Roldan's parents fraught with worry. Picon had sent tapes of Roldan playing soccer to about 30 Division 1 universities after his junior year. Not one replied.

The El Rancho team wasn't exactly a prime-time hotbed for scouts. It practiced and played on a vacant grass lot next to the school's football stadium, where the field's drainage system had given it a slope that hindered soccer performance.

Every game, soccer goal posts were installed on the vacant lot and parents and students would fill the sidelines to watch—many bringing their own folding chairs. It wasn't perfect, but it was their team.

Roldan's parents made sure at least one of them was at every game. And during one game Roldan's senior year, his mother found herself seated next to University of Washington head coach Jamie Clarke.

She had no idea who he was until Clark leaned over, introduced himself, and asked where he could find a game program so he could identify the players he was there to scout. There were no more programs, but Roldan's mother told Clark she knew of at least one player he should watch.

Clark spent about 10 minutes watching Roldan and made up his mind to offer him a scholarship then and there. Two years later, after two seasons with the Huskies, Roldan was drafted No. 18 overall by the Sounders.

Looking back, Roldan attributes his decision to the sense of loyalty and honor his family bestowed upon him, his older brother, Cesar Jr., and younger brother, Alex—drafted by the Sounders in January 2018. His parents, working-class immigrants who'd devoted their lives to shepherding the athletic-minded boys to practices and games, didn't fully grasp the politics of saying no to the academies.

"We didn't know the system at all," Roldan's father said. "We knew Cristian had talent. But we didn't know what we were supposed to do to get people to come and see him play. We didn't know anybody."

Still, his older brother says Roldan was determined to stick by his friends. And once he'd made that choice, his parents—albeit worried about the implications—were proud of the reasoning and didn't try to talk Cristian out of it.

"Playing with those kids for six-plus years together and then going to that high school together really strengthened that brotherhood bond," Cesar Jr. said, "and they were pretty good, as well. It was a once-in-a-lifetime opportunity. A perfect storm to do something the town had never accomplished before."

Now, after three seasons with the Sounders, Roldan, an emerging Major League Soccer star, says he wouldn't do things any differently.

"Long term it probably wasn't the best idea," Roldan said. "But short term, I made a lot of good memories [and] won a pair of championships there. I was really proud of the moment. It may have hindered the recruiting process in going to college and bigger schools. But I think it all worked out and I'm really proud of how it happened."

44 Listen to a Sounders Podcast

The Sounders had just been eliminated by the hated Portland Timbers in the 2013 playoffs when heartbroken fans Steven Agen and Zach Thatcher left CenturyLink Field and decided to get a drink. As the beer flowed, the longtime buddies from high school began talking about starting up a soccer podcast.

Agen was only 18 but had been a loyal Emerald City Supporters member for years and was now writing freelance articles on soccer for Prost Amerika. They both decided their podcast would be not only about the Sounders, but soccer throughout the Pacific Northwest including the Timbers and Vancouver Whitecaps.

"We figured there was this niche," Agen said. "We wanted to talk about soccer and nobody was talking about all of Cascadia at once. We thought it was worth a shot."

Prost agreed to host the podcast on its website. And by 2014, the first episode of Radio Cascadia was launched, featuring an interview with longtime Sounders mainstay Roger Levesque.

"It took a while to get it set up, but we've been going pretty much continuously since then," Agen said.

The weekly podcast features interviews from players, coaches, and journalists in the three MLS marketplaces in the Northwest. The show has also partnered with various media members in Vancouver and Portland over the years who've posted the show on their outlet's website in those markets, as well.

With Agen based in Seattle and a full-time University of Washington student, it hasn't always been easy keeping track of the Timbers and Whitecaps like he has the Sounders.

"It's definitely difficult," he said. "I try to make as many Vancouver and Portland home games a year as I can. I read all of their news online from three or four different outlets. And then I try to [talk to] our contact in that city before I record to try to make sure that I'm on-pulse as far as the topics we hit with regards to their club."

In 2016, with the Sounders coming off their first MLS Cup victory and becoming a hot commodity, Sports Radio KJR offered the podcast the chance to record the show in its studios and put it on the air. The show is called Radio Cascadia Live and features Agen, SportsPress NW contributors Andrew Harvey, and Ari Liljenwall on-air alongside KJR host Jackson Felts.

In August 2017, Agen and Prost published the book *Resurgence: How Sounders FC Roared Back to Win the MLS Cup* with contributions from Harvey and Liljenwall.

Agen says he's bumped into people at games and around town who follow his work. "I'm a radio guy, so they know the voice and not the name."

45. How Adrian Hanauer Rode a Hot Stock to an MLS Franchise

Adrian Hanauer certainly came from a family with some money. He'd grown up in a high-end home in Mercer Island, his parents having earned considerable wealth via their Pacific Coast Feather Company bedding firm. He'd been a formidable soccer midfielder in his youth for Newport Hills, then one of only three freshmen to make the Mercer Island High School team. But by age 13, he'd stopped growing and became "a pudgy little kid" while other teens around him shot up in size.

"I couldn't compete physically," he said. "I always had really good skills above my age. And I got a little bit demoralized over the course of time."

Hanauer wound up leaving the high school team and would not start playing again until his 30s. But he never lost his zeal for watching the game, which was fostered as a youth when his parents bought season tickets to watch the NASL Sounders at Memorial Stadium starting in 1974.

He began working for the family feather bedding company at age 13 and then, after graduating from the University of Washington, founded a series of companies that included a chain of pizza stores called Mad Pizza. Despite how well-off his family was, Hanauer lacked the kind of money that leads to ownership in professional sports. The process that led to that only began in 1997, when his older brother, Nick, helped found an advertising technology company called Avenue A Media.

"There were some good ones, but that was really the game-changer for me and my family overall," Hanauer said.

Hanuaer and his family members were seed investors and later took on some angel investors to get the company going. Hanauer himself owned "a lot of stock in it" and when taken public in early 2000, Avenue A quickly rocketed up to $89 per share and made "a ginormous amount of money" for him. By then, the company's name had changed to aQuantive Inc.

However, the fortune proved short-lived as the 2000 technology crash hit only months later and sent the stock spiraling down to 70 cents per share. Many owners would have panicked and bailed before the stock bottomed out. Hanauer wound up taking huge losses—all on paper—but he was determined to ride things out. Call it stubbornness, faith in the product, or plain old family pride, but he watched with hope as the stock slowly edged back up, first doubling to $1.40 per share, then $5.

Finally, by 2007, aQuantive was a $160 million business with 2,600 employees and growing by 40 percent annually. CEO Brian McAndrews was working wonders for the company and its two primary brands, Atlas and Drive PM. That's when Microsoft came along in 2007, looking to boost its advertising capabilities against Google and Yahoo! Not wanting to be outbid by competitors, Microsoft CEO Steve Ballmer offered $66.50 per share for the company—about 85 percent above its trading price.

The final pricetag? A whopping $6.4 billion. It was the largest acquisition in Microsoft history until it later bought Skype for $8.5 billion.

"It was perfect timing," Hanauer said.

Perfect for Hanauer, anyway. As for Microsoft, it never fully incorporated aQuantive and its advertising-heavy culture within its own more engineering-centered ranks. Five years later, Microsoft took a $6.2 billion writedown against aQuantive in what remains one of the biggest failures of the company's and Ballmer's legacies.

A year after the aQuantive writedown, Ballmer was out of a job.

"It's too bad," Hanauer said.

Meanwhile, Hanauer's own life passions for business and soccer were about to rocket forward. He'd already become involved in the ownership of the Sounders as the United Soccer League franchise's managing partner. But from 2003 onward, he'd looked at bringing a Major League Soccer franchise to Seattle. The numbers weren't that big at the time, with a Real Salt Lake franchise winding up being awarded a franchise ahead of Seattle in 2004 for only $5 million.

Those franchise fees would grow six times bigger by 2007, with Hanauer again making a pitch to land MLS for Seattle. Hanauer wanted to be a minority stakeholder in the ownership group, but he needed far more personal wealth. And he got it when the Microsoft deal for aQuantive went down in April 2007. Just six months later, MLS awarded the Sounders franchise.

"Ultimately, the timing worked out for me to be able to participate in the franchise that we paid $30 million for in 2007," Hanauer said. "We sold that company to Microsoft and it was right in that timeframe."

The Sounders purchase has more than paid off. Hanauer became majority owner in 2014 and as of August 2017, the franchise had been valued by Forbes at $296 million.

48 Seconds and a Tree Chop

Of all the memorable moments in the history of the Sounders-Timbers rivalry, what happened just 48 seconds into their July 1, 2009, match ranks among the biggest. The Sounders were just a few months into their debut MLS season while the Timbers were still in the USL.

The clubs met in the third round of the U.S. Open Cup at Providence Park in Portland, and Sounders midfielder Roger Levesque didn't wait long to establish himself as the rivalry's most polarizing figure. Before most people in the stadium realized what was happening, he put a diving near-post header on a Sanna Nyassi cross and sent it past Timbers goalkeeper Steve Cronin.

"Most people were probably still in the concessions line getting a beer," Levesque said. "And before anybody knew it, we were up 1–0, and so it was almost as if we started the match up a goal."

But Levesque didn't stop there. He ran over to the side of the field, where teammate Nate Jaqua joined him and pretended to chop at him like he was a tree. Jaqua had actually grown up on a farm in Eugene, Oregon, and knew exactly what he was doing form-wise. And Levesque did his best tree impersonation, keeping his hands pinned to his sides as he toppled to the ground. The gesture was meant to mock Portland mascot Timber Joey—and Timber Jim before him—who both dressed like loggers and would use a chainsaw to cut through a thick log whenever the home team scored.

Turns out, Levesque and Jaqua had hatched the plan on the bus ride to Portland. But they had envisioned it going the other way, with Levesque doing the chopping and Jaqua falling down. After all, Jaqua was starting up top at striker and Levesque was flanked out wide.

"The way we framed it on the bus was that he was going to be the one to score and I was going to chop him down," Levesque said. "But it went the other way so I just kind of took my cue off him. My mind kind of went blank after the goal but he was spot on, coming up to me and starting to chop. That sort of cemented my infamy with the Timbers Army and the Portland fans."

The Sounders went on to win 2–1 and would later that year capture their first of three consecutive U.S. Open Cups. Lamar Neagle was a Sounders rookie at the time and remembers watching the tree-chop scene from the bench.

"We didn't know it was coming," Neagle said. "I think it was Jaqua that cut him down, so obviously he knew. And those guys had planned it before. But for it to happen that quickly and for it to be Roger and his personality, the way we love him in Seattle, kind of made it all the more special."

For goalkeeper Kasey Keller, however, the antics caused him to take some heat from the Timbers faithful that day. Keller had gone to the University of Portland and played for an amateur reincarnation of the Timbers in 1989. Now he was hearing it behind his net from fans who'd once cheered him on.

"I was getting a lot of stick from the Timbers fans," he said. "When you come in there, score so early, and have a fun celebration, it just kind of puts that authority in there.

"Anytime you can be involved when you beat your biggest rival, be it the North London Derby or Gladbach-Cologne, or whatever it was in the big derby games I'd played in during my career, you took those Timbers games the same way."

Levesque would produce another memorable "scuba diver" celebration in June 2011 during a nationally televised game against the New York Red Bulls at CenturyLink Field when he stole the ball off keeper Gregg Sutton and scored on an empty net. He ran to an LED message board behind the net, sat on it, pinched his nose and toppled over backward like a diver going off a boat.

"I got the wind knocked out of me pretty good," he said of hitting the hard concrete surface backward. "There wasn't any planning that went in to that one."

Not like the pre-planned Portland antics, which made Levesque an instant hero to legions of Sounders fans and an archvillain despised for years afterward by Timbers supporters. He had already been disliked by much of Timbers Army for his strong performances against Portland, in which he amassed 10 goals over 29 matches before retiring in 2012.

During the 2007 offseason, the USL Timbers had offered Levesque a chance to play for them in an exhibition against Toronto FC. The Sounders were preparing to enter MLS in 2009 and had toyed with not fielding a USL team in 2008, so Levesque took the offer just to stay in playing shape.

"Walking out with a Timbers jersey on for the starting lineup, I heard a lot of boos," he said. "And there was this big sign in the stands that said, "Real fans hate Levesque."

And that was a year before the whole tree-chopping episode.

Two years later, in 2010, the Emerald City Supporters group unfurled a Tifo that covered the entire South End of the stadium with the words 48 SECONDS and Levesque's smiling face depicted. The Tifo is widely considered the best that ECS has ever created.

To this day, the phrase "48 seconds" remains possibly the worst taunt a Sounders fan can throw at a Timbers supporter. The goal stood as the fastest in franchise history in any competition until Clint Dempsey scored 23 seconds into a game against San Jose six years later.

47 Joevin Jones Follows in Father's Footsteps

He'd heard the stories everywhere he went. It was impossible in soccer mad Trinidad and Tobago for Joevin Jones not to be informed on a daily basis about its Socca Warriors national team and the exploits of its legendary Strike Squad that came so close to qualifying for the 1990 FIFA World Cup.

But Jones heard the tales more than most since his father, Kelvin, a police officer in their fishing village, had played on that very edition of the national team. The Strike Squad in 1989 had positioned itself to need just a victory or a tie at home against the United States to advance to its first World Cup ever.

Instead, in a nationally televised game that brought the dual island nation to a standstill, Jones' father's side lost 1–0. It would be another 17 years before T&T qualified for a World Cup. Nevertheless, the Strike Squad gained folkloric standing among the country's 1.36 million inhabitants, its players feted at dinners, banquets, and charity events for years into their soccer retirements.

"Everywhere we would go, people recognized him in the street," Jones said of his famous dad. "He got a lot of attention."

And Jones had to follow that. From a young age, he excelled in sports, although he became known as a clown in the classroom. His father the cop tried to rein in Jones and his prankster humor, succeeding occasionally if not always. Jones knew he was going to excel on the soccer field, and put most of his energy in to that.

He'd grown up watching Cristiano Ronaldo play for Lisbon, since the team's games were carried on television in Trinidad. Jones dreamed of eventually making it to Europe to play and focused his energies on training to get there. His older brother, Marvin, had played professionally in Trinidad while his younger brother, Alvin, was destined for a local pro career.

Every morning, Joevin, Alvin, and their father would head out to a vacant grass field to train. He'd have them do skill drills or sprint training.

"I did things to help all of them," Kelvin said. "They wanted me to help make them better to reach their goals."

And that they did. Joevin signed his first pro contract with the local W Connection side at age 19, played five seasons, and then was sent on a six-month loan to a team in Helsinki, Finland. That taste of international play whet his appetite for play elsewhere and his eventual goal of landing in Europe permanently like boyhood idol Ronaldo.

Jones signed with the Chicago Fire, figuring he'd use MLS as a stepping stone to return overseas. The Fire recognized in one season that Jones had no intention of a long MLS career and dealt the talented youngster to the Sounders after the 2015 season in return for the team's first-round pick in the 2016 MLS Superdraft.

The Sounders had no illusions about Jones, either. But GM Garth Lagerwey figured it was worth having him even if only for a couple seasons. That instinct proved correct as Jones provided two-way speed up and down the left flank.

Jones played a key role in the Sounders rebound midway through the 2016 season, featured more prominently after the July firing of head coach Sigi Schmid. By the time the Sounders hoisted the MLS Cup in December, Jones had already established himself as one of the game's top left backs in only his second season in the league.

His father, who watched the Sounders on television from abroad as often as he could, still tried to make his son better following every match. They'd get on the phone and dissect his play.

"I also played left back," Kelvin said. "And I used to score goals all the time. Sometimes, I'll see Joevin get inside the box and he tries to set the ball up for somebody else. I'll tell him, 'Shoot the ball! Take the bull by the horns.'"

And his son has done just that with his career. Partway through the 2017 season, among the league leaders in assists, Joevin signed a two-year contract with Darmstadt of the German second division to begin in January 2018.

48 From Gun-Toting Militia to the MLS Cup

Making it back to the MLS Cup final a year after winning a championship is no easy task. And for the Sounders to do it in 2017, they had to change some of the faces and names that had gotten them there the previous year.

And of all those new additions, arguably the most valuable was an unassuming Swedish midfielder who'd spent much of his soccer years traveling the globe in search of better competition. Gustav Svensson could have stayed in Sweden playing for his IFK Göteborg squad in his hometown of Gothenburg. He'd already won a title there, was a household name, and by 2009 had secured his first international cap with Sweden's national team.

But Svensson wanted more, so he headed off to Turkey in 2010 to play for the country's defending champion Bursaspor squad in Bursa—teaming with Toronto FC stalwart Jozy Altidore. At one point, in a game in Istanbul, Svensson played in a stadium packed with only women and children under 12 after men had been banned due to violence at games.

As if that experience wasn't enough, Svensson headed to the Ukraine in 2012 to again seek a higher level of soccer. He'd adjusted to life in the city of Simferopol, in the country's contested Crimea region. But by 2014, gun-toting pro-Russian military members had shown up, taking over city facilities, rooftops, and the local airport.

"Even when the militia came, we had a normal life," Svensson said. "My wife's parents were over there visiting Ukraine for the first time. I wanted to show it to them because it's a beautiful place, especially us being down so close to the Black Sea. They were supposed to be there for 10 days, but when they came, everything started to escalate."

After playing a friendly match at home, Svensson's cell phone began blowing up. Friends were warning him that Russian President Vladimir Putin had just announced he was sending his country's military to Crimea. Fearing for his safety, Svensson had his team arrange for a car to drive him and his wife and her family out of the region. Other foreign players asked to join him, so Svensson, a leader on the team, arranged a private bus for all.

The bus left that day for an all-night drive out of the disputed territory. But it was pulled over in the darkness at a military checkpoint. Armed men boarded the bus, demanding passports and travel plans and shining flashlights in their faces.

"I'm not afraid of things generally," said Svensson, known for his physical play. "I'll fight with anyone that wants to fight me. But at that moment, it's hard to describe. I'd never felt that way before. I had no control over what was happening."

After some of the biggest guns he'd ever seen were pointed at him and his family, they were eventually allowed to leave and made it home to Sweden. There, Svensson played once again for IFK Goteborg for two seasons before his wanderlust took him to the Chinese Super League with Guangzhou in 2016.

Newly enforced roster rules for foreigners had Svensson looking like the odd man out with his team early in 2017. But he was in luck as his good friend Erik Friberg—who'd helped the Sounders win the MLS Cup in 2016 but did not have his contract renewed—suggested the Emerald City to him.

The Sounders were more than happy to take in Svensson, as a defensive midfielder and veteran presence to replace Friberg's role as a spot duty specialist. But once the 2017 season began, right back Brad Evans went out for two months and possibly longer with a leg injury, so Svensson was pressed into starting action at an unfamiliar position.

By mid-summer, Svensson had started games at right back, center back, and eventually in the defensive midfielder role he'd been signed for. And he never complained a bit.

"I mean, yes, I've played different positions and not where I came here to play," Svensson said, "but I'm just happy to help and play where I can play."

The Sounders were so thrilled with his selfless attitude, they let him leave early to train with Sweden ahead of some World Cup qualifiers in August. Svensson hadn't been called up by the national team in eight years. He didn't know its new coach and was worried he'd be overlooked. Instead, he got playing time in those qualifiers and again in the second leg of a critical winner-take-all series against Italy.

Sweden had won the first game. In the second game, in Milan, an injury pressed Svensson into action by the 14th minute. He came on and helped his team hold off a desperate Italian attack for a scoreless draw that sent Sweden to the World Cup and knocked Italy out for the first time in 60 years.

Barely a week later, Svensson was back on the pitch for the Sounders as a starting defensive midfielder in the opening leg of their Western Conference semifinal at Houston. Early in the first half, he opened the scoring in a stunning 2–0 win by the Sounders against a Houston team that had lost only one other time at home all year.

"This was obviously one of the best weeks of my career," Svensson said. "The only thing that beats this is when my son was born and getting married. Other than that, looking back, this is going to be a very good memory."

Nine days later, the memory was even better as his Sounders qualified for their second consecutive MLS Cup in a rematch at Toronto.

49 Sounders Win Multiple USL Titles

When Adrian Hanauer became part of the ownership group of the Sounders in what was still known as the A-League, he had more on his mind than just succeeding on that circuit. Hanauer wanted a Major League Soccer franchise and would spend years laying those seeds while his A-League team demonstrated how the game could work in the Emerald City. By 2002, when the team was seeking a new head coach, Hanauer's general manager had already left the team. So Hanauer conducted the coaching search and was told by everybody around him about a former NASL Sounders midfielder named Brian Schmetzer, who'd also been part of the team's first A-League season in 1994.

Schmetzer was hired and it quickly became apparent he was quite good at his job. In his inaugural 2002 season, he was named coach of the year. By 2004, he'd reached the championship game only to lose to Montreal. And then came 2005, when the A-League rebranded as the 12-team United Soccer League First Division and the Sounders found themselves back in the championship game.

Playing under Schmetzer, the Sounders had finished fourth overall, but they had run the table in the playoffs. They defeated Portland 3–0, then Montreal 4–3 in single-elimination matches to advance to the final against the Richmond Kickers from Virginia.

A crowd of 8,011 seemed tiny in cavernous Qwest Field—later to become CenturyLink Field—but the tension was palpable.

"I think that was one of the biggest crowds we ever played in front of with the USL group," said Roger Levesque, a forward who'd played with the Sounders since 2003. "We were confident and excited. I think, for us, there was a sense that we were going to win the game. It was just a matter of when and how."

But it wouldn't be easy. Richmond grabbed a 1–0 lead in the 24th minute that held up until Maykel Galindo tied it 1–1 on a rebound from close in.

The teams headed to penalty kicks, with Seattle going up 2–0 after two rounds. But the Kickers evened it up at 2–2 by the fifth and final round.

Kevin Jeffrey had a chance to win it for Richmond but fired the ball over the net.

Then in Round 7—now sudden death—Scott Jenkins, who would retire after the match, fired the ball into the back of the net to put the Sounders up 4–3. The Kickers were running out of shooters, so goalkeeper Ronnie Pascale lined up to take the next try as Richmond's final chance. But his shot rattled off the crossbar to give Seattle the title.

"Somebody reminded me afterward that my last touch of a ball is a winning goal, and that's pretty cool," Jenkins, who spent all nine of his professional seasons with the Sounders, told reporters after the match. "It's storybook. It's a nice way to go out. How can you beat going out like this?"

Goalkeeper Preston Burpo made a half-dozen critical saves—many in the penalty kick phase—and was named MVP.

The following season proved far tougher for Schmetzer, whose team missed the playoffs entirely. "Everything that went right for us in 2005 wound up going wrong for us in 2006," Schmetzer said. "It was the most difficult year of my career as a coach."

The experience taught Schmetzer some hard lessons about preparation and about the need to shed a championship hangover and get back to work quickly the following season. He'd apply it a decade later in guiding the Sounders to their first MLS Cup title in 2016 and then taking them back to the championship match again in 2017.

After the 2006 debacle, things went much better for Schmetzer in 2007. By then, the team was doing so well on and off the pitch that rumors swirled about MLS not being able to deny Seattle an expansion franchise any longer.

"That year, we were really good," Levesque said. "We were firing on all cylinders. We had Sebastien Le Toux, Greg Howes, Leighton O'Brien, Taylor Graham. We had just this list of veteran guys who'd flirted with the MLS, and everyone was playing at their best, knowing MLS was coming to Seattle.

"It made everyone raise their game just a little bit."

With the Sounders back in the USL championship game, talk of MLS expansion was overshadowing everything else the team was doing. The title game was played at the Starfire Sports stadium in the Seattle suburb of Tukwila, where the Sounders thrashed the visiting Atlanta Silverbacks 4–0.

Indeed, within weeks of their victory, the Sounders were named an MLS expansion team for the 2009 season.

"I would say that the 2005 and the 2007 championships contributed to the growth of what we have here in the sport," Schmetzer said. "It certainly kept [Sounders owner] Adrian [Hanauer] engaged and thinking bigger things."

Schmetzer added that the MLS Cup won by the team in 2016 may have been grander in scale, but "there were a lot of diehard fans in that South End [of the stadium] that were there in '05 and '07, keeping that kind of groundswell support that mushroomed into what we have today."

50 Dempsey Dominates a Rivalry

Of all the players in the long, contentious history between the Sounders and Portland Timbers, none has enjoyed greater success than Clint Dempsey. It helps that Dempsey has always prided himself on rising to the occasion in rivalry games.

As a nine-year-old in fifth grade, Dempsey played for the Texas Longhorns youth soccer team in Dallas. It was only a three-team league, and each year they battled the powerful Dallas Texans for the title. Each game between them, be it regular season, tournament, or playoff, took on added meaning.

"It was never life and death in terms of people trying to kill each other, but it was just that you knew they would be good, competitive games," Dempsey said. "They were the teams you usually faced in the finals of tournaments, and those were the teams you needed to beat to get the points to be top of the league. So they were very important games that kind of gave you a lift during the year."

Rivalry games continue to give Dempsey that lift, and none more than the Timbers derby in which he's scored nine goals since coming back over from the English Premier League in 2013. Three of the goals have been game winners, and seven have come in the final 30 minutes of play.

Dempsey's goal in stoppage time on June 25, 2017, salvaged a 2–2 draw at Portland and is credited with helping change the team's season. The Sounders eventually went on to record a club-record 13-game unbeaten streak that propelled them to a first-round playoff bye and eventual return to the MLS Cup final.

"It's an important game for us and our fans, so you want to perform well," Dempsey said. "It's bragging rights. You look to try to get a good result. Whether it's you scoring or somebody else, it's all about trying to win and have those bragging rights."

The low point for Dempsey in the rivalry came during the infamous Red Card Wedding match during the 2015 U.S. Open Cup final. With the Sounders already about to go down two men in overtime due to a red card, Dempsey protested by tearing up the referee's notebook and earning a subsequent ejection himself.

The Sounders went on to lose the game 3–1 in a rare U.S. Open Cup home defeat at their Starfire stadium facility.

A high point came in the teams' first meeting of the 2014 season. The Timbers had eliminated Seattle in the rivalry's only playoff meeting the year before, but this was about to become the greatest regular season in Sounders history.

Dempsey was on fire that April night in Portland, scoring a hat trick to help salvage a 4–4 draw. His first goal, in the 24th minute, was a nifty left-footed drive from close range to tie things at 2–2.

But the Timbers scored a pair of goals two minutes apart in the second half, including a beautifully placed curling strike by Maximiliano Urruti inside the near post that made it 4–2 in the 57th minute. With just over five minutes left in regulation, the Sounders appeared done when a Lamar Neagle cross was flicked by Obafemi Martins straight to the foot of a charging Dempsey inside the box. Dempsey collected the ball without breaking stride, fought off a defender draped over his shoulder, and fired the ball into the net to cut the deficit to 4–3.

Then, less than a minute later, DeAndre Yedlin was tripped by Ben Zemanski and a penalty kick awarded to the Sounders. Dempsey took it and fired left as keeper Andrew Weber dove the opposite way to even the match. Dempsey smirked as he glanced at the crowd and celebrated, sealing the contempt of the Timbers Army faithful.

There had been concern about Dempsey's slow start to his second go-around in MLS since joining the Sounders the previous August. This game would erase such doubts. Dempsey that season went on to record a career-high 15 goals while adding 10 assists as the Sounders captured their first and only Supporters' Shield.

The animosity only heightened after the Sounders won their first MLS Cup in December 2016. At a celebratory rally in Seattle, Dempsey grabbed the microphone and shouted, "All I got to say is, now that we won one, Portland can't say s—!"

It was a response to the previous year when, after the Timbers won their first title, captain Will Johnson grabbed the mic at a rally and shouted "F—k Seattle!" Once again, as he had so often on the field when the teams meet, Dempsey had gotten the last word.

51 Jordan Morris Comes Home with Honors

Five games into his professional career, nobody was predicting Jordan Morris as an end-of-season awards candidate.

Morris had yet to tally a single goal, despite arriving to MLS with much fanfare as a homegrown Hermann Trophy–winner and national champion out of Stanford University. He could have played in Germany's Bundesliga for SV Werder Bremen, but he turned down their contract offer after an extended training camp and signed instead with Seattle on January 21, 2016.

But with the signing, which reunited him with his team medical director father, Michael, came expectations. It didn't help that the team's official Twitter account posted a photo of him standing side-by-side with FC Barcelona star Lionel Messi just a few hours after general manager Garth Lagerwey promised Morris would not be overhyped.

By Valentine's Day came word that striker Obafemi Martins was headed to the Chinese Super League. All of a sudden, Morris was starting up-top. Although he denies feeling extra pressure playing in his hometown, he admitted the nerves got to him ahead of his Sounders debut.

"You get nervous coming into any new environment," he said.

Especially this one. He'd grown up on Seattle's Mercer Island, just outside downtown on Lake Washington, rooting for the hometown Seahawks, who played at the same CenturyLink Field he was now stepping on. It didn't help that the Sounders got off to one of their worst starts ever, putting the focus squarely on their 21-year-old rookie.

"A lot of players gain confidence based on how you're playing, and when you're a forward and you're not scoring goals, it can be tough sometimes because that's what you're judged on," Morris said.

Finally, in the team's sixth match, at home against the Philadelphia Union, Morris took an Andreas Ivanschitz pass in the 71st minute and flicked it past keeper Andre Blake with a right-footed stab. It turned out to be the game-winner in a 2–1 victory.

"That's a big weight off his shoulders," head coach Sigi Schmid told reporters afterward. "Each week, there was probably another five pounds that got added to that."

Indeed, the floodgates opened for Morris after that. He scored four goals over a four-game stretch but still got left off the U.S. Men's National Team roster for the Gold Cup Centenario tournament in June, which would feature games in Seattle. Though disappointed, having already earned several international caps, Morris used the tournament break to regroup.

Good friend Cristian Roldan got together with Morris throughout the break and reminded him of the positives to his game that had made him such a desired commodity in the first place. "I told him not to really care about what people say and to play his game honestly.

"I thought he handled the pressure a lot better toward the middle of the season," Roldan said.

By July, with the team 10 points out of a playoff spot, Schmid was fired as coach. Then, in early August, with the team down 1–0 at Orlando, Morris made several dangerous runs that helped shift the game's momentum. Clint Dempsey went on to record a hat trick in a 3–1 win the Sounders often credit with turning around their season.

Morris never looked back after that game.

"I think for me, like a lot of players, confidence plays a huge role," he said.

He went on to score 12 goals, the most ever by an MLS rookie—six of those were game-winners. On November 10, Morris was named MLS Newcomer of the Year.

For Morris and the Sounders, it capped a remarkable turnaround in fortunes that still had some distance to go.

Morris would score the tying goal in the opening leg of the Western Conference finals against Colorado, slotting home the rebound of buddy Roldan's initial shot. Then on November 27, hobbled by a bad hamstring and the flu, Morris lifted the series-clinching goal inside the far post to send the Sounders to their first final. Two weeks later, the Sounders were league champions in one of the most stunning comeback seasons in league history.

And Morris, with the pressure of a debut season finally off, could relax and soak it in.

52 Freddie Ljungberg Arrives from Arsenal

For nearly a decade, Swedish midfielder Freddie Ljungberg helped carry British power Arsenal to two Premier League titles and three FA Cups. He became a fixture in England, ranked No. 11 on a list of the storied franchise's top 50 players in its history before later moving on to West Ham United.

But by 2008, a nagging hip problem and other injuries caused Ljungberg to retire from the Swedish national team to take a hiatus from soccer before figuring out what to do next. Numerous teams globally were interested in having him play. Naturally, wherever Ljungberg went, press accounts followed as the soccer world waited to see where he'd sign.

In August 2008, Ljungberg, nearly as famous for his tattoos as for his play, flew to Los Angeles to have another tattoo done by famed artist Mister Cartoon. While in L.A., Ljungberg's former Swedish national side teammate, Claes Elefalk, urged Ljungberg to meet with Hollywood producer Joe Roth, who was the majority owner of the newly announced Sounders expansion franchise.

That began a conversation that ended two months later in a two-year, $10 million deal between the Sounders and the 31-year-old. The Sounders had their very first designated player and quite the big name at that, drawing international attention for a franchise that had yet to play its first game. Many pundits, however, quickly expressed concern that Ljungberg didn't have much left to offer as a soccer player.

Those fears were heightened when Ljungberg underwent surgery in December 2008 to repair a slightly torn hip labrum. He wound up skipping the team's preseason training camp in Argentina but did rejoin the Sounders for training at their Starfire complex in Tukwila, Washington once they returned from South America. As expected, he missed the team's debut game against the New York Red Bulls but did suit up, just shy of his 32nd birthday, and play as a second-half substitute in their second match against Real Salt Lake.

Ljungberg's first start came on April 4 of that year against Toronto FC, in place of Fredy Montero, who remained back in Seattle to deal with the legal fallout from a rape accusation made against him. It took fewer than 15 minutes for Ljungberg to score his first MLS goal, on a quick one-two with Nate Jaqua. Ljungberg passed to Jaqua, then darted behind Reds defenders in the box, took a perfect return feed, and easily beat goalkeeper Greg Sutton to the near post.

He'd score only once more his entire Sounders career. But his overall play was strong enough to make the MLS All-Star team, MLS Best XI, and be a finalist for the league's Newcomer of the Year Award.

"Freddie has the ability to do special things on the field at special times," Sounders coach Sigi Schmid told reporters.

Ljungberg's five game-winning assists led the league that year. But for all of his on-field prowess, his off-field struggles with health received nearly as much attention. He suffered from debilitating migraines, and his physical play took a toll on his body.

During the All-Star Game in July, Houston Dynamo coach Dominic Kinnear opted to play Ljungberg the entire 90 minutes, knowing he was already suspended for an upcoming MLS match because of a prior red card. Ljungberg later told reporters he started to experience blurred vision as the game neared its end because of the onset of a migraine. He opted to skip the penalty kick round, but after the first five attempts failed to produce a winner Kinnear—not realizing how bad Ljungberg's condition was—inserted him as the team's sixth kicker.

Ljungberg couldn't see what he was doing and merely shot the ball toward the middle of the goal, hoping keeper Tim Howard would dive toward one of the corners. Howard merely stood his ground and made an easy save to seal Everton's win.

"I thought at least in the middle of the goal I can't miss that," he later told reporter Don Ruiz of *The News Tribune* in Tacoma, Washington. "I should have definitely not taken it; but it's difficult when the coaching staff don't really know how bad it is. They're like, 'Just hit it.' And I was like, 'I can't see.' But that's how it is."

Ljungberg was carried off the field on a stretcher.

Later, he attributed the migraine to trace amounts of red wine used in a sauce at the team's hotel. Ljungberg is allergic to cheese and wine.

After struggling to find cohesion up top with Sounders teammate Montero, the pair finally seemed to start clicking late in the season. "We tried to have that work," Schmidt told Todd Dybas of SeattlePI.com. "Tried to get Montero and Ljungberg on there and it was successful at times."

But Ljungberg could never display the full range of talent the Sounders thought they'd be receiving. Schmid and his coaches tried using him all over the field, but could never find the right spot.

As the 2010 season began, Ljungberg complained to the staff about the limited number of touches he was receiving. He also bickered about the quality of MLS officiating and the play of some of his teammates, who didn't take kindly to his criticisms.

Sounders veteran Jeff Parke, who'd joined the team in 2010, would later tell MLSsoccer.com that "egos" played a role in Ljungberg's strained relations with certain teammates. "If they saw each other on the street, they would walk past each other and not say hello."

Meanwhile, the Sounders, worried Ljungberg was becoming a disruptive locker room presence, quietly began shopping for a replacement. They felt they had found one in Uruguayan forward Alvaro Fernandez, who agreed to terms during the summer transfer window but did not join the team right away. The Sounders already had two designated players in Ljungberg and Montero and would have had to pay a $250,000 luxury fee for adding a third. Meanwhile, Ljungberg and his agent sought a potential escape route out of Seattle, talking with various teams internationally.

Eventually, it was the Chicago Fire that emerged willing to take on the remaining salary from his $10 million deal. Ljungberg was last seen by local fans suiting up for a U.S. Open Cup game at Starfire against the Los Angeles Galaxy in early July. He didn't play, arrived to the bench late, and spent the afternoon signing autographs.

He was held out of the team's next game and then, on July 30, 2010, his trade to Chicago was announced. The Sounders received a conditional pick in the 2011 SuperDraft, which they used on Cal midfielder Servando Carrasco. Meanwhile, Fernandez was added to the roster in Ljungberg's DP spot and the popular "Flaco" went on to play several seasons for the Rave Green.

53 Barcelona Seeing Red

Landing FC Barcelona to play a friendly match at CenturyLink Field in August 2009 had been an enormous coup for the Sounders. Barca had the world's top player in Lionel Messi, was in the midst of consecutive La Liga titles in Spain, had just won that country's open Copa del Rei tournament, and was about to capture the FIFA Club World Cup the ensuing season.

Barcelona was very, very good. And they knew it, too.

This manifested itself in various ways, the biggest being the club could get somewhat nitpicky about the venues where it played around the world. Never mind that the team charged a seven-figure appearance fee for these exhibitions. Like any good Hollywood diva, those paid appearances came with strings attached—as members of the Sounders ownership and front office quickly found out the night before the match.

Sounders owners Joe Roth and Adrian Hanauer and team president Tod Leiweke and their significant others had gathered with members of the Barcelona side's board of directors for a celebratory dinner at the Metropolitan Grill steakhouse in downtown Seattle. But what began as an elegant meal never made it to dessert.

"All of a sudden, Blackberrys started blowing up and there were crises left and right," Hanauer said.

The biggest issue: Barcelona officials had walked the surface at what was then Qwest Field and didn't like the natural grass surface. The Sounders had already replaced their usual FieldTurf with the grass at Barca's request, but there were some gaps and cracks in it.

"It wasn't perfect," Hanauer said. "But [that's] what happens when you bring in temporary grass."

Barcelona was threatening to call off the game unless the Sounders did something about the grass—and about Seattle's Space Needle. It turns out, the city had decked its most popular landmark in Barcelona team colors as a welcoming gesture. "[But] the red was the wrong shade of red," Hanauer said.

Hanauer had witnessed this type of behavior before. He'd arranged in 2005 to make Qwest Field available on short notice to Spanish side Real Madrid for a match against D.C. United after another venue fell through. Real Madrid officials were most concerned beforehand about seating arrangements at the game for the large delegation of bigwigs it had brought overseas—they did not want to insult anyone by seating them next to somebody too inferior in rank.

"I was out in the bowl personally putting little stickers on seats with the names of people from the Spanish delegation and where they had to sit in relation to each other," Hanauer said. "We had to pay attention to who was to sit closest to midfield and things like that."

So the Barcelona threats to abandon a game to which 60,000 fans had already bought tickets didn't exactly shock Hanauer. But their steak dinner was now ruined—as was any hope of sleeping that night.

"Everybody scattered and was on their phones talking to their various contact person," Hanauer said. "We basically talked them off the ledge. I think we turned the lights off the Space Needle and said we would meet in the morning and walk the field.

"We walked the field and yes, [we] solved the problems. But it was just so much drama."

If Barcelona was still unhappy at kickoff time, it certainly got its licks in, winning 4–0. But the Sounders had shown their fans the game against a world-class opponent they'd paid big bucks to see—and they survived a two-pronged crisis with nobody the wiser.

54 Inside the Emerald City Supporters

Greg Mockos remembers when he first realized the humble beginnings of the Emerald City Supporters group needed to end.

For four years, a group of soccer-minded buddies had been gathering at the Fuel Sports bar in Pioneer Square for some libations ahead of walking over to Qwest Field to see the United Soccer League version of the Sounders. Mockos, who had spent his formative years living in Italy and being exposed to supporter group culture there, joined the ECS in 2007 after moving to Seattle for a civil engineering job.

"We were so small, we'd just get up and walk all together," he said.

The group numbered about 30 people.

Among those Mockos met were the group's original founders, Sean McConnell and Eric Gilbertson. But Mockos wanted the ECS to grow. The Sounders were about to open play in a 70,000-seat NFL stadium and he realized a few dozen supporters weren't going to be anything worth noticing.

Some group members wanted to keep things small and true to their original camaraderie. But Mockos felt the group was supposed to be about supporting the players and reasoned that the bigger and louder they grew, the more their support would be felt.

He'd watched the terrace culture of supporter groups in Italy. What he wanted to change, though, was the violence often associated with those groups. He knew that would never fly in the United States.

Doing that would require some help from the Sounders, who had already reached out to the group to explore ways they could help one another. Mockos jumped at the chance, realizing it could help the group secure things it never had before—like a designated stadium section apart from other fans. It was imperative the group be permitted to get as boisterous and rowdy as it wanted without having to worry about disturbing the other fans around them. And the Sounders agreed to it. By kickoff of the team's opening match, about 400 ECS members were standing together in their new home in the South End of what was then Qwest Field.

By 2009, Mockos and Keith Hodo had become the group's first co-presidents. They began implementing a merit-based hierarchy in which volunteers to the group could work their way up the ECS ladder based on effort.

The team was jittery about the group at first. But everyone quickly saw what an attraction the energetic section had become during games and realized a highly organized group of fans could entice more people to buy tickets.

Besides writing songs and chants and organizing the singing of them during games, the ECS leadership took charge of planning the colorful Tifo banners to be unfurled in the South End prior to kickoff. Joining them was ECS member Rob Scott and a designer named Steve Collins.

By year's end, the group's numbers had swelled to more than 2,000. But it took a lot of work to grow. And in many ways, Mockos said the work still isn't done. His goal—which is aligned with the group's current leaders—is to fill the entire South End with ECS members.

"What we struggle with right now at ECS is we have a lot of young members that haven't been around a long time," he said. "A lot of new fans. And they just assume it's always been this way. And it wasn't."

But Mockos insists he's not one to think everything from the past is always better than the present. He knows change is inevitable and understands the group needs to keep evolving into whatever form it's destined to take.

These days, the ECS is on a decided youth push. One of the downsides to being a group that unleashes so much energy game-in and game-out is that members eventually grow older and get tired out. Or they have small children that the ECS warns them not to bring to the sections because of all the alcohol and rowdiness.

Mockos said that now, at age 35, he no longer stands in the South End every game like he used to.

Current ECS co-presidents Tom Biro and Heather Satterberg have tried to offset some of the dropoff by recruiting younger. Nearly a decade into the group's modern-day MLS incarnation, some type of turnover plan was always going to be needed.

Biro had always liked soccer while growing up in his native New Jersey. Upon moving to Seattle in 2009, he began living in an apartment not far from the stadium. He started going to Sounders games and grew increasingly "fanatical" about it by 2011.

He began drifting into the ECS group. What attracted him most was the opportunity to have an impact on the games themselves. That's what he felt the large, organized ECS group was accomplishing, turning the momentum far more than individual fans could by clapping, cheering, or just sitting around eating hot dogs.

"It's less like, 'Oh, that's the cool thing to do for me,' and more like, 'I can be involved,'" Biro said. "And that's the major, major difference. The difference between soccer throughout the world and being an NFL fan is, unless you're in the Dog Pound in Cleveland…for the most part, it's so watered down.

"Security has changed everything," he added. "This is a different thing that allows you to genuinely be involved and work in this space."

The group says its yearly paid membership sits just under 3,000. But it estimates between 9,000 and 10,000 fans have been paid members since 2009 and still consider themselves to be part of the group.

Biro works in marketing and advertising while also studying to be a wine sommelier and agrees that working for the ECS leadership team is like another job most of the time. But he does it because of the impact it can have. Players like Brad Evans have told the group he notices their support during the game.

"If you run an ad and it works and it's fun, you go 'I did that,'" Biro said. "This is the same kind of deal. When it comes to Tifos, people will go, 'I painted that R,' and then they'll look at it and see it in 30-foot-high letters."

The ability to work on Tifos and travel to away games in a large group are two of the biggest recruitment tools at the group's disposal.

Satterberg ought to know. Her first volunteer job at ECS in 2010 was sewing Tifos together. "We'd just use regular cotton fabric from the fabric store and sew them all together," she said, adding the first Tifo she worked on was for the 2010 season opener.

A commercial real estate manager and mother, she'd been introduced to the group by one of her soccer fanatic girlfriends. The day the Sounders were announced, she started buying up season tickets for Satterberg and a group of their friends.

"She was like, 'I'm buying them and you're all paying me back.'"

And as time went on, she and her friends weren't the exception. The demographics of the group have changed substantially.

"When ECS began, it was mostly white guys," Satterberg said. "That's not ECS anymore. There are an equal number of women throughout the leadership team, people of color. It's so vibrant. I have met so many amazing people through this."

55 Catch a Game or Pregame at a Local Pub

Pub culture is as much a part of Sounders lore as anything that commenced on a pitch. Back when the team was still in the United Soccer League, The Emerald City Supporters group got their start at Fuel Sports in Pioneer Square in 2005 because it was the only place that would set aside dedicated space for them.

"I met my wife there," said Greg Mockos, an inaugural ECS co-president in 2009. "So we became pretty intertwined. They said, 'Sure, we know what the USL Sounders are and we'll give you some space pregame to have some drinks and pump up for some soccer.'"

Celebrity Sounders owner Drew Carey took to the George & Dragon pub in Fremont to announce the team as a new MLS expansion entry in 2007. He's occasionally still seen hanging out there prior to matches, and fans have reported him to be quite approachable.

The Market Arms in Ballard was started up in 2010 by George & Dragon owner John Bayliss and has become a premier soccer hangout for all major tournaments and English Premier League matches. It's a little more upscale than the George & Dragon.

Fado Irish Pub is walking distance from the stadium, on the outskirts of Pioneer Square. It usually gets packed pretty quickly by dedicated fans who show up to drink prior to marching to the match. Further away, to the north, The Atlantic Crossing in Roosevelt is more for fans planning to stay and watch the game on television. It features a popular large outdoor deck with a 70-inch TV screen.

Also, the St. Andrews Bar and Grill in North Seattle has become a mainstay hangout for soccer devotees. The bar features more than a dozen televisions, including a giant projector, to show the game.

The Sounders quickly realized the importance of incorporating pub culture into their business plan. The March to the Match became popular because it heads straight past numerous bars in Pioneer Square, where patrons arrive early for a drink or two and then join the procession to the stadium.

The team partners with pubs like The Atlantic Crossing and Fuel, but also Allstadt, Doyle's Public House, Flat Stick Pub, Ozzie's, The Westy, Rhein Bar, and others to offer food and beverage discounts to season-ticket holders who show their digital pass. And those discounts are applicable daily, not just on match days.

56 Blaise Nkufo Records First Sounders Hat Trick

Plenty of expectations surrounded the July 2010 arrival of Swiss forward Blaise Nkufo to the Sounders. He'd played for Switzerland in that year's FIFA World Cup in South Africa and spent the prior seven seasons with Holland's FC Twente, where he'd been their all-time scorer. Earlier on, in March, he'd agreed to become the second designated player in Sounders history and would join them two months later during the summer transfer window.

But once he arrived, things didn't go quite so well for the Zaire-born Nkufo in Rave Green. By the time the Sounders rolled into Columbus Crew Stadium in Ohio on September 18, 2010, Nkufo had gone 415 minutes without scoring for his new team. That would change on what had been dubbed Silence the Sounders night by the Crew's public relations team.

Instead, it was Nkufo who would break his scoring silence and record the first hat trick by a Sounders player since the team's MLS arrival. By the time the whistle sounded, the Sounders had also recorded the most lopsided victory, 4–0, of their brief history in the league.

"For me, the team is most important," Nkufo told the *Seattle Times* after the match. "We needed to win tonight."

That much was true, as the three points would help the Sounders ultimately qualify for the playoffs. But for Nkufo, they provided some hope in what had been a worrisome stint with his new team to that point.

It didn't take him long to get going, scoring in the game's fourth minute by slotting home a rebound on a wild goalmouth scramble off a corner kick. His teammates leaped atop him in celebration, knowing how big the goal was for a striker feeling the pressure of his designated player contract.

Then in the 39th minute, he scored again, outmuscling defender Ronnie Carroll along the left side of the box and firing a low, left-footed liner past goalkeeper William Hesmer just inside the far post. It was everything the Sounders had hoped for in signing the World Cup star—a talented playmaker with a scorer's natural instinct.

But his night wasn't done. In the 75th minute, Steve Zakuani made a strong run down the left side, darting past defenders and working the ball all the way to the end line. From there, Zakuani threw it back up toward the top of the box, where Nkufo was waiting to deliver a blistering drive from distance past Hesmer and into the top right corner of the net.

Three goals, all very different and demonstrating the range of Nkufo's talents. The Sounders, it seemed, had found the man they'd been searching for.

"Any time a goal-scorer scores, it's huge," Sounders coach Sigi Schmid told reporters. "They sometimes measure their games by different standards than we do."

But Nkufo would score only twice more the rest of the season to finish with five goals. And by the following March, his Sounders career was done almost as quickly as it began. At age 35, he'd been plagued by minor injuries throughout the preseason and Schmid had wanted him to be more physical up top than Nkufo was prepared for.

Also, if Nkufo stepped on the field for a preseason game, the Sounders would have to guarantee his $480,000 salary. Instead, wanting to make a deeper postseason run that year and not sure Nkufo could get them there, they agreed to renegotiate his contract and part ways.

By dumping Nkufo when they did, the Sounders shed $335,000 worth of salary against the league's $2.67 million cap per team. He left town without speaking to reporters and retired two weeks later.

For the Sounders, the franchise's first hat trick would be as good as they got from Nkufo.

57 Can't Stop Wondo

Every sports franchise has a nemesis it just can't seem to shake. For the Sounders, no opposing player has tormented them so often, for so long, than San Jose Earthquakes striker Chris Wondolowski.

With Wondolowski's 11 career goals in 19 games through the 2017 season, no other player has inflicted as much scoring damage over a prolonged period. In fairness, "Wondo" has hurt many teams, scoring 134 career goals to sit just 11 behind all-time MLS leader Landon Donovan.

Not bad for a player selected 41st overall by San Jose in the 2005 MLS Supplemental Draft out of Chico State University. He'd spent five seasons with the Earthquakes and Houston Dynamo, scoring just four goals. The Dynamo traded him back to San Jose midway through the 2009 season and his very first goal for the Earthquakes would come against—you guessed it—the Sounders.

Wondolowski had been a second half substitute in that game. With the Earthquakes already ahead 3–0 and the Sounders gassed from playing down a man most of the way, Wondolowski took a perfect pass from Shea Salinas in the 84th minute and converted a fourth goal to complete a 4–0 rout.

"It was a great pass from Shea, and I am glad I finished it because I am not sure he'd find me again if I'd missed that," Wondolowski told reporters afterward.

Instead, having flashed some of his natural finishing ability, he got more playing time. And in 2010, his career finally took off.

Wondolowski scored 18 times that year to lead the league. He's managed at least 10 in every season since and there's usually one or two popped against the Sounders.

"He knows how to fly under the radar and all of a sudden pop up in the right spot," said Sounders goalkeeper Stefan Frei, who, like Wondolowski, attended De La Salle High School in Concord, California, albeit a few years after the striker. "I think he has that striker's nose if you will, to kind of get a feel for where the rebound or the deflection may go. And then he'll just clean it up."

Sounders midfielder Cristian Roldan agreed. "Wondo's a clever player. For me, he's very sharp in the box."

Roldan said the Sounders constantly warn themselves to keep track of Wondolowski on crosses and not give him an opening. "All he needs is one."

Indeed, Wondolowski had been a non-factor most of an April 2017 meeting between the teams until someone left him unguarded in the waning minutes. A Nicolas Lodeiro goal in the 85th minute had given the Sounders a late 1–0 lead. But Wondolowski found himself standing all alone in the box as a 90th minute cross came through and he easily one-timed a deflection into the net off his right knee for his 11th career goal against the Rave Green.

It was the second straight matchup between the teams in which Wondolowski had scored the only San Jose goal in a 1–1 draw. He'd done the same the previous September in a match also played at Buck Shaw Stadium.

In the Sounders' second game of the 2015 season, he'd scored a pair of goals at CenturyLink Field to guide the Earthquakes to a 3–2 comeback victory. During the Sounders' record-setting 2014 campaign, Wondolowski nonetheless got the better of them in an August game at CenturyLink, tapping home a close-range shot in the 66th minute to salvage yet another 1–1 draw in which he was his team's only scorer.

"That's what Wondo does," Earthquakes coach Mark Watson told reporters afterward. "He makes something out of nothing. He knows where to be, and he just has that instinct to be in the right spot at the right time. It was a goal that we really needed."

The previous year, at San Jose, Wondo's goal in first half stoppage time gave the Earthquakes a 1–0 victory over the Sounders. And in 2012, with Wondolowski en route to a league-record 27 goals and league MVP honors, he scored the winning goal of a 2–1 victory at CenturyLink Field.

"He's been a thorn in our side for many years," Sounders coach Brian Schmetzer said. "We have shown the film, we've worked on it. We're hoping we can shut him down. But it seems like Wondo's getting better with age."

58 Clint Dempsey Scores Fastest Goal in Sounders History

Getting to CenturyLink Field early the night of March 14, 2015, was paramount for any Sounders fans wanting to witness history. Unfortunately for those fans, staying late wouldn't send them home happy.

The Sounders were playing their second game of the season against the San Jose Earthquakes and took possession right from the opening kickoff. They worked the ball upfield along the left side where Lamar Neagle tried to center it through the box only to have it deflect back to him off a defender.

Neagle then looked up high and spotted defender Tyrone Mears standing alone about 25 yards out. He sent a long ball back through the box and out to Mears, who laid into it on the run. The blast was knocked down by diving goalkeeper David Bingham, but Clint Dempsey was standing right on his doorstep and headed home the rebound.

Only 23 seconds had ticked off the clock. It was the fastest goal in Sounders franchise history. No other early strike has been managed in fewer than three minutes.

Unfortunately for the Sounders, it would be the highlight of their night. Longtime franchise nemesis Chris Wondolowski tied the game just 13 minutes later, then put San Jose ahead to stay early in the second half. Both times, the goals came as a direct result of misplays by converted Sounders center back Brad Evans.

Then, with 20 minutes to play, Innocent Emeghara slipped past Evans to the inside and beat Stefan Frei to the far post for a 3–1 lead. The Sounders got a late goal to make things interesting but wound up taking their first defeat of the 2015 season.

59 Fan Protest Reverses League Policy on Championship Stars

By day, Stephanie Steiner creates merchandising and marketing strategies to help better connect grocery stores with shoppers. But after hours, she heads up the Alliance Council fan group that connects about 35,000 Sounders season-ticket holders with the team's leadership.

And never before did that fan-team connection come together more than when the Sounders convinced Major League Soccer to reverse a merchandising policy with regards to putting championship gold stars on team jerseys for sale.

Championship clubs worldwide have long sported gold stars above the team crest on their jerseys. But moments after the Sounders defeated Toronto FC to win the MLS Cup, Steiner began hearing from irate fans via social media that stars would only be put on authentic Sounders jerseys and not the replica home and secondary ones favored by much of the fan base. "The authentic jersey...is designed for professional soccer players," Steiner said. "How many people in the fan base fit the body type of a professional soccer player? Kids don't. They're too small. Women develop breasts—it's an inevitable event. And men have to be incredibly athletic for that to fit.

"So what's the percentage of the population that can fit well in authentic jerseys? They were saying, 'Nobody else gets that star.' And that's kind of ridiculous."

The league controls such merchandising decisions in conjunction with member clubs. Adding stars to jerseys had never really been an issue until the more rabid fan bases in the Pacific Northwest began seeing their teams capture championships.

It started in 2015 when the Portland Timbers won the MLS Cup. Timbers fans, knowing their soccer history and tradition, began clamoring for stars. Without notice, the team simply began sewing the gold stars on all jerseys, which were quickly snatched up by appeased Timbers fans.

That sparked a league crackdown. MLS marketing officials had wanted to create more value for authentic team jerseys by only adding the stars to those jerseys. The Timbers decision effectively undermined those efforts. Going forward, MLS told its member teams that its policy had to be upheld.

But a year later, when another Pacific Northwest team won the title, the same situation unfolded where fans began besieging the Sounders with requests for stars. Sounders officials promptly contacted MLS headquarters in New York and opened discussions on what to do. Those talks were fast-forwarded when Steiner's group entered the fray and applied more pressure on the team.

The Alliance sent an official letter to MLS demanding the stars. Steiner and others also kept in regular contact with the Sounders for updates on ongoing talks with the league.

Sounders chief operating officer Bart Wiley said the pressure certainly helped. "Many fans expressed to us their concerns with the previous championship star policy, and we applaud Alliance Council leadership for representing their constituents to address those concerns with MLS and our organization."

By late February 2017, the league reversed its prior decision and allowed the Sounders to add the stars to all home and Pacific Blue jerseys as well as a Heritage Kit unveiled in 2017 to commemorate the franchise's first North American Soccer League season in 1974.

MLS also agreed to review its policy on gold stars on a season-by-season basis following each championship. Steiner said her group will keep the pressure on, wanting all fans—especially women and children—to be able to have the stars on clothing that actually fits them.

"The important thing for me is, if you're going to build this [sport] in the U.S., you've got to build it for kids," Steiner said. "These are their heroes. These are the people they look up to. So let them celebrate the championship."

60 Homegrown Gems

While ramping up for MLS entry in 2009, the Sounders quickly realized they'd only go as far as their ability to sustain a pipeline of homegrown talent. Sure, the team's Hollywood ownership could spend some big money early on to keep the franchise competitive. But they'd eventually need to offset costs with young, cost-contained players who could both help the MLS club thrive and also be sold off via transfer fees to leagues in other countries.

So the team's very first employee, Chris Henderson, was tasked with creating the Sounders youth academy. Henderson knew about young talent, having captured the Gatorade National High School Player of the Year Award growing up in the Seattle suburb of Edmonds. By his early twenties, he was playing for the U.S. Men's National Team and became an 11-year MLS professional with several teams.

Henderson looks for kids with talent but also a willingness to put in work to reach their full potential.

"There's a certain level of desire and commitment that you need if you're going to make it as a pro," Henderson said.

He found that in DeAndre Yedlin, who was spotted at age 11 by Sounders youth director Darren Sawatzky. Yedlin had been raised by his grandparents in the Lake Forest Park section of Shoreline and became a fixture on Crossfire youth teams. By 2010, Yedlin had joined the fledgling Sounders' youth academy, soon to head to Akron University to play for coach Caleb Porter. Henderson was impressed with Yedlin's raw speed but also his uncanny ability to read what was happening in front of him and make the needed play.

Three years after joining the youth academy, Yedlin was starting for the Sounders as their first ever Homegrown player signing. He'd go on to be their most successful Homegrown ever, becoming a starter not only with their MLS team but also with Newcastle United in the English Premier League.

Next up was midfielder Aaron Kovar, who joined the Sounders academy the same year as Yedlin in 2010 after playing his youth soccer in Seattle. Kovar went on to play at Stanford University, then returned to sign a pro contract with Seattle in 2014. By the end of the 2017 season, his fourth as a pro, he'd made 13 starts for the first team and appeared in 32 games.

But an even bigger signing was still to come in forward Jordan Morris, who'd grown up on Mercer Island and whose father, Michael, had been the Sounders' team physician since 2006. The Sounders got Morris into their academy in 2012 after his youth career with Eastside FC.

By 2014, he was off to Stanford where he won two national titles and a Mac Hermann Trophy his junior season as the nation's top college player. From there, he broke in as a starter with the Sounders in 2016. He'd go on to lead them to an MLS Cup, earning Rookie of the Year honors.

The next Sounders homegrown to play in MLS wasn't as explosive as Yedlin or Morris, although his older brother was friends with Yedlin and they lived in the same Shoreline neighborhood. But midfielder Henry Wingo, like Yedlin, had speed and the type of in-game smarts that folks like Henderson were watching for.

Wingo attributes his in-game awareness to his college days at the University of Washington when coach Jamie Clark moved him further back into a defensive midfielder's role.

"You understand the game and how to defend, individually and as a team," Wingo said. "You watch players differently. When you step on the field, you need to know whether he's right-footed or left-footed. Whether he likes to pass and move, whether he likes to dribble. Those are things I didn't really pay attention to prior to that."

Wingo signed with the Sounders in January 2017 and so impressed out of training camp that he was given some early playing time. He appeared as a late game substitute at Houston in the 2017 opener and in 11 games by season's end.

Not all Homegrown signings have worked out quite as quickly.

"I think just so many things can happen from when you're 17 until your early 20s," Henderson said. "People get sidetracked with girls, school. Maybe you don't get the breaks. Injuries. I think there are guys who were much more talented than me at 14 or 15 coming up and they just didn't stick. We want to make sure they do."

Victor Mansaray was signed as the team's fourth Homegrown player in 2014. But unlike Yedlin and Kovar before him, he never appeared in a single MLS game. He was loaned to Cincinnati's USL club in 2017, but was returned early due to disciplinary issues. Two weeks later, the Sounders waived him for good.

Henderson doesn't spend much time chatting up the young recruits about what it takes. He mostly hangs around the first-teamers, hitting balls with them and discussing his prior MLS experiences.

"There are some times where I'll go out with the academy, with a team or two, and pull out some guys to shoot with one-on-one," he said. "But those kids have no idea that this old guy once played soccer. Until after you shoot with them a couple of times and they'll go 'Hey, this old guy's pretty good.'"

He's good at picking players, too. To date, his Homegrown hits have far outweighed his misses.

61 Seattle Hosts MLS Cup Championship Game

For the first 16 years of existence, Major League Soccer held its annual championship game at a neutral site. And as a perk of being awarded an expansion franchise in November 2007, Seattle in March 2009 was named as host city of that year's MLS Cup final before the Sounders had even played their first regular season game.

For a while, fervent Sounders fans hoped the final might become a home game for their team. The Sounders enjoyed a strong debut season, finishing third in the Western Conference with a 12–7–11 record, just one point behind the Los Angeles Galaxy and Houston Dynamo.

But the dream died in the conference semifinals when the Dynamo battled the Sounders to a scoreless draw at Qwest Field, then took the second leg 1–0 at Houston to advance on aggregate. Houston would get knocked off by a star-studded Los Angeles lineup in the conference final to advance to the MLS Cup championship for the sixth time—the most of any club in the league.

The Galaxy boasted David Beckham, Landon Donovan, Omar Gonzalez, Edson Buddle, and Mike Magee, and they were viewed as a potential dynasty in the making.

The Eastern Conference playoffs, meanwhile, featured an upstart Real Salt Lake squad that had finished sub-.500 at 11–12–7 and only made the playoffs on the season's final day, but they knocked off the defending champion Columbus Crew in an opening round stunner. RSL clinched the series with a 3–2 win at Columbus, which was also somewhat shocking since the team had performed poorly on the road all season, at just 2–11–2.

RSL then upset the Chicago Fire to advance to the MLS Cup final. "We were underdogs in every single game, so we were viewed as a fluke," said Garth Lagerwey, general manager of RSL at the time prior to assuming the same post with the Sounders.

So with the L.A.-RSL match set, the only question became how many fans would go to see a neutral site game. Qwest Field was the eighth venue to host the MLS Cup final, and Sounders season-ticket holders were given automatic seats to the big game. That took care of some initial apprehension, since the club had the biggest season ticket base in the league at more than 22,000. By the Thursday prior to a Sunday kickoff, only $20 upper level seats remained for sale.

Come game time, a crowd announced at 46,011 had made its way into the stadium. It was the largest crowd for an MLS Cup final since 2002 when the New England Revolution played and lost the title game at Gillette Stadium in Foxborough, Massachusetts.

The game itself was fairly exciting, with the teams playing to a 1–1 draw through regulation and overtime. Magee opened the scoring for Los Angeles in the 41st minute, knocking home a Donovan feed from close range on a play started on a good ball by Beckham. But Robbie Findley tied it up 1–1 in the 64th minute, corralling a loose ball in the box and slotting it past the keeper with a left-footed shot to the near post.

The game went to penalty kicks. In the seventh round, RSL keeper Nick Rimando made a diving stop to his left on a blast by Galaxy striker Buddle. That left it to Robbie Russell—who had no goals all season—to try to win it. And win it he did, firing a ball just inside the left post as keeper Donovan Ricketts dove the opposite way.

Russell fell to his knees, pumped his fists, and dropped his head into his hands as teammates stormed off the bench to congratulate him. The crowd erupted as if it were an RSL home game. For the devastated Galaxy, they would have to wait two more seasons before their star-studded roster produced consecutive title wins over the Houston Dynamo.

But for now, the night belonged to RSL and to the city of Seattle and the Sounders organization for putting on a title show few would soon forget.

62 Sounders Rout FC Dallas for Biggest Margin of Victory

By mid-July of 2016, there wasn't much for the Sounders to celebrate. They were in last place in the Western Conference and two weeks away from firing head coach Sigi Schmid. Nicolas Lodeiro had yet to be brought on and any mention of winning an MLS Cup was a quick ticket to being ridiculed.

First-place FC Dallas was visiting CenturyLink Field with the league's top record overall, while the Sounders were 1–6–1 their previous eight games. On paper, it appeared the mismatch of the year. Instead, the warm and sunny evening would end with the most lopsided victory in Sounders history.

It helped that Dallas was coming off a heavy schedule and about to embark on U.S. Open Cup and CONCACAF Champions League play. Thus, coach Oscar Pareja opted to rest starters Mauro Diaz, Fabian Castillo, Michael Barrios and Maximiliano Urruti. The Sounders were not impressed by the apparent slight.

"I had a couple of words for my team on that, and they reacted appropriately," Schmid told reporters afterward.

Indeed they did.

An early penalty kick awarded for a Maynor Figueroa hand ball was converted by Clint Dempsey in the sixth minute before many fans had taken their seats. Figueroa was also ejected, leaving the Sounders up by a man. They seized on the opportunity, with Osvaldo Alonso sending a long through-ball to Andreas Ivanschitz, who chipped it past goalkeeper Chris Seitz in the 18th minute to make it 2–0. Then Dempsey and Jordan Morris completed a nifty sequence of passes four minutes later with Morris slotting it home for a 3–0 lead.

The Sounders hadn't managed three goals in a game all year. Now they had a trio midway through the opening half. Dempsey evened things out by taking a red card before the half for putting his hands on Juan Esteban Ortiz's face. But the Sounders kept on scoring in the second half, with Joevin Jones beating keeper Seitz with a blast from outside the penalty area in the 61st minute.

Dallas was trying merely to escape further embarrassment and mounted a next-to-nothing attack. But they could not avoid one final Sounders goal, this one in the 73rd minute when Cristian Roldan headed home a perfect set piece from Ivanschitz for the first goal of his MLS career.

When the final whistle sounded, the Sounders had a 5–0 victory and a rare moment to celebrate in a difficult season. The largest victory ever by the squad would be short-lived in terms of accolades.

The Sounders lost to Portland 3–1 just four days later and then were embarrassed 3–0 at Kansas City ahead of Schmid being fired. Very quickly, the 5–0 win over Dallas was dismissed as a fluke—consequence of the visitors resting half their team.

It wasn't until months later, when the Sounders upset FC Dallas on aggregate in the Western Conference semifinals, that some attitudes may have changed. Once the Sounders shocked all of MLS by winning their first championship, that anomaly game in July was looked at somewhat differently—more like a title-winning club showing flashes of the potential that was to come.

Most memorable from that night was left back Joevin Jones stepping into his own as one of the premier players at his position, dominating the left side of the field in addition to scoring his second goal of the season. If anything, this was the game that vaulted Jones to another level and ultimately saw him play a pivotal role in leading the team to its first title.

63 For Drew Carey, the Price Was Right

Comedian Drew Carey grew up not knowing much about soccer, nor caring for it. What he did like, however, was sports photography. And when his decade-long run on *The Drew Carey Show* came to an end in 2004, he took some time off and pursued his hobby of photographing sports events.

Since soccer wasn't nearly as popular as the other big-time professional leagues, he found he could get sideline passes to games rather easily. Los Angeles Galaxy games became a favorite hangout. That led to a job for a wire service photographing the 2006 FIFA World Cup in Germany, which truly opened Carey's eyes to the wonders of soccer on a global stage.

He became fascinated by the sport and especially an idea to "democratize" it. He knew that Spanish clubs Real Madrid and Barcelona FC allowed their fan bases to elect the team's president and wanted to attempt the same thing in the U.S. He felt that if he could become an owner, he could introduce the idea of letting the masses have a say in how teams are run. Tim Leiweke was the Galaxy's president and frequently came into contact with Carey at games.

"He was following the Galaxy around and literally was like a team photographer for us," Leiweke said. "He was really in love with the sport. So we threw Drew into the conversation with Joe [Roth] and Adrian [Hanauer]."

Leiweke had brokered a 2013 meeting between Hollywood producer Roth and MLS commissioner Don Garber. Later, Leiweke arranged another sitdown between Roth and Tod Leiweke, president of the Seattle Seahawks and his younger brother, which led to a subsequent introduction to Hanauer and the forming of a Sounders ownership group that would land an expansion franchise by November of that year.

But before that group was announced, Carey wanted in. So Leiweke approached his friend Roth, by then the group's majority owner, asking whether a stake could be given Carey.

A last-minute lunch meeting was arranged between Carey and Roth, but it took weeks to finalize. Roth was one of the more powerful men in Hollywood and getting a sitdown with him was no easy task. On the morning of the meeting, Carey lacerated his hand on a prop while taping a segment of *The Price is Right*, the longstanding TV game show he now hosted.

Carey knew that if he missed the lunch with Roth, he might never get to be a soccer owner. So he wrapped his bleeding hand in a bandage and scurried off to the meeting.

"We were meeting for lunch close to where *The Price is Right* is," Roth said. "So, he walks in, and his hand is wrapped and bleeding. I'm like, 'What's wrong with you? Let's go to Cedars.' And he's like, 'We'll go afterward. I have to own a piece of this team.' And I said, 'Okay, but don't you have to go to the hospital first?' And he says, 'No, no. I have to own a piece of this team.'"

Roth said he wrote a figure down on a napkin and slid it across the table to Carey. The comedian said the terms were acceptable and that he'd seal the deal then and there under two conditions: that the team have a marching band and that the team would allow fans to elect the club president.

The first condition was easy. But Roth wasn't sure about allowing the club president to be voted in or out on a whim. They negotiated and arrived at a compromise of allowing fans to vote on confirming or dismissing the general manager every four years.

Carey became founder and honorary chairperson of what became known as the Alliance Council. The group's membership encompasses all season-ticket holders attending at least 50 percent of Sounders home games and holds an annual business meeting to review club decisions. During its first GM vote in 2012, the Alliance agreed overwhelmingly to retain then minority owner and GM Hanauer for another four years.

Carey became a fixture at Sounders matches and could frequently be seen marching to games and drinking with fans at nearby pubs. And his "Democracy in Sports" mantra became a Sounders ideal espoused by ownership and fans alike.

"This was all him and it works," Roth said of Carey's vision. "This isn't just some marketing thing. We really wanted to give the fans a say."

But Gary Wright, the team's longtime vice-president of business operations, said Carey provided something more—instant star power.

"He understood what the fans wanted, but he gave us a celebrity ownership," Wright said. "All along, our goal wasn't just to be real good in MLS. Our goal all along was to be a world stage player and to get the whole world's coverage.

"To have an owner that was a celebrity, that kind of opens up some doors," he added. "His picture, touting the Sounders, was on the front page of the *L.A. Times* one day. Not the front page of the local section. But page one of the *L.A. Times* talking about the Sounders."

64 Stefan Frei Becomes a U.S. Citizen

Stefan Frei had moved to Concord, California, as a teen, earning the nickname "Swiss" from his soccer teammates at De La Salle High School. He'd been raised in Alstaetten, a historic rural town in Switzerland's Rhine Valley, founded in the year 853 and known for the plethora of castles on its outskirts.

Through many of his formative years, however, he grew to identify with the United States. He'd played for University of California Berkley, then the San Francisco Seals and San Jose Frogs in the USL Premier Development League. Although he'd represented Switzerland on its U15 team, he'd thought about donning the colors of the U.S. Men's National Team. The only problem was that Frei didn't have U.S. citizenship. And that would become more difficult after he was taken by Toronto FC in the 2009 MLS SuperDraft.

Frei effectively was a Swiss national and permanent U.S. resident now, spending the majority of the year working for a team based in Canada. And when he nearly won MLS Rookie of the Year honors that 2009 season, the city of Toronto became his de facto home and thoughts of citizenship were pushed aside. They drifted further from his mind when Frei spent a couple of seasons battling injuries ahead of his December 2013 trade to the Sounders.

It would take Frei the full 2014 season to regain his previous goalkeeping form. But once he did, he'd by 2014 established himself as one of the league's formidable netminders. And again, the citizen thoughts loomed. By now, it made sense since Frei was living and working in the U.S. full-time again.

And it especially made sense when USMNT coach Bruce Arena called him in for training in January 2017, fresh off his iconic save just weeks earlier in the MLS Cup final against his former team. Though Frei left the camp early due to an injury, his taste of the national squad hastened his urge to seek citizenship.

But there were complications, mostly related to his time with Toronto and the days spent living outside the country. Frei said in February 2017 his application had been delayed as a result, but his lawyer was working through it. "They're trying to streamline the process, and you have to make sure everything is perfect," Frei said. "We're making sure every kink is ironed out. I should have [citizenship] very quickly.

"Sometimes when it comes to departments working, it's on their schedule. If somebody is in a good mood and has had their lunch, maybe it's a week. If not, it's maybe six months. I'm hoping for the best, and it's not something that's going to take years, that's for sure."

Finally, by June 13, 2017, his paperwork was ready and he took and passed his citizenship test. He was sworn in as a U.S. citizen that day. The Sounders celebrated the occasion in a halftime ceremony during their July friendly against Eintracht Frankfurt. Frei says the experience has given him a deep appreciation for what it means to be a citizen by choice and not just birthright.

He said he struggled with the decision, not liking the direction some of the country had taken politically. But ultimately, he added, he believed that "a lot of Americans are good people, are inclusive, are open, and are respectful.

"And maybe I have a platform to show that the majority of Americans think the way that I do," he added. "That's how I viewed it, and that's why I became a citizen. But first and foremost, it's a huge honor."

65 Attend a Sounders2 Game

The creation of the Major League Soccer incarnation of the Sounders in 2009 meant that the United Soccer League version stopped playing on that circuit after 2008. Initially, the team's ownership pondered disbanding after 2007 to focus on the MLS entry, but the team played that one final campaign as defending champions and finished sixth at 10–10–10 before being eliminated by Montreal in the first round of the playoffs.

Then, in 2014, the Sounders announced they would field a USL entry for the upcoming season as a reserve team for their MLS squad. Dubbed Sounders2—or S2 for short—the team would begin play at the Starfire Sports stadium, site of the MLS team's U.S. Open Cup matches.

One of the benefits of attending games at Starfire, in the Seattle suburb of Tukwila, was that it offered an intimate environment in which to watch matches. This contrasted greatly with watching the MLS team play in an NFL stadium in downtown Seattle. In fact, Starfire was a little too cozy; its capacity was well below the USL-mandated 5,000-seat minimum. And with USL no longer giving out exemptions to that rule, the Sounders announced plans to have Sounders2 begin playing at Cheney Stadium in Tacoma in 2017.

The ballpark is home to the Class AAA Tacoma Rainiers. The Sounders had already announced a joint venture with the Rainiers to build a soccer-specific stadium for S2 in Tacoma for the 2020 season, so this temporary switch to Cheney Stadium while that stadium is being built merely hastened the moving process.

Whether it's watching S2 in a Class AAA baseball stadium or a state-of-the-art, soccer-specific facility in a few years, the USL squad offers professional-style soccer at a lesser cost with more intimacy and player access.

In its three seasons of existence, S2 has reached the playoffs once, finishing sixth in the 12-team Western Conference in 2015 with a record of 13–12–3. They were eliminated 2–0 in the sudden death first round of the playoffs by Colorado.

The last two seasons, with the USL expanded to 15 teams, S2 finished 12th in the conference both times with a record of 9–13–8 in 2016 and 9–19–2 in 2017.

But again, as with farm teams in any sport, the idea behind S2 isn't only on-field results. Fans attending matches will see future MLS players up close, some of whom will be splitting time between the Sounders and S2 all season. That happened in 2017 with Sounders midfielders Henry Wingo and Jordy Delem. The prior year, S2 supporters were able to see Cameroonian left back Nouhou break in as a professional for a full season before moving up to MLS with the Sounders as a 20-year-old rookie in 2017.

66 Obafemi Martins Bolts to China

For three standout seasons, Nigerian forward Obafemi Martins carried the Sounders through some of their most successful times. He scored 40 goals in 72 appearances and was the player most feared by opponents until Clint Dempsey arrived midway through 2013.

By 2014, the Sounders were enjoying their best season ever and Martins was completing the top individual performance the franchise had seen yet. He scored a club record 17 goals and added 13 assists to set the franchise mark with 30 points.

Martins would finish runner-up to Robbie Keane in league MVP voting. Combined with 15 goals by Clint Dempsey that year, the Sounders boasted one of the most feared one-two punches in the league. But things slowed considerably during a disappointing 2015 campaign, which ended with the Sounders eliminated by FC Dallas in the conference semifinal. Then, in February 2016, rumors began circulating that Martins was being pursued by multiple Chinese Super League teams. Though the Sounders had him locked up contract-wise through 2017, Martins quietly approached the front office to let them know he was seeking a new challenge.

"When a player comes to you like that, there isn't really a whole lot you can do," general manager Garth Lagerwey said. "You can fight and claw to keep the player, but then you'll have a guy that's unhappy and he'll start talking to other players and before you know it, your franchise gets an international reputation as being a difficult place to play.

"So in my experience, you try to do your best to get the most you can out of the situation. But ultimately, if the player wants to leave, trying to keep him is the worst thing you can do."

Also, the Sounders were being handed a taste of their own medicine in a way. They'd signed Martins in March 2013 from Spanish La Liga squad Levante—which had been reluctant to lose him and even threatened to file a tampering lawsuit.

But Lagerwey had nothing to do with that and was now in a tough spot. He'd joined the Sounders the prior season as GM replacement for owner Adrian Hanauer and watched them decline from their 2014 high point under his watch. Now arguably his best player wanted out with the season just weeks away. And no wonder, as CSL teams had been throwing their money around, dropping $250 million in transfer fees during that winter's window alone.

Shanghai Shenhua was offering Martins a $6.6 million net amount for the 2016 season, nearly triple the $3.6 million he'd make with the Sounders once taxes were deducted from that.

Lagerwey did what he could to negotiate a strong transfer fee, but Martins wanting out had hampered his leverage. Ultimately, the Sounders received $2 million for parting ways with a franchise icon.

By mid-February, with the MLS season just nine days away, Martins put out a message on Twitter that read, "Thanks to all who made these last three years an amazing experience. Seattle has a special place in my heart."

Sounders fans promptly flew in to a panic. After all, their top scorer of the past three years had bolted with the season about to begin. Lagerwey chose to view it as a glass half-full. After all, much of his offseason had been spent hearing fans worry about how rookie Jordan Morris was going to find playing time.

"For me, it wasn't the worst thing in the world that could have happened," Lagerwey said. "Did I want a guy like Martins to leave right before the season started? Um, no. I'm not crazy. But ultimately, when you think about it, this followed along the lines of what we were already planning to do anyway—move out some more senior players and bring in new ones.

"This just accelerated that process for us. But it was something we were ultimately going to have to do on multiple levels anyway."

Lagerwey would take more lumps as the 2016 season began and Morris got off to a slow start on a last-place team. But by season's end, Morris would win MLS Rookie of the Year honors and the Sounders would claw their way to an unexpected first MLS Cup title.

67 Sounders Play First Friendlies Against Two World Powerhouses

One of the perks of having an MLS franchise is that the Sounders had become part of a first division league and could thus lure other such clubs from around the world. And they didn't aim low in that regard, inviting two of the world's most storied franchises—Chelsea FC and FC Barcelona—to Seattle in 2009 to play exhibition friendlies and gain exposure for the sport locally.

"When we started the franchise, one thing [majority owner] Joe Roth always talked about was we wanted to be competitive in the international arena," Roth's fellow Sounders owner Adrian Hanauer said. "You can't necessarily compare a friendly to actual competition, but there are only so many opportunities we get to play against foreign teams."

It helped that Qwest Field would be the site of that year's MLS Cup final back when the league still made its title match a neutral-site affair awarded in advance. But landing the squads was a coup. Chelsea was enjoying some of the best times in its 104-year history, having won two Premier League titles that decade in 2004–05 and 2005–06 and preparing to embark on another one that 2009–10 season.

Similar to Chelsea's recent domestic success, FC Barcelona had also won Spain's La Liga in 2004–05 and 2005–06. They were the reigning champions from 2008 to 2009, and would add a second consecutive title that upcoming 2009–10 season. They had arguably the world's best player in Lionel Messi and were the defending European champions. They had also just won their country's annual open competition, the Copa del Rey (King's Cup). Later that year, they'd add their first of a record three FIFA Club World Cup wins to their ledger.

A crowd of 65,289 showed up for the July 18 contest against Chelsea, which just two months earlier had captured the FA Cup with a 2–1 win over Everton at Wembley Stadium. They were led by Nicolas Anelka, who'd scored 19 goals in league play and 25 in all competitions. Future Montreal Impact forward Didier Drogba was also in the lineup that day.

"I remember sitting in my dorm before I'd even signed, hearing the Sounders announced for MLS and the Chelsea game soon afterward," said Lamar Neagle, whose first game in a Sounders uniform wound up being the Chelsea match. "And later, I suited up and walked out into Qwest for that game. It was kind of nerve-wracking as it was my first time walking out there in front of 60,000 or 70,000 people."

Buoyed by the rambunctious crowd, the Sounders went right at Chelsea throughout the match—not acting intimidated by the perennial powerhouse. "It was really back and forth," Neagle said. 'Chelsea was one of my favorite teams so it was surreal. But it went back and forth. I had a shot and it went way over. But I got a shot off."

But it was Chelsea scoring first in the 12th minute, with Daniel Sturridge beating Kasey Keller with a close-range shot from the left side of the box.

The teams traded chances from there before Chelsea added to its lead in the 35th minute as club scoring leader Anelka slid a pass from the right side of the box over to Frank Lampard, who chipped it in for the one-touch goal.

That 2–0 score held the rest of the way. But the Sounders kept pressing. Sounders coach Schmid would tell reporters afterward, "We didn't come to sit back and defend. We came to play soccer."

Chelsea manager Carlo Ancelotti would say after the game, "The players are of good quality."

A few weeks later, defending European champion FC Barcelona arrived and was greeted by an even bigger crowd of 66,848 at CenturyLink. This time, the Sounders were somewhat less competitive, with Messi scoring a pair of eye-catching first-half goals while Jeffren Suarez and Pedro Rodriguez added two more in the second half to hand the Sounders a 4–0 defeat.

"We're realistic," Schmid told reporters postgame. "We know where we're at, and we're an expansion team that's getting to know each other. There were some positive things for us to gain. It's not punishment; it's learning and continuing to get better because someday they might want to play at that level. Tonight we played the elite of the elite."

But the Sounders proved they could put on a show. Barcelona manager Josep Guardiola came away impressed by the huge crowd and atmosphere at the match. "It was amazing. Yesterday the owner of the Sounders explained to me the support for his team and we saw that tonight. It was a pleasure for us and for the players to play in the marvelous stadium."

For the Sounders, the learning experience of both matches provided a taste of where they ultimately hoped to be as a franchise.

"It was a great way to expose our fans to the top teams in the world," Hanauer said. "We are in the entertainment business, so it was high-level entertainment."

68 DeAndre Yedlin Heads Overseas

It was supposed to be a fun-filled family reunion for Sounders right back DeAndre Yedlin, the grandparents who raised him, and his birth mother. In the summer of 2014, Yedlin had been selected to play in the MLS All-Star Game in Portland, so his mother, Rebecca, drove down there with him in early August. They were met there by her father, Ira Yedlin, and stepmother, Vicki Walton, who'd flown up from their retirement home in Tucson, Arizona.

But the weekend was immediately turned upside down. Rumors had percolated in previous weeks that DeAndre was being pursued by Tottenham Hotspur of the English Premier League. For Seattle's first homegrown player, still only 21, the opportunity represented the fulfillment of a childhood dream. At age 16, he'd written down his three biggest soccer goals in the kitchen of his grandparents' Shoreline home.

They were: "Play in Europe." Then "Become a 'Pro' (on and off the field)," and, finally, "Become accustomed to European Culture."

Now, in one stroke of a pen, Yedlin was about to fulfill all three. He'd already become a professional with the Sounders the prior season, earning an All-Star nod in his first try at U.S. soccer's top level. Earlier that summer of 2014, he'd also made his World Cup debut for Team USA in Brazil.

But this was different. No soccer player from Seattle had ever made it to the EPL. Yedlin was already fast becoming known as a star both locally and nationally. He'd been named grand marshal of Seattle's annual Torchlight Parade and could be seen on billboards around the city. After the World Cup, he'd made the media rounds on ABC's *Good Morning America* and other talk shows.

Now, the international spotlight beckoned.

But he wouldn't come cheap. The Sounders had poured resources into their youth academy for this very reason. They knew some players would go on to help them win titles. But others would reap the lucrative transfer fees needed to keep their operations growing for years to come. In addition, the Sounders were in the midst of their best season yet and would go on to capture their first and only Supporters' Shield with the league's best record that 2014 season.

The last thing they wanted was to disrupt the current team's momentum.

"Things got pretty intense," Sounders owner Adrian Hanauer said. "There was a lot we were trying to do at once."

Yedlin spent much of that All-Star weekend in Portland on the phone with his agent.

"We hardly got to see DeAndre at all," his grandmother, Walton, recalled. "Usually, he'd come to us for advice. But this time, it was all pretty much beyond our scope, and he had to make some important decisions in a short amount of time."

Yedlin had to negotiate a deal with Tottenham apart from the transfer fee. But within a week of that All-Star game, everything was in-place. The Sounders would receive a $4 million fee for transferring Yedlin's rights to Tottenham. It was the largest sale ever of a homegrown player from MLS, topping the $3 million paid for D.C. United winger Andy Najar by Belgian side Anderlecht the previous year.

"I was thrilled," Yedlin said. "It was the opportunity I'd always wanted. But the whole process of getting there was pretty draining."

Yedlin got a four-year contract worth a reported $4 million.

The Sounders achieved what they'd wanted, not only by earning the big payout from Tottenham but by delaying the transfer until after the MLS season. Yedlin went on to play the remainder of 2014 for the Sounders, who were upset by Los Angeles in the Western Conference final.

Yedlin began training with the Spurs in January 2015, making his EPL debut in April. He struggled adapting to the pressures of playing in big city London, where locals were skeptical about an American coming over for big money to play their national sport. It had been the same for Clint Dempsey in his initial EPL foray with much smaller Fulham.

But just as Dempsey found his way, so did Yedlin. He was loaned to Sunderland for the 2015–16 season, where he thrived away from the pressures of London. Then in August 2016, he was sold to Sunderland archrival Newcastle United, where he inked a five-year, $6.5 million pact with a second division club that had been relegated the prior year.

Yedlin helped lead historic Newcastle—founded in 1892—to the 2016–17 championship, with a goal and five assists in 21 league starts. That bumped them back into first division play, where Yedlin has been a featured regular.

69 Sounders Give Up Fastest Three Goals in Team History

Some of the worst defensive games in Sounders history have occurred at Gillette Stadium in Foxborough, Massachusetts. There was the 5–0 defeat suffered there in 2014 during what was otherwise the best regular season the team has ever known. And then there was the September 4, 2010, game when the Sounders gave up three goals in just 11 minutes to the New England Revolution late in the contest to turn potential victory into ugly defeat.

In hindsight, the quickest collapse in team history should not have surprised. The Sounders had flirted with disaster all match long, but the snakebit Revolution players kept missing the net or having shots blocked. Then the Sounders grabbed a 1–0 lead on a 59th minute goal by Steve Zakuani. But New England continued to crash the box with attackers and the Sounders, struggling desperately to hang on, were fortunate not to get a red card against them when defender Patrick Ianni appeared to kick at Revolution captain Shalrie Joseph.

In the 67th minute, goalkeeper Kasey Keller mistimed his leap for a bounding ball in the box and two defenders had to come to his rescue to deflect it away from a sliding Chris Tierney in close.

But the team's luck ran out in the 70th minute when a ball was flicked across the goal mouth and Tierney headed it back across the crease and just inside the far post to tie the score. It was Tierney's first-ever MLS goal in three seasons with his team. The home crowd of 13,124 went wild and celebratory muskets were fired off by the team's Revolutionary honor guard. But they'd have to reload quickly because the New England side struck again in the 73rd minute.

Tierney started the play with an attempted pass blocked by a Sounders defender. But the loose ball found its way past everybody and into the box. Serbian midfielder Marco Perovic sprinted for it while Keller charged out to try to beat him to the ball. But Perovic got there first and—with a classic finish—tapped it just beyond Keller's reach to his right and into the net.

A stunned Sounders squad tried to recover and press forward. But in the 81st minute they got caught flat-footed in their own end as Kheli Dube took a nifty give-and-go feed from Ilija Stolica and rocketed a blast home just under the crossbar from 18 yards out.

The Sounders have never again allowed three goals that quickly. But they earned a measure of revenge against the Revolution nearly seven years later, scoring three second-half goals in just 13 minutes to erase a 3–0 deficit and salvage a draw in front of a rabid crowd at CenturyLink Field.

70 Sounders-Timbers Rivalry

A lumberjack mascot likely best summarizes the longstanding rivalry between the Sounders and Portland Timbers.

The Cascadia derby is one of the fiercest in Major League Soccer with its origins dating back more than four decades to the North American Soccer League days.

"They remind me a lot of what we had back in England when I played over there," former Sounders coach Alan Hinton said.

Overall, the Sounders are 48–35–14 against Portland, including 8–5–6 in MLS play. But that record doesn't begin to describe the emotions of the games themselves.

"I think once that whistle blows on the field, it's a rivalry in the sense of, 'I will do anything I can to win the game,'" said Roger Levesque, one of the most polarizing figures in the rivalry's long history. "As far as the players go, there's a healthy respect. But outside of that, the organizations, the fans—Timbers Army and Emerald City Supporters—I say really don't like each other. And that competitive edge I would say is greater in this rivalry than a lot of others in sports."

The teams first played on May 2, 1975, at Providence Park in Portland during the Timbers' franchise opener. The Sounders won 1–0, the first in a series of big road wins each team would notch against each other throughout the course of their rivalry. Portland beat the Sounders just two months later in Seattle and later eliminated them from postseason play in the opening round.

On June 30, 1979, the Sounders handed Portland the rivalry's biggest defeat, a 5–1 setback at the Kingdome. A year before that game, Portland came to have a mascot named Timber Jim whose claim to fame was sliding down a 110-foot pole and sawing through some thick 12-foot logs whenever the Timbers scored. Naturally, over the decades, the Sounders grew to despise Timber Jim because he seemed to be cutting through a lot of trees at their expense.

"I wasn't really as you would say a logger," said Jim Serrill, who created the original mascot and remained until retiring in 2008. "I was more of a line-clearance tree trimmer and moved into other work within the utility industry."

After the NASL folded, the rivalry resumed in the A-League and United Soccer League. By 2004, the teams met in the playoffs for the first time since 1975 and the Sounders came out on top.

The Sounders eliminated Portland again in 2005, then the following summer, a match between the sides featured eight yellow cards and one red.

Serrill was still sawing through logs by then but would be replaced by Timber Joey—a lumberman from Philomath, Oregon, named Joey Webber. It was Timber Joey on the sidelines in 2009,when the Sounders and Timbers met in the opening round of the U.S. Open Cup. The Sounders were in their inaugural MLS season, while the Timbers were still a USL franchise. But the clubs still despised one another.

Just 48 seconds into the game, Levesque potted a near post header to open the scoring in an eventual Sounders win. But what happened next is all anyone remembers. Levesque stood still on top of the Timbers penalty area and teammate Nate Jaqua—who'd planned this out with Levesque ahead of time in the event one of them should score—pretended to chop him down like a tree. Levesque completed the goal celebration by toppling to the ground.

Sounders fans went wild. But the hometown Portland spectators were not amused at all.

Levesque's gesture earned him the lifelong disdain in Oregon and helped fuel the rivalry in later years.

"It reminds me of some of what I experienced playing in England," Clint Dempsey said. "Over there it gets pretty intense. I get up for these games the same way."

Through 2017, Dempsey had scored nine goals in 10 games against the Timbers since 2013, the most in the rivalry of any player. Three of those goals have been game winners and six came in the final 30 minutes.

"It's an important game for us and our fans, so you want to perform well," Dempsey said. "It's bragging rights. You look to try to get a good result, whether it's you scoring or somebody else. It's all about trying to win and have those bragging rights."

But Dempsey's return from overseas during the 2013 season wasn't enough to push the Sounders past their hated rivals in their only MLS playoff meeting so far.

Portland finished atop the Western Conference while the Sounders were fourth. In the conference semifinals, in their first MLS playoff game, the Timbers stunned the Sounders 2–1 at CenturyLink Field behind goals by Ryan Johnson and Darlington Nagbe. The Sounders didn't get on the board until the 90th minute, frustrating the 38,507 fans in attendance.

The victory plus the two away goals proved a huge lift. Just five days later, the Timbers completed the playoff victory with a 3–2 win at home, taking the series 5–3 on aggregate.

"I still haven't forgotten losing that playoff game at home back in 2013," said Sounders coach Brian Schmetzer, then an assistant under Sigi Schmid. "That one stuck with a lot of us."

The following year, Dempsey scored a hat trick against the Timbers in their first game since the playoff encounter. Then, during the 2015 U.S. Open Cup, Dempsey infamously tore up a referee's notebook to protest a red card ejection of a teammate in what became known as the Red Card Wedding match. The Sounders were already down two men due to a prior Brad Evans red card and an injury to Obafemi Martins. They finished the game with only seven players to Portland's 11 and took a 3–1 defeat in overtime.

The Timbers went on to win their first MLS Cup that winter. At a celebratory rally in Portland, midfielder Will Johnson grabbed a microphone and said "F__ Seattle!"

Not to be outdone, after the Sounders captured their first MLS Cup a year later, Dempsey grabbed a microphone at a rally and shouted, "All I got to say is, now that we won one, Portland can't say s__!"

But they can and they will keep talking. And shouting. And chopping plenty of wood.

71 Sounders Score Fastest Three Goals

The Sounders achieved many milestones during a memorable 2014 season in which they captured a Supporters' Shield by posting the league's best regular season record. But the team got off to a slow start and didn't really begin to pick up speed until winning five consecutive games in April and May. More than anything, that stretch of games ignited what would become one of the league's most lethal attack pairings in Clint Dempsey and Obafemi Martins.

Right in the midst of that streak, the Sounders hooked up with the Colorado Rapids for a sun-filled Sunday afternoon contest on April 26, 2014, at CenturyLink Field. For most of the first half, the 38,582 fans on hand had no idea they were about to witness history. The game remained scoreless through the opening 45 minutes, which was hardly a surprise since the 3–1–1 Rapids had allowed just five goals their opening six matches. But that all changed very quickly once stoppage time began as Martins gathered the ball in Colorado's half and fired a pass to a streaking Dempsey.

Rapids goalkeeper Clint Irwin charged out to beat Dempsey to the ball. But Dempsey slipped by him to the keeper's left and slid the ball toward the open net. The ball deflected off defender Drew Moor, who'd scrambled back to cover the unguarded net, and went right to Lamar Neagle who drilled it home to open the scoring.

The late goal right before halftime left the Rapids deflated. And they remained that way early in the second half as Dempsey scored twice in the first seven minutes. Just 69 seconds into the half, he back-heeled a flick to Marco Pappa. An initial shot by Pappa was stopped by Irwin, but Dempsey was perfectly positioned to slam in the rebound for a 2–0 lead.

The stunned Rapids were still recovering five minutes later when Dempsey struck again. Sounders defender Chad Marshall headed a ball Dempsey's way and keeper Irwin came well off his line in an attempt to cut down the angle. But Dempsey managed to head the ball over Irwin's outstretched hands and into the vacated goal.

The three goals in just over seven minutes—counting the first half stoppage time strike—remain the fasted trio ever posted in franchise history. Martins would add a fourth goal in the 75ᵗʰ minute as the Sounders cruised to a 4–1 victory.

"The two guys up top really made a difference," Rapids coach Pablo Mastroeni said. "Martins and Dempsey really caused us a bit of grief."

72 Doctor in the House

Dr. Michael Morris never set out to make professional sports history. In fact, the orthopedic specialist had no intention of ever working in soccer until becoming a soccer dad to his two boys. One of those boys, younger son Jordan, ultimately joined the Sounders in 2016 alongside his team physician father.

"I didn't know soccer at all until my kids started playing it," Morris said. "Jordan's brother, who is four years older, started playing. And then, I knew a guy who knew soccer and coached their U7 team so I got interested in it. And then Jordan kind of followed and our whole family started getting into it. That's when I learned it and became interested in it through my kids."

His eldest son, Christopher, would go on to play three seasons for Seattle Pacific University from 2009 to 2012. By then, Jordan was enrolled in the Sounders' youth system, where he'd go on to score 28 goals in 32 matches to become the nation's top academy player and earn a full ride to Stanford University.

His father had a front-row seat to that ascension. The physician had always been interested in pro sports, graduating from the University of Washington's orthopedic residency program, followed by the Kerlan Jobe Sports Medicine Program. By 2006, a spot became open with the Sounders franchise of the United States Soccer A-League.

"It's a joy, it's a gift, it's a blessing," Morris said. "I don't know if this has ever happened before. I know there's been some coaches in some sports that had sons who played for them. But I don't know of this situation."

"I've been a soccer dad for a lot more years than most dads get to do it."

A whole lot more.

By the time son Jordan was done at Stanford, he'd led the Cardinals to consecutive national titles. In his final season, as a junior, he captured the Mac Hermann Trophy as college soccer's top player. The Sounders were anxious to sign him and—after Morris flirted with a German squad for several weeks—they did.

Father and son were reunited.

In the two seasons since, they've tried to keep their relationship professional when at work. That's not always easy, given Morris in 2017 was still living with his father and his mother, Juliette, at their Mercer Island home. But his dad knows things aren't the same as when Jordan was five or six years old and he was coaching his teams.

"Oh yeah," the elder Morris says with a laugh. "Every once in a while, I check on things. But I check on things with the other players, too."

He said Jordan "usually leans on me" for medical advice and they rarely disagree. The 2017 season was especially rough on Jordan in that regard. He suffered an ankle injury at training camp and struggled in the early season. Then, in the team's home opener, he collided with New York Red Bulls keeper Luis Robles and aggravated the ankle problem. His father wanted him pulled at halftime.

Jordan refused.

"He's always in there trying to figure some things out," Jordan said of his father, laughing. "We were going to stay and try for 10 minutes and see, and it felt fine. I felt a little pain but nothing too bad. I was ready to keep playing and didn't want to come out of the game."

He did, and wound up scoring in the second half of a 3–1 victory.

Reminded of the halftime head-butting, his father quipped, "I said he *usually* leans on me."

Soccer Royalty Serves Up Humbling Lesson

Manchester United has long been considered an elite English Premier League franchise, capturing a record 20 league titles, 12 Football Association Cups, five League Cups, and a record 21 FA Community Shields. Playing at the hallowed grounds of 75,000-seat Old Trafford since 1910, the 139-year-old Red Devils franchise has blown out many opponents.

But the Sounders were a confident bunch as they prepared to face Man U in a July 20, 2011, friendly at CenturyLink Field. They had captured their second consecutive U.S. Open Cup, had made the playoffs their first two seasons, and had already established themselves as Major League Soccer's premier attendance-drawing franchise. They were also riding a nine-match unbeaten streak in regular season play.

Hence, it wasn't surprising to see 67,025 fans turn out to CenturyLink Field for the exhibition match. Many were anxious to see the storied visitors in person. But others still were intrigued by what they viewed as a game that would test where the Sounders and their league stood in terms of direct competition with a global powerhouse.

The day's events would prove a harsh lesson that they still had a ways to go.

For the first 45 minutes, the Sounders held on as best they could. Fan favorite Fredy Montero nearly scored twice on Anders Lindergaard in the early going but failed to convert his chip-attempts.

United came back the other way and opened the scoring in the 15th minute as Ashley Young fed defender Patrice Evra down the left side. Evra then put a stellar cross through the box that Michael Owen nodded home for the first half's only goal.

By halftime, the Sounders had reason to be encouraged. They trailed by only a goal, had nearly scored one or two themselves, and the Red Devils seemed to be wearing down physically on the blistering hot artificial pitch. Sounders goalkeeper Kasey Keller had also made a late-half stop one-on-one off Owen to keep the deficit to just a goal.

"In the first half we did well. We were able to hold the ball, we were able to get in on them. We had some chances," Sounders coach Sigi Schmid told reporters afterward. "Montero had some good chances. A little more cleverness and a little more sharpness and we might have had a goal or two. Overall, I wasn't displeased with what we did in the first half. I thought the first half was good."

Then the Sounders took the field for the second half. And the proverbial roof caved in on them.

Schmid made what he later admitted was a tactical mistake in trying to use as many substitutions as he could, wanting all of his players to get a chance to play against a legendary side. But his team's rhythm suffered because of it.

Two United substitutes, Mame Biram Diouf and Wayne Rooney, scored on backup Sounders keeper Terry Boss within the first six minutes. Rooney had been England's Footballer of the Year in 2009–10 and was the player fans in attendance wanted most to see. And he didn't let them down.

The Sounders pressed up looking to get on the board, but Man U countered and Rooney again found the net with a left-footed blast in the 69th minute for a 4-0 lead.

The Sounders by now were merely trying to finish the match without further embarrassment. But it was not to be as the visitors added another goal two minutes later and Rooney completed his second-half hat trick—his three goals scored within 21 minutes—soon after. Gabriel Obertan closed out the scoring in what ended as a 7-0 rout.

"I felt we had an equal amount of good chances, but that's the difference in the quality in the level of play—the ability to finish," Schmid said afterward. "I need to apologize to our fans because I thought we embarrassed ourselves in the second half. Not to take anything away from Man United because they're a great team. For me, I know it's my most embarrassing loss, personally."

74 Sounders Draw All-Time Largest Crowd

"Clint Dempsey Watch" had been in full effect for nearly a month by the time the Sounders and archrival Portland Timbers squared off at CenturyLink Field on August 25, 2013. That would be the night when Dempsey made his home debut in the midfield, having already appeared in two road matches for the team.

More than 6,000 tickets to the game were sold right after Dempsey's signing was announced.

The Timbers entered with just three losses and in second spot in the Western Conference standings and unbeaten in three matches, while the Sounders were trailing Vancouver by two points for the final playoff position. In a prior meeting the second game of the season, the Sounders led 1–0 before a goal by Rodney Wallace in stoppage time knotted things 1–1.

The Sounders had been feeling their way ever since and hoped Dempsey would give them a needed spark. The Timbers would go on to capture the conference title that season and meet the Sounders in the second round of the playoffs. But on this night, it was all about Cascadia Cup positioning, a fierce rivalry, and the launch of the Dempsey era in Seattle.

"It's great things are moving in that direction," Dempsey told the Associated Press in the days leading up to the match, as ticket sales continued and a milestone crowd was anticipated. "The game is growing here, as you can see—more franchises popping up, more soccer-specific stadiums. It's awesome to be a part of, helping continue the growth of the game here. The most important thing is to make sure we're successful here in Seattle and we get the job done."

By the time kickoff rolled around, a crowd of 67,385 had made its way into the stadium. It would be the largest crowd in Sounders history, seventh biggest in MLS, and second-largest for the league in a standalone match. Members of the Emerald City Supporters, seated in the end zone, unfurled an epic BUILD A BONFIRE Tifo. The display was a play on the fan group's chant that begins "Build a Bonfire, Build a Bonfire, Put the Timbers on the top!" and featured Eddie Johnson, Michael Gspurning, Osvaldo Alonso, and Brad Evans.

But it was the Timbers that turned up the early heat. The Timbers' biggest scoring chance came when Argentinian import Diego Valeri saw his 25-yard shot ring off the near post and out of harm's way. Valeri was all over the field in the opening half, creating multiple opportunities the Sounders managed to repel.

Dempsey wasn't nearly as dominant and at times seemed sluggish.

By halftime, coach Sigi Schmid decided to change tactics and press the pace. He subbed in Mauro Rosales roughly 10 minutes into the second half as the Sounders pushed up field aggressively.

Then, in the 60th minute, Rosales took a free kick and sent it angling into the box. Dempsey's national team cohort, Johnson, was there to head the ball home just inside the far post. The record crowd let out a thunderous roar as Johnson leaped in celebration, having notched his fourth goal in five career games against Portland.

The Timbers tried to rally, with Kalif Alhassan getting a shot off from in close that Gspurning had to be careful with. From there, the tension turned up as Gambian defender Pa-Modu Kah kneed Johnson in the head and got away with just a yellow card. Osvaldo Alonso then went after Darlington Nagbe minutes later and was fortunate not to have been ejected.

Dempsey tried to put the game away with 10 minutes to go, getting off a shot that beat Timbers goalkeeper Donovan Ricketts but sailed just off target beyond the net. The crowd was on its feet, seemingly willing the Sounders to victory as the final frenetic seconds ticked away in stoppage time.

The whistle finally blew and the Sounders had a victory over their hated rival. But for Sounders coach Schmid, the crowd itself had already delivered a win for his team and the sport of soccer.

"Today I drove in around 2:15, 2:30 and I already saw all green walking around…. It was fantastic," he told reporters postgame. "When you're out there as the team marched out for the national anthem, you just looked and saw everything full. I still pinch myself every time I see that.

"I think we're moving forward. I think we're getting there.... You never really thought this was going to happen. You see our league moving forward, you see the continued support. I was watching TV, the Montreal game, and the fans there were fantastic in that game. But nobody compares to our fans. Turnout in numbers like that is indescribable to me."

75 The Memorial Stadium Years

When the Sounders were launched as a North American Soccer League franchise in 1974, they immediately needed a place to play. The most logical was Memorial Stadium, opened in 1947 during a high school football jamboree. It was named in memory of Seattle armed service members killed during the Second World War.

The stadium initially held 12,000 and was located on the site of what became the Seattle Center campus for the 1962 World's Fair. In 1967, it became the first high school stadium in the country to have artificial turf. Despite its location, the venue wasn't operated by Seattle Center but owned by the Seattle Public Schools District so it could remain a focal point for high school sports.

By the time the NASL franchise was awarded, the stadium sat in the shadow of the city's Space Needle and was later expanded to accommodate more than 17,000 spectators by the 1975 season.

"They took it up to close to 18,000 by putting in bleachers," said former Sounders communications director and historian Frank MacDonald. "There was bleachers just about anywhere you see grass or a dead spot there now. So the open end on the West Side was a big bank of bleachers. There were bleachers up on either side of the scoreboard. There were bleachers below those and more toward field level. And there were bleachers that extended past the concrete of where the stands are now."

The team's opener was played May 5, 1974, against the Denver Dynamos, with Willie Penman scoring the franchise's opening goal less than two minutes in. When the final whistle blew, the Sounders had a 4–0 victory and many of the team's mostly British and European players were unsure of what to do in front of the appreciative crowd.

So they stood in a circle, turned outward toward the fans, and waved their thanks in what soon became a postgame tradition that helped bond the team with its supporters.

And as the Sounders grew in popularity, so did the crowds.

"After the first couple of games, they changed the configuration so more folks could go watch," said Dave Gillett, a Sounders defender in those early years.

By 1975, the stadium expanded to fill in both end zones, and the Sounders set an NASL attendance record by drawing three crowds each totaling an announced 17,925. "The stands at both ends would be full, so it was like a bowl," Gillett said. "There were very steep sightlines, 18,000 per game, and the atmosphere was white hot."

The Sounders became such a box office success at Memorial Stadium that MacDonald says there was debate amongst those running the team about whether a planned relocation to the new, more spacious Kingdome in 1976 would hurt ticket demand.

"They had that conundrum," MacDonald said. "Do they keep making it a tough ticket by staying at Memorial and maybe invest in repurposing that stadium? Or do they move into the bright shiny place where the Mariners and Seahawks were ultimately going? So they decided to go big time and go downtown.

"The season tickets probably went from 12,000 down to about 8,000 or 9,000 after a couple of years. Because you knew you could walk up any day of the week and get a seat because it's a huge stadium."

The Kingdome just didn't have the same intimacy or sightlines. And the team would struggle with crowds the rest of its existence through 1983, averaging the same 18,000 or so in per-game attendance that it could have fit in to Memorial Stadium and its forever expanding bleachers.

After the NASL's demise, it was back to mostly high school events for the stadium until the Sounders were reincarnated as an A-League product in 1994. The 1995 season would see the Sounders finally crowned as champions, playing with a core of mostly homegrown players largely from the Seattle Pacific University soccer powerhouse.

One of those homegrown stars was Sounders goalkeeper Marcus Hahnemann, who played a pivotal role in deciding arguably the most important professional soccer game played on Memorial Stadium turf. In the best-of-three A-League final that 1995 season, the Sounders dropped the first game to the Atlanta Ruckus on the road but took the next one at home to set up a winner-take-all Game 3 at Memorial.

The Sounders trailed 1–0 until Jason Farrell tied it in the 82nd minute, electrifying the crowd with one of the biggest goals in franchise history. With the match still even after regulation and overtime, it headed to penalty kicks where the Sounders grabbed a 2–1 lead. Ruckus specialist Lenin Steenkamp, who rarely missed a penalty kick, had one final chance for the visitors.

But Hahnemann stopped him. The longtime resident of the Seattle suburb of Bellevue leaped in celebration and headed to the sidelines, mobbed by players, coaches, and fans that stormed the field on one of the wildest nights the aging stadium has known.

The Sounders remained at Memorial until 1999 when they agreed to move for two seasons to a venue in the suburb of Renton. Though they'd later return to Memorial, players complained about its artificial turf being dated and permanently etched by football lines.

By 2003, the team moved to freshly built Qwest Field. The NFL facility used FIFA-approved FieldTurf more suitable for soccer, and Hanauer wanted the challenge of playing in a larger venue.

Memorial Stadium is still used for pro soccer by the Seattle Reign of the National Women's Soccer League. But its earlier years, especially when the NASL Sounders first captured the city's hearts, won't soon be forgotten by those who were there.

"It was a pretty special time," MacDonald said. "It was a team that connected with the fans the way we hadn't seen before, and the stadium had a lot to do with it."

76 Buy Pitchside Seats

Soccer fans enjoying a little dinner and wine with their action can get all that and more at CenturyLink Field with the team's Slalom Experience pitchside seats package. For a price of between $250 and $350 per person, fans can sit along the sideline and dine on fine food and wine while hoping not to get a ball in their white truffle risotto.

All-inclusive meals have to be ordered in advance and can't be changed come game day. Each table gets an appetizer of fresh fruit and assorted cheese and charcuterie plate. From there, entrée choices include burgers made from grass-fed beef, a gluten-free St. Helen's Skirt Steak, or a Pacific salmon BLT sandwich on brioche bread. Other options include grilled portabella mushroom paninis, Asian tacos, lemon chicken lettuce wraps, and halibut and chips.

Dessert is served at halftime and includes cookies and brownies. The beverage package includes beer, wine, soft drinks, bottled water, coffee, and tea. Alcoholic beverage service ends in the 70th minute.

But best of all, the tables and comfort seating are located along the sideline directly opposite the team benches. There is a waist-high sign barrier separating fans from the action, but they are still just a few yards off the sideline—close enough to hear players cursing at each other after a hard tackle.

The seats have been available since 2012, when Slalom Consulting of Seattle partnered on them with the team and billed it as "one of the most up close and personal experiences fans can purchase at a professional sports stadium in the U.S."

That part is accurate. Other than becoming a professional athlete, it might be the closest a fan can get to feeling what it's like to be on the field with 40,000 fans staring down on you. As long as it doesn't get too close to the real thing. A warning on the team's website advises fans buying pitchside seats that "soccer balls flying in to spectator areas can cause serious injury" and to "be alert for objects leaving the field of play at any time."

Sounders owner Adrian Hanauer says no one dining in pitch-side seats has gotten run over by a player or flattened by a deflected ball.

"We've come close a few times," he said. "But fortunately, nothing's happened yet."

Fans seeking to purchase the seats can go to the Slalom Experience page on the team's website at https://www.soundersfc.com/tickets/tickets/premium-seating/pitch-side-seating. Or they can call 877-MLS-GOAL and speak to a representative.

77 Ljungberg First Sounders Player Named to MLS Best XI

Swedish star Freddie Ljungberg had a short, sweet tenure in his first Major League Soccer go-around with the Sounders. But the former Arsenal star did make franchise history during his 1½ seasons with the Rave Green, becoming their first player ever voted by media members to the MLS Best XI side following the end of their 2009 debut season.

The postseason award recognizes the league's top 11 players at each position, and Ljungberg was one of five midfielders chosen despite the fact his own coaching staff had struggled all year to find the right place for him on the field. Still, when he wasn't recovering from offseason hip surgery, or struggling through migraines and minor injuries, Ljungberg managed to make a huge impact on the team's attack.

His five game-winning assists led all of MLS, and he and Fredy Montero provided a lethal one-two punch up top once they finally found some cohesion. Ljungberg also had four assists the final two games to capture MLS Player of the Month honors for October and help the expansion Sounders make the playoffs.

The Sounders had entered the final month with a 9–7–11 record and on the playoff bubble. But they won all three October matches for nine crucial points to finish as the Western Conference's third seed. In the second of those three October games, down 2–1 with 25 minutes to play in Kansas City, Ljungberg assisted on two Sounders scores to pull out the victory. The winning goal saw Ljungberg feed a streaking Nate Jaqua in the penalty area in the 76th minute.

In the season finale at Qwest Field, the Sounders trailed FC Dallas 1–0 in the second half when Ljungberg and Montero assisted on Jaqua's equalizer. Then in the 85th minute, Ljungberg found Brad Evans at the near post and saw him rifle home a close-range shot for the game-winner.

Only four other Sounders have since made the Best XI list: Kasey Keller in 2011, Osvaldo Alonso in 2012, Chad Marshall in 2014, and Obafemi Martins in 2014.

78 Stalking the L.A. Galaxy

From their franchise debut in 2009, the Sounders have used one opponent to measure where they want to be. The Los Angeles Galaxy had been the marquee MLS franchise since the league's 1996 debut, their best years having come under Sigi Schmid. Now, Schmid was running the Sounders and telling them what it would take to measure up to their foe.

It wouldn't be easy. Buoyed by the signing of David Beckham just two years earlier, the Galaxy were about to embark on their next dynasty. Into that fray came the Sounders, the first-year team lacking the Galaxy's overall talent but with aspirations of making things difficult on them.

"They were always the team we tried to measure ourselves against," said Sounders head coach Brian Schmetzer, then an assistant under Schmid.

Indeed, for the next nine seasons, the Sounders and Galaxy would post the two best win-loss records of any MLS teams over that period. The Sounders having two L.A. residents as owners—Joe Roth and Drew Carey—didn't hurt the rivalry any. Roth's inspiration for buying an MLS team had come from seeing what the Galaxy had done in L.A. and wanting to emulate it.

"They had shown how you could do things the right way," he said. "And when I invested in the Sounders, that's how I wanted us to be."

Another factor that played into things was the early rivalry dominance by the Galaxy. The Sounders, good as they were, had met an opponent that seemed to constantly have their number.

Things didn't start off that way in 2009.

The two sides first met on Mother's Day in 2009 at what was then still known as Qwest Field in Seattle. A crowd of 29,025 saw Sebastien Le Toux score his first MLS goal in the 22nd minute, only to have the Galaxy equalize in what ended a 1–1 draw.

But what really opened eyes three months later was the Sounders heading into what was then the Home Depot Center in Carson, California, and stunning the Galaxy 2–0 behind goals by Steve Zakuani and a clean sheet from Kasey Keller.

The following season, though, the Galaxy began tilting the rivalry heavily in its favor. They'd lost the 2009 MLS Cup final to Real Salt Lake in a neutral site game at Qwest Field and now were back at the same stadium five months later. And what a result it was—a 4–0 demolition of the Sounders behind a goal and three assists from Landon Donovan.

"You lose 4-nil at home, it can never be good," Zakuani told reporters afterward.

Schmid called it his toughest defeat as a Sounders coach. Sounders owner Adrian Hanauer announced a refund for the team's 32,000 season ticket holders and promised changes would come.

But in the next matchup between the sides, on the Fourth of July, the Galaxy again supplied the fireworks in a 3–1 win at home. The teams would meet in their first of four playoff series that year, with the Galaxy taking the Western Conference semifinal clash 3–1 on aggregate with a 1–0 win at Qwest Field and a 2–1 victory at home.

Though the Galaxy would lose in the conference final, their much anticipated dynasty finally took shape the following two seasons. They opened 2011 with a 1–0 win over the Sounders at CenturyLink Field, then played them to a scoreless draw at home in July.

L.A. went on in December to win their first of two consecutive MLS Cup finals over Houston. The Sounders, meanwhile, struggled against their foe. By May 2012, when they met in Seattle, the Sounders had gone winless in the teams' last six clashes including playoffs. That finally changed with a 2–0 Sounders win, then a 4–0 home win against the Galaxy in August. But the Galaxy beat the Sounders 1–0 at home the final day of the regular season. And when the teams met in the conference final—the first time the Sounders had made it that far—it was a familiar story. The Galaxy waxed the Sounders 3–0 at home, then cruised through a 2–1 loss at CenturyLink Field to win the series 4–2 on aggregate and go on to claim another title.

But perhaps the most crushing playoff blow was delivered by the Galaxy in 2014. The Sounders had beaten them in an emotional, winner-take-all match for the Supporters' Shield the final day of that season, only to lose again in the conference final.

After the Galaxy took the playoff opener 1–0 at home, the Sounders returned to a sea of supporters at CenturyLink, hoping to make their first MLS Cup final. Riding that wave of support on a chilly late November night, the Sounders grabbed a 2–0 lead by halftime on goals by Brad Evans and a shot by Clint Dempsey that deflected off keeper Jaime Penedo and in.

From there, the Sounders tried to hang on. But in the 54th minute, Brazilian star Juninho—who hadn't scored all season, but always saved his best for the Sounders—got his leg into a bounding ball from distance and rapped it home off the near post. The crowd was stunned and the frantic Sounders, try as they may, could not score again. Dempsey fired a shot over the net in the 90th minute and the Galaxy held on through stoppage time to take the 2–1 loss, but they won the tied aggregate series by virtue of their away goal. They advanced to the MLS Cup final against the New England Revolution and won a league record fifth title.

For the Sounders, they were denied an unprecedented treble of winning the U.S. Open Cup, Supporters' Shield, and MLS Cup in the same year.

They got some revenge in 2015, defeating the Galaxy 3–2 at CenturyLink in the knockout phase of the playoffs. That loss is largely viewed as the end of the Galaxy dynasty that had produced three titles in five seasons and four finals appearances in six campaigns.

By the time the Sounders won their first title in 2016, the Galaxy were headed to a rebuilding phase. Head coach Bruce Arena had left in-season to take over the U.S. Men's National Team. While the team finished third in the West, it was beaten by Colorado in the conference semifinal.

Meanwhile, the Sounders had fired Schmid in July, leaving both teams without the two longtime coaches that had fueled the rivalry. The Galaxy struggled throughout the ensuing 2017 campaign, with the Sounders blowing them out 3–0 at the StubHub Center in April. By late July, with the Sounders preparing for another visit, the Galaxy made a surprising move by firing coach Curt Onalfo and hiring Schmid to replace him in his second go-around with the squad.

Just two days later, the Sounders arrived for what became an emotional scoreless draw against their former coach. For the first time since the rivalry began, it was the Galaxy that was trying to keep pace with the Sounders, using them as a measuring stick for their own progress.

"That's something I want our team to understand—we didn't tie a lesser team in our league," Schmid said afterward. "We tied, in my mind, one of the best teams in our league."

Weeks later, with the Sounders en route to another MLS Cup appearance, the Galaxy fought them to a 1–1 standstill at CenturyLink Field. While the Galaxy's talent may have waned as the Sounders' soared, the rivalry was still in full force.

Sounders midfielder Cristian Roldan, who grew up in the L.A. suburb of Pico Rivera, summed up nicely where things stand today by saying, "I think Seattle and L.A. have been top notch teams, I guess since their existence. Both clubs have a history, a pretty good history, and when you play two big clubs like that it means a lot. There's a higher standard that comes into the organization and also in the play on the field."

79 Sounders Get Championship Rings

When the Sounders defeated Toronto FC on penalty kicks to win the 2016 MLS Cup title, they were given championship rings from Jostens by the team.

Sounders owner Adrian Hanauer said that, in working with Jostens to design the 10-karat white gold rings "We looked to not only recognize a singular moment of victory, but to commemorate the journey that brought us to that point."

The ring top features the club's primary logo set with custom Sounders Blue and Rave Green enamel. The logo is accented with eight diamonds and an additional 30 diamonds surrounding the crest.

On the ring's bezel are the words MLS CUP CHAMPIONS with a yellow gold star accenting the topmost bezel.

The ring's left side features a detailed skyline of Seattle against a backdrop of mountains. They are surrounded by the player's name and the number below the skyline. On the right side sits the Seattle Sounders FC woodmark and a depiction of the league's Phillip H. Anschutz trophy with the year 2016 on its base.

Finally, the inside of the ring has the December 10, 2016, date of the game, the Sounders and Toronto FC logos as well as the final score of the game and penalty kick rounds.

The rings were presented by the team to all players, technical staff, and front office personnel during a private ceremony on May 23, 2017, at the team's Starfire training facility in Tukwila, Washington.

80 Carry a Team and a Tune

Nobody can sit through a Sounders match without hearing chants that often linger in their heads for days. The sound of more than 40,000 people singing in unison is quite an earful and doesn't happen by accident.

The Emerald City Supporters group leads the singing and chanting from the South End sections of CenturyLink Field, and its choices are quite deliberate. Some new songs are added to the mix as years go by, but there are traditional ones that continue to be sung at every match.

The group encompasses local musicians and artists, many big into the punk rock scene. They helped adapt several well-known tunes into the updated Sounders chants heard today. They try to be witty and funny in their song adaptations—sometimes over a few beers.

Their punk influences are notable in their use of chants from "Take 'Em All" by 1970s British group Cock Sparrer and "Us vs. Them" by 1980s band Sick of It All from Queens, New York.

The ECS hands out song cards to fans seated in their sections. They are expected to follow a "capo" (captain) at the front of the section with a megaphone directing them on the song selection and pacing. There are physical gestures that go with each song, and ECS encourages members to study YouTube videos to familiarize themselves with the timing.

The game day repertoire always begins at kickoff with the opening verse of the 1969 Perry Como classic "Seattle" that starts off "The bluest skies you've ever seen are in Seattle...."

From there, at 11:02 of the first half, the chant "Roll on, Colombia" from an old Woodie Guthrie tune begins in recognition of when Colombian forward Fredy Montero scored the franchise's first ever goal against the New York Red Bulls in March 2009.

Then, in the 74th minute, "Sounders 'Til I Die" is sung to commemorate the birth of the original 1974 franchise in the North American Soccer League.

"Depending on whether the capo is paying attention or how much wine she's had, we'll either sing those on time or slightly late," ECS co-president Heather Satterberg said.

Everything else from the ECS-approved song list is up for grabs and depends on how the match is progressing. "You tend to hold back a few that you know the hard core love," Satterberg said. "You kind of want to hold those until you absolutely need them."

"Take 'Em All" and "Us vs. Them" fall into that category, as is "Born in '74"—commemorating the first Sounders franchise in the NASL. ECS members also love doing the "Seattle Sounders Ole" pogo chant, when they bounce up and down in unison as if on a pogo stick.

"I can't tell you how many times the team scores when they pogo," Satterberg said. "It's insane."

One song the group has learned to avoid is "Come on Sounders, Score a Goal!" Apparently, the team is prone to losing possession the minute those lyrics are uttered. Full-stadium chants like "Fight and Win!" are used by the group to try to shift momentum at key moments.

"Every capo has their favorite song that they want to hold for a special moment," Satterberg said.

81 Sounders Suffer Biggest Defeat

There was little to indicate beforehand that the glorious Mother's Day afternoon of May 11, 2014, in Foxborough, Massachusetts. would go down as the worst regular season result in team history. After all, the Sounders were 7–2–1, had won five in a row, and were about to record their best regular season ever. Not to mention a charged up Clint Dempsey was making his return to Gillette Stadium, where he'd played for the New England Revolution the first few seasons of his career before heading to the English Premier League.

But on this day, nothing went right. And after a Chad Marshall own goal in the opening minute of the second half, the Sounders trailed 5–0 and would finish with that same score.

"We played soccer. But I think, psychologically, maybe we weren't as alert as we needed to be in certain occasions like around the box and maybe defensively," head coach Sigi Schmid told reporters afterward. "Our positional defense was not good."

Obafemi Martins and Lamar Neagle had direct chances on goal in the opening minutes but failed to score. The Sounders would not manage another shot on goal until the 54th minute. And by then, the game was long over with.

The Sounders were in control early until Chris Tierney broke in 2-on-1 with Diego Fagundez down the left side in the 14th minute. Tierney put a cross into the box toward the far post that Teal Bunbury got an initial crack at. Stefan Frei made the stop, but Patrick Mullins was there to poke home the rebound for a 1–0 lead.

Fagundez then made it 2–0 in the 29th minute, taking a lead pass from Tierney and ripping a shot past Frei to the far post. The Sounders were still looking competitive to that point, but the back breaker would quickly come in the 37th minute.

Lee Nguyen got a pass to Bunbury that split the defense. Bunbury's initial shot was stopped, but his rebound attempt deflected off Frei's hand and rolled slowly into the net.

Down three goals, the Sounders merely tried to survive the half and regroup. But it was not to be as teenage midfielder Fagundez took a Bunbury pass down the left side in the 41st minute and lined a low shot past Frei.

The stunned Sounders were still trying to figure out what hit them when a fifth goal went in less than a minute into the second half. Bunbury took a shot that deflected off Marshall and into the net to close out the day's scoring.

"I think four in the first half is tough to bounce back from," Sounders midfielder Brad Evans said after the game. "You do your best to fight and claw back. Then we get unlucky with the deflection and it's five at the start of the second half."

The five goals tied for the most given up in franchise history, since the Sounders had lost 5–1 at Colorado the previous year. Ultimately, the loss in New England would go down as one of those anomalies in an otherwise stellar season. The Sounders had actually controlled possession for much of the game but just couldn't keep the ball out of their own net whenever the Revolution took hold of it.

"We will bounce back next week," Schmid told reporters. "There isn't any other option."

Indeed, the Sounders did bounce back six days later, defeating San Jose 1–0. They would go unbeaten in five—winning four— in the weeks after the New England debacle and finish with the league's best record.

82 Alliance Council Votes to Retain Hanauer

Comedian Drew Carey's idea of democratizing American sports when he first became a Sounders owner had some folks worried. Namely, what if his plan to have fans vote every four years on retaining or firing the general manager somehow went haywire?

Professional sports are a shrewd business in which teams need to be well-managed or they could pay a price for years. Allowing fans, whose decisions were often influenced by emotion and alcohol, to make critical franchise-altering choices had left folks somewhat nervous. The first big test of Carey's idea was to come at the end of the 2012 season.

Adrian Hanauer, former owner of the second-division Sounders in the United Soccer League and now minority owner of the MLS team, had served as its GM since 2009. The first four years of franchise existence had gone rather well, with the Sounders making the playoffs and leading the league in attendance all four seasons.

Hanauer's position seemed like it should be safe. But still, this was a decision being left to the masses.

"I've always, as the owner and full-time employee who has never taken a salary, I've always wanted to make the right decisions for the organization," Hanauer said. "And if stepping away from day-to-day operations of the club makes the organization stronger, I still own 35 percent of it."

Ultimately, he had nothing to worry about. He was retained via a vote of 96.3 percent. Any potential for a fan-induced crisis of emotion was averted.

"I think it served me and the club well," he said of the vote. "Again, I'm not trying to protect a job. I'm not trying to maximize my income."

Still, Hanauer wasn't sure he should continue as GM much longer. The Sounders were moving toward breaking away from their business arrangement with the Seahawks and pushing towards financial self-sufficiency. Up until then the Seahawks, via minority Sounders partner Paul Allen, had managed all of the Sounders' ticket sales and marketing. But by 2014, the Sounders were ready to venture off on their own. Hanauer was to become the team's majority owner and Joe Roth a minority partner.

Hanauer had helped guide the Sounders to a Supporters' Shield crown in 2014 only to suffer a heartbreaking Western Conference finals setback to the Los Angeles Galaxy. So ahead of the 2015 season, Hanauer decided to voluntarily relinquish his GM duties and hire Garth Lagerwey to fill the position.

The Alliance Council had already re-confirmed Hanauer through the 2016 season, so it held a meeting to review rules and figure out when another retention vote was to take place. It was decided that Lagerwey would get four full seasons and that the retention vote would be pushed back from 2016 to 2018.

Further firming up the voting rules stated that a supermajority of at least 67 percent of the vote would be needed to terminate a GM and only if at least 40 percent of the membership voted.

Also, it was decided a recall vote of any GM could be held after a minimum of two years if enough of a "question of competence" could be raised. The process of having a GM recalled was deliberately made difficult, with a similar 67 percent of all Alliance Council leadership required to support holding a vote before it could be held with members. And then, the membership itself had to be at least 20 percent in favor of moving forward before an official recall vote could be taken.

It sounds complicated, but again, that was a recognition of the high stakes involved. It's one thing for a team owner like Hanauer to say he doesn't mind stepping aside if fans don't like him. But it's quite another for a GM like Lagerwey or somebody else down the road who isn't involved in ownership and draws a paycheck strictly via the one job to be removed by a fan vote.

Allowing fans to remove a GM after four, or even two years could not only harm the team, it could also make it difficult for the squad to attract the best GM candidates going forward, knowing their job could depend on the whim of fans.

"This is what we agreed to do," Hanauer said. "We have to let the process take its course."

83 Send Your Child to a Sounders Camp

There used to be only a few outdoor soccer camps nationwide that offered the possibility of meeting professional players. Now the Sounders offer a variety at various levels of skill.

There's a two-hour, $180 emergence camp for players ages three to five looking for a basic introduction to the sport. The Sounders also offer a basic $195 half-day camp for players ages five to fifteen and a $270 full-day camp for those six to sixteen who are "recreational to intermediate players" wanting to work on technical and tactical skills. And there is a $300 advanced technical camp for "serious" young soccer players ages 10 to 18 looking to continuously improve their game and take it to the next level via highly focused training.

The camps typically run in late August in Seattle and the suburbs of Bellevue, Kirkland, and Tukwila. Registrants receive a ticket to a Sounders match, an official team soccer ball, and a T-shirt. They go through a curriculum created by the team's staff and also get to meet and receive autographs from players as well as various prizes.

For $2,000, teams of all ages can have a Sounders FC Youth Programs coach customize a 10-hour training program for all players. Each participant receives a Sounders camp shirt. The customized camps are usually held outside the peak months of June through August.

Finally, a $175 matchday dream camp offers youngsters ages five to sixteen the chance to get three hours of instruction from Sounders coaches on the pitch at CenturyLink Field in the hours before a match. There are also 90-minute emergence camps for three- to five-year-olds for $90 and three-hour team versions of the camp for $2,000 offering the same chance to train at CenturyLink before a game.

84 The Mission of Gorilla FC

While the Emerald City Supporters are undoubtedly the best-known of the plethora of organized Sounders fan groups, the much smaller Gorilla FC averages about 300 annual members and tries to distinguish itself through community activism.

The group is political in nature, declaring itself as "anti-facist, anti-sexist, anti-racist and anti-homophobia" in the tradition of the St. Pauli supporters group in Germany initially founded by anarchists. CNN once declared St. Pauli as "soccer's coolest club," while the *Washington Post* was impressed that it had welcomed all "free spirits, left wingers, outcasts, punks, dockworkers, the homeless, and transvestites."

There's even a St. Pauli supporters group in New York calling itself the East River Pirates.

Founded in 2009, Gorilla FC supports, of course, the Sounders and not a faraway German club. But its mission is similar. Its name is derived from the idea of guerilla tactics, but its methods are decidedly non-violent. Indeed, the group works with the Sounders to eschew the violence that can often engulf politicized supporters groups overseas.

Instead, the group attempts to improve the community and raise awareness of various issues through soccer. It claims to have raised more than $150,000 for various local charities, including Seattle Education Access, Rainier Valley Food Bank, Friends of the Children, Bikeworks, and Skate Like A Girl.

Its origins date back to when its politically like-minded founders were playing in a recreational league soccer club. From there the group grew, but its members can often be found hanging out at the Fado pub on the outskirts of Pioneer Square.

The group's founder, former punk rocker Kevin Zelko, is a stadium vendor who gained notoriety using Twitter to sell beer at Seattle Seahawks football games. After being diagnosed with Hodgkin's lymphoma in November 2014, he raised $40,000 to donate to the Seattle Cancer Care Alliance with a 4,000-foot climb of Mount Rainier with the Sounders' 46-pound Supporters' Shield trophy in tow.

85 Steve Zakuani Draft and Injury

Through his first two stellar seasons of an all-too-brief career, Sounders winger Steve Zakuani became a fan favorite. Perhaps part of it was because he was the team's inaugural draft pick, taken No. 1 overall in the 2009 MLS SuperDraft. That cast him in an immediate spotlight and the Zaire-born, British-raised Zakuani certainly did not disappoint.

His bolstered the team's attack on the wing, using his uncanny speed and gifted touch to finish third in Sounders scoring his first year with four goals and adding four assists to become an MLS Rookie of the Year finalist and lead all first-year players in both categories. His first career goal had come in the season's second game at Toronto, adding an insurance marker in a 2–0 victory that was the club's inaugural road win.

That summer, Zakuani helped the Sounders become just the second MLS expansion team to win the U.S. Open Cup. In the semifinal against Houston, the Sounders tied the game 1–1 in the 89th minute, then saw Zakuani assist on the winning goal by Stephen King four minutes into extra time. They went on to defeat D.C. United to claim their first of three consecutive U.S. Open Cup trophies.

Just 10 days after that final, facing D.C. United again at the same RFK Stadium site, Zakuani added MLS Goal of the Week honors by outsprinting defender Bryan Namoff from midfield for a loose ball. Zakuani finally caught up to it and made a nifty left-footed tap to send it by keeper Josh Wicks and into the net.

After appearing in all four playoff games that year, Zakuani continued his progress in 2010, scoring 10 goals and adding six assists. Zakuani twice was named MLS Player of the Week, and added three assists in U.S. Open Cup play to lead the Sounders to their second consecutive title. He also scored his first playoff goal against the Los Angeles Galaxy in that year's Western Conference semifinal.

By 2011, Zakuani had shown signs of morphing into a true star. He managed at least a goal or an assist in his first four games, then scored the winner in a 2–1 victory at Chicago on April 19.

Just three days after that, playing at Colorado on April 22, disaster struck.

Rapids midfielder Brian Mullan challenged Zakuani with a two-footed lunge. The hard tackle broke Zakuani's tibia and fibia. He had to be airlifted to the hospital and for some tense days, there were fears his leg might have to be amputated.

Mullan, a decorated veteran with five MLS Cup wins to his credit and typically renowned for his good character, inflamed the situation by telling reporters postgame, "It was never my intention to injure him in the least. It's a tackle that I've done hundreds of times and would probably do again."

Though Mullan reiterated that he hadn't meant to hurt Zakuani and wished him a speedy recovery, the damage was done. Fans on social media tore in to Mullan and the Rapids organization.

Rapids coach Gary Smith would later write a column about the incident for *Prost Amerika* magazine, saying the team was in-between media relations officers for just that one game and that Mullan should never have been allowed near a reporter.

"I have no doubt that had it happened at any other time, Brian would not have been allowed near the media and would not have uttered those words that quite understandably angered Seattle fans," Smith wrote. "Any hope that the anger at his tackle might display some sense of proportion went right out the window. He had made things worse."

A major backlash ensued on social media against Mullan for his comments. Smith wrote that Mullan grew so distraught over what was happening and what he'd done to Zakuani that he later needed therapy for it.

Mullan was handed a 10-game suspension, the largest in league history. MLS executive vice-president Nelson Rodriguez said the kind of tackle Mullan used needed to be eliminated from the game and that the suspension's length was meant as a deterrent.

Mullan quickly announced that he would not appeal.

Zakuani, meanwhile, would miss 15 months as he tried to salvage his career. His return came on July 7, 2012, against Mullan and the Rapids, when he was inserted as a substitute with five minutes to go. The CenturyLink Field crowd gave him an emotional round of cheers. After the game, Zakuani, who had already publicly forgiven Mullan, hugged him and the pair exchanged jerseys.

But Zakuani was never the same. He scored only one more goal in the final 33 games of his career, the final 17 of those matches played for Portland after the Timbers selected him in the 2013 MLS Re-Entry Draft.

Zakuani retired after that, unable to get his game going again. He went to work for the Sounders as a television commentator and spent the next two training camps working out alongside his former teammates.

In January 2017, the workouts grew serious enough that rumors swirled about a possible comeback. After all, Zakuani was still only 28 years old. But then, in February, two days before his 29th birthday, he posted on his Instagram account that he was aborting what indeed had been a comeback try because he felt he couldn't get in shape for the season quickly enough.

"It would not be right for me to occupy a roster spot if I don't feel I could contribute as much as someone else I'm keeping the spot from could," he wrote.

86 The Starfire Training Facility

Those watching the Sounders from a distance often assume they work out at their CenturyLink Field home stadium. While that does happen on occasion—more to re-familiarize players with its FieldTurf surface early in the season—the vast majority of the team's workouts occur about a 20-minute drive away in the suburb of Tukwila.

Therein lays the Starfire Sports complex, home to 12 outdoor and two indoor pitches as well as the 4,000-capacity Starfire Stadium. There is also a high-end, 85,000-square-foot athletic center, a restaurant and retail shop, a sports performance center, and a place for physical therapy.

It's the room for all the extras that made the move necessary, as CenturyLink Field could not possibly accommodate a single tenant team with those needs. The abundance of fields also allows the MLS side to train alongside its United Soccer League reserve squad, Sounders2, on a regular basis to keep players acquainted.

New fields, offices, and workout and technical areas were created for the Sounders' arrival during a 2008 expansion of the facility. The lands had been taken over by the non-profit Starfire Sports group in 2003 at a time when King County had considered closing what was then known as Fort Dent Park.

The non-profit group negotiated a 40-year lease with the City of Tukwila to operate and manage the lands while being allowed to develop them. Its mission was to create a soccer haven for those who played the sport or wanted to learn more about it.

More than 100,000 visitors per year partake in the facility as players or spectators, be it in league play, summer camps, or the more than 15 youth and adult tournaments held there annually.

The campus plays host to thousands of games, including U.S. Open Cup matches featuring the Sounders.

Through the 2017 season, its stadium had also served as home to the Sounders2 reserve squad of the United Soccer League since 2015. S2 announced late in 2017 that it was moving to Cheney Stadium in Tacoma while it awaits construction of a larger, soccer-specific stadium in that city. But S2 will continue to train at Starfire alongside the MLS Sounders.

One feature of the facility is that Sounders players have to walk from the practice field and are fairly approachable. They can also be spotted in the indoor training center walking up and down stairs or through its hallways to the weight room and lunchroom. Most training sessions are open to the public, and fans can often stand just a throw-in from the sidelines to watch the players at any point in their season.

It's no accident that players and fans are close enough to literally walk into one another. When the Sounders were launched, they'd wanted a facility where it would be easy to bond with the soccer community and fans at large.

Games featuring the MLS Sounders are some of the biggest draws. There have been notable U.S. Open Cup matches played at the stadium, including the largest victory ever by the Sounders against a professional side when they beat the Chicago Fire 6–0 in the 2014 semifinal.

Starfire's stadium also played host to the 2015 penalty-filled clash between the Sounders and Portland Timbers that later became dubbed the Red Card Wedding.

87 Sounders Take the Lead on LGBT Rights

Shortly after assuming majority control of the Sounders in 2015, owner Adrian Hanauer looked at his calendar and pinpointed a date. Hanauer knew that June was Pride Month in Seattle and wanted to dedicate a Pride Day game in which lesbian and gay rights could be celebrated.

A June 24 match against the San Jose Earthquakes was designated. But that wasn't all. Hanauer wanted other events leading up to the match that would help raise awareness of the issue. For Hanauer, soccer was a sport of inclusion, encompassing players worldwide. It also had a younger fanbase that tended to gravitate more toward social issues

Former NBA center Jason Collins, that league's first openly gay player, was invited to speak to fans in a fireside chat at The Ninety, a team-owned event facility in Pioneer Square. Collins was also presented with a traditional Golden Scarf by the team ahead of the game.

Sounders captain Brad Evans wore a pride-themed armband throughout the match. A crowd of 39,971 fans turned out at CenturyLink Field, many sporting the rainbow red, yellow, orange, green, blue, and purple colors associated with the pride movement.

A year later, the team held its second Pride Day match, this time against New York City FC in a nationally televised showdown that drew 47,537 to the stadium. Evans told the *Seattle Times* why the event meant so much to him. He'd come up at Columbus with Robbie Rogers, who would later go on to become the first openly gay athlete to compete in a top North American professional sport.

"Anytime something hits a little closer to home, it's going to change the way you think about things," Evans said. "If you're an advocate for guns and a close family member or your child is killed by somebody with a gun, it may change your views a little bit.

"Robbie is living his life and living free now, and that's the most important thing to take away from it. He's performing at a very high level. He's in a locker room with no issues and no problems.... He's been a focal point, and it takes somebody like that to start a movement."

By the following year, Hanauer and Evans wanted to take things further. The third annual Pride Day match was looming, but this time they wanted to push the inclusion aspect of what they were doing beyond just soccer. So they invited all of the city's professional sports teams to participate in a press conference at The Ninety to discuss lesbian and gay issues in sport.

Seattle Mariners owner John Stanton participated. So did Seattle Seahawks vice-president and general counsel Ed Goines. Seattle Reign women's soccer star Megan Rapinoe, who is openly gay, spoke at the press conference and said her team has "a big, gay locker room."

Sounders captain Evans was also there, joined by teammate Chad Marshall. Evans admitted things could get difficult in a soccer locker room for outwardly gay players if their teammates fail to provide the proper support. That's because players come from multiple continents and "backgrounds where being gay is not just frowned upon but can be dangerous."

Rapinoe told the gathered crowd that athletes can make a difference because of their prominence. "Sports has so many eyes on it, all the time anyways in this country. It's obviously a very popular profession and it goes into pop culture and politics and many different things, so I think the opportunity to have a positive impact can be very tremendous."

88 The Golden Scarf Tradition

One of the often-overlooked elements to the Sounders success was their partnership with the Seahawks football team. With Seahawks owner Paul Allen serving as a minority Sounders partner—and the team turning over its business staff to the new soccer franchise—it was inevitable that some football traditions would find their way into the soccer sphere.

And so it happened that the Golden Scarf tradition was born. The Seahawks had started a tradition years earlier where they'd invite upstanding citizens or well-known football figures to hoist the 12th Man Flag. The Sounders wanted to begin something similar and thus introduced the Golden Scarf.

Prior to each game, they would present a selected member with a special gold scarf which they'd raise above their heads. The very first recipient prior to the club's inaugural March 19, 2009, home opener was MLS commissioner Don Garber. After that, longtime Sounders great Jimmy Gabriel—an original from 1974—was given the honor, followed by Microsoft executive Robbie Bach and Seattle native Jimmy McAlister, another Sounders legend from the 1970s.

As the 2009 season wore on, the club began including more non-soccer personalities as recipients. Notables include former Seahawks coach Jim Mora, NBA legend Bill Russell, and glass artist Dale Chihuly. Alan Hinton, the former Sounders coach and so-called "Mr. Soccer" in the region, was honored in September of that year.

At first, with so many soccer community contributors having gone without such formal recognition for years, the Sounders were handing out scarves left and right.

By season's end, they'd given scarves to 17 individuals. That number would be reduced in following years as the club chose to be more selective with who would be honored.

Between 2011 and 2016, only 25 more scarves were handed out. Popular former players to receive them included Kasey Keller, Roger Levesque, Steve Zakuani, and Zach Scott, while first Sounders coach John Best and original broadcaster Bob Robertson were also honored.

89 Go to a Road Game

One of the disadvantages of going to a road game in any sport is being outnumbered. The Emerald City Supporters group eliminates that by arranging for discounted trips to Sounders road matches for its members who—of course—sit in groups big enough that nobody messes with them. Non-members can also buy tickets at the ECS online store and still sit with the group.

"There are a lot of fun West Coast and East Coast cities to go see a soccer game at," ECS co-president Heather Satterberg said.

ECS has a "lead travel monkey"—named for the monkey-work or grunt-work these volunteers must do to work their way up in the ECS chain—who co-ordinates travel to every competitive match the Sounders play. They had 60 fans go to Houston for the 2017 season opener in March and more than 600 go by bus to a June contest in Portland.

The group splits trips into drivable ones—like Vancouver and Portland and sometimes even San Jose and Salt Lake City—where cars are taken separately and members meet up once they arrive. There are also quick weekend trips to mainly West Coast cities where members leave on a Friday evening and return Sunday. For destinations where a little tourism might be needed—usually on the East Coast—the flights leave Thursday and return Sunday.

And finally, there are week-long trips where the group is either taking in multiple games or going to other countries, like it has for Central American CONCACAF Champions League matches.

ECS leaders keep tabs on travel deals or group discounts on airfare. For bigger matches, they'll do a hotel room block for playoff games or special trips where there's a new stadium or some other special circumstance to the match.

Sometimes, if there's enough demand for Portland or Vancouver games, they'll charter busses instead of just driving. The busses also allow for ECS members to party a bit pregame—something the group's leadership would prefer happen there than outside Providence Park in Portland or B.C. Place Stadium in Vancouver. Those stadiums are surrounded by numerous local watering holes where rival supporter groups congregate for their own drinking.

"We really want to keep them separate," Satterberg said. "Because it really only takes one knucklehead to ruin everybody's day."

Otherwise, the group does usually arranges a pregame meet-up at a local bar, or a tailgate outside the stadium.

They also negotiate with the home team's front office for tickets, and for supporters' group exemptions to bring drums and other items into the stadium. They'll work with the local security team to make sure items get in and out without being confiscated.

A big thing they work on is getting Tifos into away stadiums, using "leads" to negotiate getting ECS members in early to set them up. MLS encourages teams to work with opponents' supporter groups, figuring it's good for PR and league growth.

Of course, traveling with the ECS also means adhering to their code of conduct during the game. That means staying attentive, cheering and chanting on demand, and following the lead of others telling them how to support the club.

But it's definitely safer than going to many away sporting events alone and decked out in your team's colors.

90 Rare Violence Between Sounders and Timbers Fans

Supporter groups for the Sounders and Portland Timbers are notorious for not liking one another. Members of the Emerald City Supporters and Timbers Army will hurl insults at one another, both in person and over the Internet. But rarely does animosity between fans of both teams ever lead to outright physical violence.

An exception occurred in March 2010 following an exhibition Community Shield match at then Qwest Field between the Sounders—about to enter their second MLS season—and the second division Timbers. The game was played on a rain-soaked evening and hyped up in advance, since the Timbers would be entering MLS the following year.

Despite it being just a friendly, both teams fielded top lineups. But it would be a trialist, OJ Obatola, who scored the only goal of the evening to give Portland a 1–0 lead and eventual victory. The Timbers Army fans inside the stadium were going crazy. As the majority of the 18,606 drenched fans filed out of the stadium disappointed, the Sounders fans weren't in the mood for smack talk by visiting spectators.

It just so happened that, not far from the stadium, a 28-year-old Portland fan was walking in search of a bus back to his hotel. Three Sounders fans clad in team scarves saw his Timbers scarf and they began jawing at one another.

The Timbers fan later told police he thought he'd been engaging in "friendly rivalry banter" with the men, who wound up following him. Shortly after, they caught up to him, their faces now covered by their scarves. He told police they tried to grab his scarf and pull it off him. They also punched him in the face and later dragged him around on the sidewalk by his scarf, choking him in the process.

Police said the man wasn't seriously hurt. But they were unable to locate his assailants because there were dozens of other young men in the vicinity all wearing team scarves.

To this day, despite the ferocious on-field rivalry, there have been no other reports of serious violence between fans of both teams. The ECS and its leadership oppose violence of any kind and have worked vigorously to defuse potential flareups involving its members. There remains no evidence that ECS members were involved in the assault on the Timbers fan.

91 Leerdam Solidifies a Second Title Shot

The unbelievably short honeymoon period following the Sounders' inaugural MLS Cup championship had worn off completely by June 2017. Opponents had figured out the Sounders were too weighted toward the left side of the field, where Joevin Jones and a revolving door of wingers created what limited attack the team had.

As a result, teams merely sat back and let the Sounders take the play to them. And when they did, those teams would throw up a wall against the left side, wait for a turnover, and then try to burn the Sounders on the counterattack. It worked more often than not, even though by late June the Sounders had started to see Clint Dempsey return to form and give them some offensive options.

What they needed was balance. An early injury in training camp to right back Brad Evans became a recurring theme as the season progressed. General manager Garth Lagerwey knew that gaining stability at the position would help the team go a long way. Gustav Svensson and Jordy Delem had done an admirable job of filling in, but they weren't the types of players the position required to make another title run.

One thing was for certain—Evans was dealing with an assortment of hurts and couldn't be counted on. The Sounders had a replacement in mind, a Surinamese native named Kelvin Leerdam who'd been playing for Vitesse over in the Eredivisie in The Netherlands. A gifted two-way player, Leerdam had at one point been targeted by Manchester United of the English Premier League before some internal politics prevented that squad from acquiring him via loan.

Meanwhile, Leerdam had experienced his own problems with Vitesse early in 2016 when he spoke his mind to a Dutch soccer magazine about the direction of the team and its new interim manager. Leerdam was dropped by the first division side and demoted to its reserve squad. Although he returned the following 2016–17 season under a new manager, the general consensus was that Leerdam was primed for a fresh start someplace else.

His had already been an interesting life. He was the son of Marlon Grando, a household soccer name in the tiny South American nation of Suriname. Those in the know like to call Suriname the greatest soccer power nobody has ever heard of. Famous international stars Ruud Gullit, Frank Rijkaard, Patrick Kluivert, and Clarence Seedorf all hailed from the former Dutch colony. But the country's strict laws prohibited players who'd earned their soccer livings abroad from holding dual citizenship to return and play for the national team. That's the reason Suriname has never been to a World Cup.

The country has also been beset by coups and long stints of military rule since its 1976 independence. Grando and his national squad teammates had been poised to play in the 1980 Olympics in Moscow after the United States boycotted to protest the Soviet Union's invasion of Afghanistan.

Then, having already accepted an invitation to the Games, Suriname pulled out only weeks later. An official reason was never given—the country had undergone a coup only months earlier—but the result was that Grando never got to go.

"It was very hard," Grando said. "Because it would be the first time that [independent] Suriname would participate in an Olympic event and show the world what we had. I was very disappointed about that. Suriname is such a small country in soccer. The moment you have a chance to be there, you've got to be there."

A decade later, he and his girlfriend, Juliette, a schoolteacher who'd also been a talented club level soccer player, gave birth to a son, Kelvin. The year was 1990 and Suriname had just fallen back under military rule. Like many Surinamese, Grando left for the Netherlands a year later, hoping to find greater prosperity for his family there.

One year later, Juliette left to join him, leaving young Kelvin behind with his grandparents but hoping to bring him overseas soon.

It would be seven years before that happened.

"I had no brothers or sisters, so I was on my own in Suriname," Leerdam said. "I had my grandparents, my aunts and uncles, but you learn to be by yourself and how to handle being on your own."

Leerdam would see his mother during her yearly visits, when she'd give him backyard soccer lessons. He grew quite talented at the sport.

He never saw his father during those years, and their phone conversations were infrequent. But when Leerdam was finally brought overseas to live, Grando tried to be a bigger presence in

Kelvin's life. Though Grando and Juliette had split up by then, Grando would still visit on weekends and he and Leerdam would bond while going to watch soccer games.

"We were together almost every day on the pitch and away from it," Leerdam said. "We talked about soccer but a lot of other things, as well."

Eventually, Leerdam proved good enough that he earned a tryout with the famed USV Elinkwijk youth club where Marco van Basten had gotten his start.

The Sounders didn't need to know that whole backstory. They'd scouted Leerdam for the better part of two years and had seen enough on the field to know he'd fit.

When they signed him in July 2017 for Targeted Allocation Money, Sounders fans were a tad underwhelmed. They'd had their minds set on a Designated Player signing of Paraguayan midfielder Derlis Gonzalez from Dynamo Kiev. But the Ukrainian side wouldn't relent on their high transfer fee demands. Lagerwey had been prepared to sign both players, feeling the team needed a combination of improved offense and defense.

He'd later add Spanish midfielder Victor Rodriguez in lieu of Gonzalez. But in Leerdam, Lagerwey had his defensive game-changer. And the impact was instant. The Sounders did not allow a goal the first four consecutive games started by Leerdam, eventually setting a club record with 421 shutout minutes.

Leerdam locked down the right side to such a degree that it became almost an afterthought. The Sounders posted clean sheets their final two regular season games to clinch a playoff berth and first-round bye. Then they blanked the opposition four more times in the playoffs to reach the MLS Cup final once again.

"He's had a huge impact on our team just based on the level of play he brought to that fullback position," Lagerwey said. "That's something we haven't seen."

By the time the Sounders stepped on the pitch at BMO Field in Toronto for their MLS Cup rematch, they'd set a new league playoff record for consecutive shutout minutes at 647.

"It isn't easy coming to a new team and playing in a new country," Leerdam said. "It took me time to get to know the style of play of my own teammates and the rest of the league. But after a while, it all clicked."

And the Sounders had another title shot.

92 U.S. Open Cup Dynasty

During the two years before the Sounders launched their Major League Soccer franchise, their United Soccer League version had made the semifinal of the Lamar Hunt U.S. Open Cup both times. In doing so both in 2007 and 2008, the Sounders had beaten a number of MLS teams in the process.

When they entered the 2009 tournament with six carry-overs from their USL squad and a roster filled out with mainly MLS players, they naturally expected to win. Trying to gain a bigger foothold in the Seattle sports market, the team realized that securing trophies of any kind would give them a boost.

The U.S. Open Cup had been around since 1914 and now was competed for by MLS, USL, NASL, and amateur teams. Only one non-MLS team had won it since the league was founded, meaning the Sounders making it to the final four the prior two years had been a huge accomplishment.

But now, they wanted more.

"Everything was just about continuing momentum and trying to be relevant from day one," Sounders goalkeeper Kasey Keller said. "The USL Sounders had made some good runs in the U.S. Open Cup, so there was some history there."

Only the top six MLS squads from the prior season gained automatic entry, so the Sounders—in their first season as an expansion squad—had to win a pair of qualification matches to get there. But they did and then they defeated hated Portland 2–1 in the opening round with help from the fabled Roger Levesque goal only 48 seconds into the match.

For the third straight year, they made the semifinal, this time against Houston at the Starfire Sports stadium, where the team had chosen to play its U.S. Open Cup home games.

"I think playing the games at Starfire also kind of gave a bit of a throwback to the faithful that had come out during the times when the team was playing at smaller venues," Keller said. "It was a lot of fun. I remember some of the MLS coaches would say to me, 'What are you doing playing in these Open Cup games with everything else you've done?' But that's what you're here to do. I'm here to play. I'm not here to watch."

It was 1–1 after regulation and then, five minutes into extra time, Stephen King scored the eventual winner to send the Sounders to their first-ever final. King had scored only three MLS goals in four seasons but bagged two in U.S. Open Cup play that summer.

The final was against D.C. United at RFK Stadium. Back then, MLS ran a private bid process to see who would host the championship match and the Sounders weren't thrilled when they lost out.

"I'd be lying if I didn't say I was frustrated and somewhat skeptical of the process," Hanauer told Don Ruiz, a reporter with *The News Tribune* in Tacoma. "I don't think D.C. has played a game in the Open Cup on the road in two years. They had a road through all lower-division teams to get to the Open Cup Final. I'm not in the know…enough to be able to raise any real issues, but

I'm frustrated and I wish U.S. Soccer would explain why one bid wins over another."

He added, "Our fans deserve some answers. And by the way, U.S. Soccer has been trying to raise the profile of the U.S. Open Cup. A game in front of 10,000 fans at RFK I don't believe is going to raise the profile as much as a game in front of a sold-out Qwest Field."

Ticket sales had been sluggish at 45,000-seat RFK Stadium, and Hanauer's comments sparked a frenzied public relations push by D.C. United to fill the venue. Celebrities pitched the game on local TV, and the team offered promotions and discounted seats.

But by game time, only 17,329 fans—about 38 percent stadium capacity—were in attendance. After a scoreless opening half, Fredy Montero drilled home a rebound in the 67th minute by diving feet first at the ball. After the goal, D.C. United keeper Josh Wicks lashed out in frustration by stomping on Montero's leg while he was still on the ground.

Wicks received a red card, leaving his team down a man the rest of the match. Levesque then made it 2–0 in the 86th minute, and although D.C. United managed to snap the shutout a few minutes later, the Sounders held on for their first U.S. Open Cup victory.

Fans greeted the team upon its return to SeaTac Airport, and the trophy was displayed around town at various events.

A year later, MLS made sure the Sounders were awarded the chance to host the final and the Sounders made the most of it, defeating the Columbus Crew 2–1 in front of 31,311 at Qwest Field—the highest attendance for a U.S. Open Cup game in 81 years. The Sounders had become the first MLS team to defend a U.S. Open Cup title.

"We were so disappointed to not be awarded the right to host the final the first year," Keller said. "And then winning in D.C. and [being] able to come back the next year and win it in front of our fans was again one of those progressions."

But they weren't done yet.

By October 2011, the Sounders were gunning for the three-peat and again made the final, this time against the Chicago Fire. A crowd of 35,615 showed up to what is now known as CenturyLink Field and saw Osvaldo Alonso play the game of his life.

It was the fourth straight U.S. Open Cup final for the Cuban defector, who'd made it there with the USL Charleston Battery in 2008—defeating the Sounders in the semifinals—before joining the Rave Green for their victories in 2009, 2010, and now their three-peat quest.

Alonso defended ferociously throughout the night, smothering the Fire attack and limiting their chances against keeper Keller. The game remained scoreless until the 78th minute, when Jeff Parke put a header into an Erik Friberg cornerkick. Though the initial save was made, the ball came loose and Montero cranked home the rebound for the latest goal ever scored in the modern professional era of the tournament for a match decided in regulation time.

In the waning moments, Alonso sealed a 2–0 victory by dribbling through the Chicago defense and past the keeper before slotting the ball into the open net. The crowd went crazy and Alonso had the signature goal of his career.

Alonso's team became the first MLS squad to win three straight trophies of any kind. Though the Sounders would add another U.S. Open Cup title in 2014, the 2011 three-peat was the last one for goalkeeper Keller, who retired just a few weeks later.

"I think we took that tournament seriously, and that's the reason we had so much success in it," Keller said. "And again, once you build that kind of momentum, everybody else kind of follows suit. The fans were excited about it and we were excited to give it to them."

93 A Sounder at Heart

When Dave Clark was just a child, he played on a youth soccer team near Kent, Washington, coached by his father. His dad wasn't that into sports but had taken the job because nobody else would. To supplement his soccer knowledge, he'd invested in a bunch of tactical books about soccer that young Dave eventually read.

"They'd be sitting out on the table at night and I'd read the books," Clark said. "That might be why my tactics are outdated, but it's also why I view the game from a tactical rather than a ball-at-your-feet kind of thing. I mean, I was reading soccer books when I was six, seven, eight years old."

Later he joined the Army and served as the intelligence asset for a special forces unit as a Arabic linguist and signals interceptor. He was stationed in Kuwait during the run-up to the 1998 FIFA World Cup and got to take in two qualifying matches when that country played Saudi Arabia and Qatar.

Upon returning home, he followed the Sounders during their A-League incarnation and later their United Soccer League days. By then, he started working as a producer for Sports Radio KJR and asked if he could go to games and report on the team.

"They told me, 'Sure, but we'll never use any of it,'" he said.

That initial soccer reporting gave Clark the experience he'd sought. He'd been doing some part-time blogging about base-ball on sites run by Jason Churchill, who later founded Prospect Insider. Churchill kept pushing Clark to blog about soccer.

"He said, 'You have to blog. You have a voice,'" Clark recalls. "And that way, I'd stop calling him and trying to talk about soccer because he didn't like it. So it was a way for him to get rid of me."

The Sounders in November 2007 had announced they were joining Major League Soccer, so Clark started blogging a full year ahead of the team's launch. By then, he'd left KJR to work for Starbucks full-time, so writing about the Sounders became his full-time sports passion.

Churchill hosted Clark's new Sounder at Heart blog on his servers for 16 months, well into the team's inaugural 2009 season.

That's when SB Nation approached Clark about running one of the first pro soccer team blogs on its network. Sounder at Heart moved under the SB Nation umbrella. Clark's first live game blog was November 8, 2009, during the second leg of the team's conference semifinal against Houston, ending in a 1–0 loss to the Dynamo.

Eight years later, Sounder at Heart has grown to nearly one million monthly page views. It employs three full-time staffers, a network of about 20 freelance contributors, does occasional road trips, and offers fans some of the most comprehensive coverage about the team that can be found anywhere.

Clark tries to strike a balance on the site that maintains a fan's exuberance while offering serious content that includes player, coach, and front office interviews and delves heavily into tactics and strategy. He insists Sounder at Heart is not the same as print media outlets covering the team; it isn't pretending to be neutral in its reporting.

"We've never turned our backs on being fans," he said. "That's something that we believe in."

Clark does, however, try to have the site maintain a professional approach to all aspects of its work, something he attributes to his prior radio job. His lead writer and senior editor, Jeremiah Oshan, had worked as a copy editor for the *Oakland Tribune* and various other Bay Area outlets.

Clark says the biggest change to the blog is that it now covers all daily news stories just as a newspaper would. That wasn't always the case.

When he first jumped to SB Nation, the Sounders were covered daily by the *Seattle Times*, *The News Tribune* of Tacoma, and the *Everett Herald*. "We struggled to find unique angles," Clark said. "I wouldn't really refer to us as a thought feeder then."

But by 2017, the *Times* was the only newspaper still covering the team regularly.

"Early on, I would interview a lot of backups because I'd avoid the stuff that everybody was doing," he said. "Now I don't have that luxury. We have to do what everybody's doing because there isn't everybody. We can't avoid a mainstream story because if we don't do it, that big story may only be done by people employed by the team."

In 2011, the Sounder at Heart website began doing a podcast called *Nos Audietis*—a Latin phrase meaning "You will hear us"—and selling sponsorships for it to local businesses. It was a way to generate extra income; Clark's deal with SB Nation only allows the company to sell ads directly on Sounder at Heart. But the podcast as a side component to the site itself was under no such restriction.

Remaining salaries and money for stories are paid out through a regular SB Nation stipend. Clark more recently has resisted offers for a raise in order to use any additional funds to hire more writers.

"It's getting more and more difficult to find paying jobs in this writing world of ours," Clark said. "So the more people I can pay to do stuff for us, the better."

And the more his site can keep on growing.

94 Soccer's Rare Marching Band

Sounders owner Joe Roth couldn't believe his ears when comedian Drew Carey gave him one of his conditions for buying an ownership stake in the team. The pair had just finished a power lunch in which Carey, bleeding profusely from a cut to his hand suffered that morning during an accident on the set of *The Price Is Right*, had made a passionate case for why he should be involved with the group headed by majority owner Roth.

But now, Carey had conditions.

"He says to me, 'We've got to have a marching band,'" Roth said.

Roth had to keep himself from rolling his eyes, since soccer teams typically don't have marching bands the way they do in college football. But the request seemed simple enough. It was a bit easier than Carey's other condition—that fans be allowed to vote out the team's management every year. That was later negotiated down to a vote every four years on retaining the general manager.

But the marching band idea would stick.

And that's how Sound Wave, a 53-member ensemble of traditional marching percussion and brass instruments, was born. Each year it holds tryouts for local musicians and plays arrangements including pop, rock, Latin, big band, and funk.

The team at first wanted to place the band alongside the Emerald City Supporters section in the South End of Qwest Field, but that idea didn't fly.

ECS members worried the band would make a mockery of the team and MLS because marching bands were not part of traditional soccer in Europe and South America. And they believed it was their responsibility as a supporters group to keep up the stadium energy, not some artificial band noise they believed to be a corporate symbol.

"Drew was like, 'We want this marching band,'" said Greg Mockos, the first ECS co-president along with Keith Hodu in 2009. "And I actually thought it was kind of an interesting idea. But later on, they actually tried to place the band in our section, which I didn't think would work.

"I always thought it would be a halftime thing, as you'd expect," Mockos added. "But it ended up not going that route."

Instead, Mockos pitched the idea for what became the March to the Match, at which Sound Wave now plays an integral role. Hundreds and often thousands of singing and chanting fans march the half-mile route from Pioneer Square down to the stadium, with the band helping to pump them up.

It didn't go smoothly at first.

"There were problems with drowning each other out," Mockos said. "But the march grew. They went first, then we went first. There were a variety of ways to try and tweak it."

Inside the stadium, Sound Wave is now positioned in the North End side of the stadium alongside the North End Supporters group. Though Carey calls it a "marching" band, it is actually more of a stationary pep band during games. The only marching it does takes place pregame, while during games the band will try to work off the energy dictated by the crowd, rather than compete with supporter group fans. When ECS and other groups start chanting, the band lowers its instruments. But during lulls in the chanting, it will start playing to keep the crowd pumped up.

Eventually, an uneasy beginning led to a truce. And it gave the Sounders one of the only marching bands in all of professional sport.

95 A Favor Returned

Plenty of folks in and around the soccer world had asked Garth Lagerwey for favors before.

But this one seemed at first like it would be more of a headache than others. The Sounders general manager had taken a call from an old friend, longtime soccer agent Leo Cullen from the renowned James Grant agency. Cullen had played alongside Lagerwey while they were both with the Miami Fusion and was now starting a tryout camp in Cameroon. The idea was for players from some of the African nation's poorer communities to be seen by professional scouts when they otherwise might get overlooked.

Lagerwey was skeptical. But he wasn't going to tell Cullen no. So in late 2015, Lagerwey and team director of player personnel Kurt Schmid hopped on a transatlantic flight. They arrived and were driven for hours to a remote field set against a jungle backdrop.

There, for the first time, they saw a teenager named Nouhou Tolo.

"He was raw, but he was really, really good," Lagerwey said.

Schmid concurred. "His athleticism really stuck out. His ability to get up and down the line, his speed, his jumping ability—even though he's still working on his heading technique. You'd see some good starting points that we could build on."

Nouhou's biggest battle to get to that point in his soccer development had been inside his own house. He'd grown up the second oldest of a family of five children in the port city of Douala. His mother, Aissatou, died after a lengthy illness when he was just 14, leaving Nouhou's father, Issiaka, a currency exchanger, to raise his kids alone.

His father was strict, preferring Nouhou—he likes to go by his given name only—drop soccer altogether and focus on his studies. They quarreled over it and Nouhou kept trying to juggle both. Then, at age 15, he got an invitation to play for Cameroon's U17 squad.

A couple of years later, the Sounders spotted him in Cullen's tryout camp. Nouhou was flown overseas in April 2016 to play for the Sounders2 reserve squad, having to learn basic things like how to boil water in a kettle and fasten a seat belt in a car.

Also, his game had to develop.

"In Cameroon, it's much more about being athletic and physical," Nouhou said. "But over here, it's a lot more technical and tactical."

But he developed quickly. And by early 2017, the Sounders were ready to try him in an MLS game. He made his Sounders debut in a friendly against Mexican side Necaxa, then he played his first MLS game on May 31 as a substitute late in a 3–0 loss at Columbus.

Nouhou was playing behind Joevin Jones at the time, and the left back was enjoying a phenomenal start to the season. But behind the scenes, contract talks between Jones and the Sounders were at an impasse. That led the Sounders to start Nouhou in a couple of games to see how he'd handle the position and whether they'd have a left back when Jones inevitably departed. That summer, Jones would nearly sign an advance deal for 2018 with the second division German side SV Darmstadt.

Nouhou handled his starts better than expected. His physical prowess helped him defend nearly as well as Jones, and his offensive game was a sight to behold. Nouhou was deceptively fast for his size and would barrel downfield with seeming disregard for whoever got in his way. He'd literally run over opponents, then protest in disbelief when the referee called a foul. But it all somehow worked.

Then, in a move that undoubtedly helped the team reach a second consecutive MLS final, the Sounders began experimenting by starting Nouhou at left back and pushing Jones up to the attacking midfield on left wing. Later, as the playoffs approached, the move became a permanent fixture. A late-season quadriceps injury to midfielder Victor Rodriguez, who had been used primarily on the left side, meant the Nouhou-Jones combo was again in play.

The left-side speed generated by the duo was about the best the Sounders had ever seen. And by the time Rodriguez was healthy enough to start the second leg of the Western Conference final against Houston, he was placed on the right wing instead of the left so Nouhou-Jones could remain intact.

Jones would notch an assist in a 3–0 win over Houston, while Rodriguez would score the game's opening goal to help send the Sounders back to the MLS Cup in what had been one of the best playoff performances the Sounders had ever produced. The team was now lethally dangerous on both flanks.

And had Lagerwey not boarded that plane to Cameroon, the whole thing—including that return trip to the championship match—might never have happened.

96 The Best of Beginnings

Launching a North American Soccer League franchise in Seattle was going to require more than just solid on-field play. It was going to take plenty of off-field work to convince the sporting populace that pro soccer was worth going to see.

And the Sounders made sure they brought in the right guy to get that work done. Liverpool native John Best had been an American pro soccer pioneer, a five-time All-Star with the Dallas

Tornado who became a fixture in that community and spread the word about that team.

Then, with the Sounders preparing for their 1974 NASL debut season, general manager Jack Daley hired Best as the team's first coach.

"We made him basically the face of the franchise," Daley told the *Seattle Times*. "He was a great public speaker. He was a good-looking guy. He almost had a Pied Piper personality. I can't recall anybody who John Best ever met in Seattle that was turned off by him."

Former Sounders defender Dave Gillett remembers Best as "a real cool character and an honest guy."

Gillett said a lot of the English coaches at that time were authoritarian and prone to bullying players. Not Best, he added, who was methodical, tactical, and supportive of players.

"He was the first guy I had who was thoughtful of the way the team played, thoughtful about how he managed and coached players he knew would get better in a different environment. He was a very calculating and smart guy."

Those early Sounders teams quickly forged a bond with the fans. They set league attendance records with sellout crowds in the 13,000-to-17,000 range at Memorial Stadium, depending on its ever-changing capacity.

"A lot of the veteran guys were used to playing a couple of hours and then would piss off and go play golf," Gillett said. "But he made it completely different and got us doing coaching clinics, school assemblies. He made us do a lot of hard work building the crowds."

Gillett said Best was very selective about new players added, bringing in guys "of good character" like Jimmy Gabriel and Dave Butler who would go the extra mile in building the game. By 1976, the Sounders moved to the Kingdome where they averaged 23,828 fans per game.

"There was always this wonderful rapport between the players and the fans," said goalkeeper Tony Chursky, who joined the Sounders under Best that 1976 season. "A lot of it had to do with the fact we were one of the few teams that initiated the idea of lapping the field and waving to the fans after the games. And that was always encouraged and fostered."

Even with the big crowds now secured, Best kept pushing his players to get out into the community.

"We did so many public appearances," Chursky said. "Not only during the season, but in the offseason. Players were actually hired on contract in the offseason to do tons of assemblies at schools and that kind of thing."

And Best's teams were competitive.

The Sounders went 43–26 during their three seasons under him before he left for the Vancouver Whitecaps, where he won a Soccer Bowl championship in 1979. He then returned to the Sounders as general manager in 1982, watching coach Alan Hinton lead the team to the Soccer Bowl that season before bowing to the New York Cosmos.

While in Seattle, Best helped sell the team by writing a newspaper column about soccer. He also hosted a primetime weekly TV program.

"I always found John to be a very personable fellow," Chursky said. "He struck me as always taking a kind of cerebral approach to the game. A real calm demeanor and was very articulate. He broke down the game very well."

But more importantly, he broke it down and sold it to the fans. And that set a course to where the Sounders find themselves today.

Best continued living in the Seattle area after he retired from soccer, undergoing three kidney transplants. He died in October 2014 from a lung infection while visiting overseas in Ireland. His death came the same week the Sounders had planned 40th anniversary celebrations commemorating the arrival of Best and the first Sounders team in 1974.

"You look at those people who were going to those early games, [and] some of them have kids who are going to Sounders games today," Gillett said. "[Best] had a long-term vision."

97 Getting Their Man

With their first Major League Soccer season fast approaching, the Sounders were determined to make a splash with their inaugural head coach selection. But they nearly belly-flopped in the process.

The Sounders wanted Sigi Schmid, who'd just won the MLS Cup championship with the Columbus Crew. Earlier in that decade, he'd won another title with the Los Angeles Galaxy in 2002, making him the league's only coach to win championships with two different teams. This was the winning face they wanted stamped on a franchise destined to go places.

And for the reigning champion Crew, that stamp was coming a little too fast. After all, it had been only two weeks since Schmid had won the title with them. They wondered how the interview process and a contract offer could have been made so quickly.

So before the Sounders could even announce Schmid as coach, the Crew filed a formal tampering charge against them with the league. They accused the team of having talked to Schmid while he was still under contract during the season, causing him to violate a vaguely worded non-compete clause they claimed prevented him from coaching elsewhere in 2009.

Schmid had wanted to be closer to his Los Angeles–based family, and direct flights from Seattle certainly offered that. He also claimed the Crew's ownership, notoriously frugal, had not met his contract demands.

But the Crew claimed differently and said both sides had been close. They claimed Schmid was predisposed to joining the Sounders.

The league investigated and ruled there had been no tampering. But the Sounders were urged to pay the Crew financial compensation to settle the dispute and get around the non-compete clause. They did and a week later, with Schmid contractually released by the Crew, the Sounders had their man.

"We want to be competitive from day one," Schmid told reporters. "I'm not a big believer in saying we want to win a certain number of matches. And we have to be realistic. We're an expansion team, and players play better once they have 20 or 30 games under their belt."

Midfielder Brad Evans had played for Schmid in Columbus and had been picked up by the Sounders in the MLS Expansion Draft.

"I think I got a call in late December for Sig and he told me, 'We've already got 5,000 season tickets sold,'" Evans said. "He told me, 'We're doing something special up here, the ownership is second to none, and the GM is willing to do whatever it takes to get this team off the ground and running.'"

Indeed, the Sounders were immediately competitive under Schmid, finishing third in the Western Conference at 12–7–11 and making the playoffs before losing to Houston in the conference semifinals. They also won the Lamar Hunt U.S. Open Cup for the first time in Sounders history, defeating D.C. United 2–1 at RFK Stadium in Washington, D.C.

The Sounders would make the playoffs again in 2010 and win another U.S. Open Cup. But after a slow start in 2011, some fans wanted Schmid gone. They questioned his tactics and handling of younger players. Also, the team's designated player signings under Schmid had been fleeting.

After an eight-match unbeaten streak vaulted the team's record to 9–4–8 by July 2011, the Sounders offered Schmid a contract extension and praised his professionalism and results.

"From the moment we hired Sigi, I knew it was the right decision and that he was the right man for this particular club," Sounders owner and general manager Adrian Hanauer told reporters. "I feel that even more strongly today."

Such would be the pattern that followed Schmid throughout his seven and a half seasons with the club. By 2014 Schmid was arguably the marquee face of the franchise, as recognizable to the average sports fan as any player. He'd even earned an endorsement deal from a local Volkswagen dealership, something fairly common for the city's NFL and MLB players but unheard of for the relatively new MLS team.

But in a way, Schmid's early success merely raised the bar of expectations. And eventually, the lack of an MLS Cup left Schmid vulnerable. Whenever the Sounders slumped, the critics were back out. That was the case in 2013 when the Sounders were ousted by rival Portland in the only playoff series the two squads have had. Never mind that the Sounders that year had become the first MLS squad in a decade to eliminate a Mexican side in CONCACAF Champions League play, making it all the way to the semifinals of that tournament. For some fans, he'd overstayed his welcome.

Even majority owner Joe Roth had seen enough and summoned Schmid and Hanauer to a meeting in Los Angeles. "We sat down for a couple of hours," Roth told reporter Matt Pentz of the *Seattle Times*. "And I thought, 'Well, I could fire this guy, who, to me, is one of the two best coaches in the league. He's won a championship in L.A. and in Columbus. You've either gotta fire him or fire the players.' So I fired the players."

After that season, Schmid had met with veterans Evans, Osvaldo Alonso, and Clint Dempsey to get their take on the team. He asked them about locker room discord, a huge concern for management since striker Eddie Johnson had gone public with his salary demands in embarrassing fashion. The players also told Schmid the team should pursue a commanding center back presence to solidify the back line.

Now Schmid relayed those concerns to Roth.

Johnson was soon traded to D.C. United. Mauro Rosales was jettisoned, as well. And Schmid pursued a center back he'd coached previously and knew could be a Sounders mainstay for years to come, eventually landing Columbus Crew franchise cornerstone Chad Marshall.

The Sounders added goalkeeper Stefan Frei, winger Marco Pappa and midfielder Gonzalo Pineda, as well.

Schmid got a second chance as well that 2014 campaign, a dream season for the Sounders in which they compiled the league's best regular season record. For a while, Schmid's critics were silenced. But after a devastating conference finals defeat to his former Galaxy squad, the critics were back out in force.

"As things go in sports, everything's micromanaged," Evans said. "You ultimately try to find faults in people, and when we do fail, we have to be the first ones to admit it. And sometimes, Sigi's good at that. But sometimes, his record's been so good throughout his whole career that maybe he wasn't the first one to raise his hand and say, 'S—t, that was my bad.'"

The Sounders failed to sustain their level of play in 2015. Schmid by then had a new general manager looking over his shoulder in Garth Lagerwey, who had replaced Adrian Hanauer so the latter could focus more on his responsibilities as the team's new majority owner.

When the Sounders got off to a slow start again in 2016 and were languishing in the league's basement by mid-season, a change was finally made.

Two days after the firing, dozens of Emerald City Supporters members gathered at a Pioneer Square sports bar to thank Schmid for what he'd done for the team. "That was something I'll never forget," he told the *Los Angeles Times*. "It was something that has a very special place in my heart."

The Sounders would go on to rally their first MLS Cup victory that 2016 season. "I had some great years in Seattle. I really enjoyed myself," Schmid said. "Being part of the group that established the foundation of the club...I'm very proud of that."

In July 2017, Schmid was hired by the Galaxy for a second go-around as their coach. His first opponent, coincidentally, was the Sounders, who visited the StubHub Center for an emotionally charged scoreless draw. After the match, one by one, the Sounders who had played under Schmid greeted him with hugs on the field.

"I think the record speaks for itself," Evans said. "As one of our great assistant coaches, Ezra Hendrickson, would always say, 'They never ask how they just ask how many?'"

The final Sounders scorecard for Schmid: 109 victories, four U.S. Open Cup titles, a Supporters' Shield, and seven straight postseason appearances.

"Ultimately," Evans said, "he'll be a Sounders legend."

98 Brad Evans Becomes Mr. Versatility

Brad Evans was as much a part of the Sounders expansion launch as any player could be. He'd won the MLS Cup with the Columbus Crew and coach Sigi Schmid on November 23, 2008, defeating the New York Red Bulls.

Three days later, Evans was selected by the Sounders as their 10th and final pick in that year's expansion draft. Within weeks, he'd be reunited with Schmid in Seattle when the Sounders named him their first head coach.

Evans would go on in March 2009 to score the second goal in franchise history, playing against the same Red Bulls team he'd beaten for the championship a few months prior. His 24th minute shot between the legs of Red Bulls keeper Danny Cepero in the Sounders' season opener gave the home side a 2–0 lead in an eventual 3–0 victory.

But as time wore on, finding a secure position for the Sounders captain and U.S. Men's National Team member became a challenge. Evans started off alternating between center midfield and right wing, then began seeing temporary defender action at center and right back in 2012.

Playing in June 2013 for the USMNT, Evans started at right back in a World Cup qualifier against Jamaica and scored the game-winning goal in stoppage time. Come 2014, he made his first two career starts at left back in May, planting a seed in the club's head about using him on full-time back-line duty.

In the playoffs that year, he'd score one of the biggest goals of his career in the second leg of the conference finals against the Los Angeles Galaxy. In just the 26th minute, Evans was there to smash home a loose ball in the crease to even the aggregate series at 1–1. The Sounders would even take the series lead before halftime, but a Juninho goal in the second half put an end to Seattle's MLS Cup dreams.

That offseason, the team approached Evans about dropping into a defender's role at center back so they wouldn't have to sign an expensive player to fill the void.

Evans agreed, though the adjustment proved difficult. The San Jose Earthquakes badly exposed Evans on all three goals of a 3–2 comeback win at CenturyLink Field early in the 2015 season. But Evans kept working to learn the position and by that summer felt he had gained command of it.

"I feel like I had a good two-thirds of the year," he told the *Seattle Times*. "I built into that position and felt like, save for a few mistakes, I thought that I was playing well."

But the Sounders put an end to the experiment that summer by signing Panamanian center back Roman Torres for targeted allocation money. Immediately after, they inserted Evans into the defensive midfield following an injury to Osvaldo Alonso.

"We've got to try to get our best team on the field," Seattle coach Sigi Schmid told *The Times*. "There might be a little bit of variety there, and we'll try to find the position [for Evans] next year again."

Evans was 30 at the time. The team had said the switch to center back would add years to his career, but now things were uncertain again. Then Torres tore the ACL in his knee almost immediately after arriving in Seattle and Evans was thrust back into the center back role once again.

He remained there the following season, which began slowly for the Sounders until a mid-summer turnaround following the firing of head coach Sigi Schmid. By September, Torres was ready to return after a year-long absence and Evans knew he'd be switching positions again.

"Ultimately, I think I'm a guy who can play multiple positions and he's a guy who can play one position, so I think I understand the situation at hand," Evans said. "Nothing will ever change my mindset going into a training session or a game. I think I've adapted to multiple positions fairly well."

Torres came on and helped solidify a team poised to make an unexpected playoff run. Evans, meanwhile, was used in the midfield and at his preferred right back position, helping to keep a banged-up club from falling completely apart.

"In Brad's case, the pundits can say, 'Brad doesn't have a position.' I don't look at it that way," interim Sounders coach Brian

Schmetzer told reporters. "If I play Brad [anywhere], he'll do whatever it takes to help the team win. That, to me, speaks volumes about his character."

The Sounders unexpectedly gutted their way in to the MLS Cup final against a heavily favored Toronto FC side. But the Sounders held the Reds off the scoreboard until the penalty kick round.

There, Evans led things off by scoring for the Sounders. And it would be Torres who finished it, burying his final try to give the Sounders their first league title.

99 Mr. Sounder Finds a Home

As their 2017 training camp loomed, Sounders head coach Brian Schmetzer felt he needed a new trick to pull out of a bag he'd largely used up a couple of months earlier. Schmetzer had taken over a cellar-dwelling Sounders team and guided it to a stunning MLS Cup title victory over Toronto, using every coaching and psychological tactic at his disposal to hold the squad together.

But now, with players about to return from a short offseason, Schmetzer knew what a disaster the approaching 2017 season might become. As coach of the United Soccer League second-division version of the Sounders, he'd won a championship in 2005 and then endured a terrible season in 2006. There were things he'd promised himself he'd do differently in that situation again. Now here he was, having to explain to players the perils that a championship hangover might carry and that nothing more than hard work would carry the day.

Rather than have the message come from him, Schmetzer dialed up a favor from one of those USL players who'd won a pair of titles with him and had come over to the MLS squad. Zach Scott had just retired from the team a few weeks earlier, but Schmetzer felt that he alone could convey what needed to be said.

Scott was now working for Slalom Consulting in Seattle, and Schmetzer had agreed to speak at a corporate event only a couple of weeks prior. Now he figured Scott owed him one and placed a phone call.

"He wanted me to explain to the guys a bit about what life looks like outside of soccer," Scott said. "How lucky they have it to be in the position they are. Being…in a unique situation of coming off of a championship and now, how are we going to answer that with a renewed focus and vigor for 2017?"

Scott had never been one who could afford to take a day off. The Maui native had fought to get a shot at playing Division 1 college soccer with Gonzaga University, then was told afterward he didn't have what it takes to be a pro.

After rejections by Major League Soccer teams and the A-League Portland Timbers, Scott tried out for the second division Sounders in 2002 and their new head coach, who just happened to be Schmetzer.

"The thing I always liked about Zach was he may not have been the most talented player on my teams, but he was always willing to put in the work to make himself better," Schmetzer said. "And sometimes, at this level of play, that can make all the difference in the world."

Scott was a mainstay on Schmetzer's A-League and USL squads, winning a Commissioner's Cup trophy in 2002 for the Sounders after having posted the best regular season record. The Sounders made it all the way to the finals in 2004, losing to the Montreal Impact. But the following year, back in the championship game, the Sounders ultimately prevailed.

Roger Levesque was Scott's teammate with the Sounders through all but his rookie year. "I think initially what separated him was his drive, his fight, his athleticism," Levesque said. "Those are the things that come to mind from his early days. His edge. I know it could be a little bit reckless, but it became the same progression you saw later in MLS. He just continued to work at it and got better and better each year—not just technically, but in his approach to the game and how he saw it."

After the mess of 2006, the Sounders won another title in 2007 that was largely overshadowed by the expected announcement they'd soon be awarded an MLS franchise. Once that happened, the Sounders agreed to play one more USL season in 2008, which turned into an audition for the MLS team as players jockeyed to be picked for the expansion launch.

By season's end, Scott was preparing for life after the Sounders. But then, he got an invitation to training camp and dazzled the expansion team's new head coach Sigi Schmid with his work ethic.

Scott was in the starting lineup at right back as the Sounders beat the New York Red Bulls in their season opener. But starts would be sporadic for Scott, who had to keep working and looking for openings.

He kept training as hard as ever.

"I never took my position on the team for granted," he said. "I knew it could come to an end at any time."

But few players knew the history of the Sounders like Scott did, having spanned multiple incarnations of it. Though the emergence of DeAndre Yedlin in 2013 relegated Scott to a reserve role, he kept working. Then Yedlin left in 2014 to play for the U.S. Men's National Team and Scott had some additional starting time. That time increased when an injury to center back Djimi Traore opened another spot for Scott, despite being undersized for the position.

Center back actually suited Scott, since he didn't have to cover as much ground as he previously had.

Scott would manage double-digit starts from 2014 through the 2015 season. And by 2016, he was still around and on the field to win an MLS Cup alongside longtime coach Schmetzer—the only remaining member from the team's pre-MLS days to do so.

He'd retire that winter having played eight MLS seasons and seven more with the A-League/USL version of the team, earning the nickname "Mr. Sounder." And when he spoke to players the following Janaury in training camp at Schmetzer's request, Scott didn't hold back his blunt assessment of what they needed to do.

"No one cares about mistakes if you get on with it," Scott said. "But I told them, 'There's going to be moments throughout the year when you've felt like you've made it. That's when you're about to [screw] up.'"

So he told them, "Don't get into a situation where you think you're here, you've made it. Where you think you're talented. Where you're given this amazing opportunity and you take your foot off the gas. Because 15 years, for me, has gone in the blink of an eye."

But he made them last all the same.

100 Brad Evans Finds Penalty Kick Perfection

Back when Brad Evans was playing soccer for Mountain Pointe High School in Phoenix, his coach had a can't-refuse offer for his players—make your penalty kick try during drills and you won't have to do post-practice fitness work. And Evans was definitely not a big fan of the wind-sprints and shuttle runs.

"My goal was always to never be a part of that fitness group," Evans said with a chuckle. "So I think it started a long time ago and was always something I took seriously at practice. I try to stick with the same technique. I don't do anything fancy."

That technique now sees Evans a perfect 11-for-11 on MLS penalty kick tries. He's also 17-for-17 in all competitions, including U.S. Open Cup and friendlies. He'll pick a corner of the net to shoot at and focus on executing the kick. Only once has he ever deviated from his choice at the last second.

It was the 2012 U.S. Open Cup final against Sporting Kansas City, and Evans had been chosen to lead off the penalty kick round after the teams were tied 1–1 following regulation play and overtime. He'd never shot for the left-handed corner before.

"For some reason, my brain was telling me, 'Go right! Go right!' And then at the very last millisecond, I went left. It was a little bit higher than I thought I was going to kick, but I ended up scoring on that one."

Evans did his part, but the final three Sounders shooters missed and cost the team a fourth consecutive U.S. Open Cup title.

He went left twice more, shooting left on penalties in his career. He did it again at home against the Portland Timbers in 2015. Then in October 2016, he notched an 81st minute penalty kick game-winner at Vancouver that proved instrumental in helping the Sounders make the postseason that year ahead of their first title.

"It's only a handful of times," Evans said, "but you have to mix them up ultimately to keep them guessing."

That he did in the 2016 MLS Cup final. The Sounders hadn't registered a shot on net in regulation play or extra time, then Toronto FC striker Jozy Altidore put the first ball in the net all night to open the penalty kick round.

But Evans coolly tied it up on the very next try. Toronto keeper Clint Irwin, perhaps having reviewed beforehand the most recent Evans penalty tries, guessed he might go left again and dove for that corner. But this time, Evans went right and his hard blast along the ground easily found the open side.

Minutes later, a successful Roman Torres handed the Sounders their first title.